Greater Miami

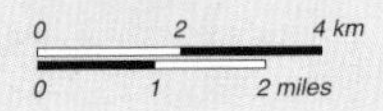

PLACES TO EAT

1 JD's Pizza & Subs
2 Turn Bagel
3 Unicorn Village Market Waterfront Restaurant
6 Rascal House
15 Versailles
16 Hy Vong Vietnamese Restaurant
17 Daily Bread
22 Johnny Rockets

OTHER

4 Borders Books
5 Aventura Mall
7 Bal Harbour Shops
8 Immigration & Naturalization Service
9 Caribbean Marketplace
10 Haitian Refugee Center
11 Churchill's
12 Black Archives Historical & Research Foundation of Southern Florida
13 The American Police Hall of Fame & Police Museum
14 Bacardi Imports Headquarters
18 Miami Museum of Science & Space Transit Planetarium
19 Sailboards Miami
20 Vizcaya Museum & Gardens
21 Miami Seaquarium
23 CocoWalk Mall
24 Coconut Grove Playhouse
25 Fairchild Tropical Gardens

NICK SELBY

Fontainebleau Mural

Miami

a Lonely Planet city guide

Nick Selby
Corinna Selby

Miami
1st edition

Published by
Lonely Planet Publications
Head Office: PO Box 617, Hawthorn, Vic 3122, Australia
Branches: 155 Filbert St, Suite 251, Oakland, CA 94607, USA
10 Barley Mow Passage, Chiswick, London W4 4PH, UK
71 bis rue du Cardinal Lemoine, 75005 Paris, France

Printed by
Colorcraft Ltd, Hong Kong

Photographs by
Nick Selby, Corinna Selby, Kenneth Dreyfuss, Kim Grant
Front cover: Kenneth Dreyfuss, Greystone Hotel, Miami Beach
Title page: Corinna Selby

First Published
October 1996

National Library of Australia Cataloguing in Publication Data

Selby, Nick
Miami.

1st ed.
Includes index.
ISBN 0 86442 373 X.

1. Miami (Fla.) – Guidebooks. I. Selby, Corinna
II. Title. (Series: Lonely Planet city guide).

917.593810463

Nick Selby

Nick Selby was born and raised in New York City. He worked for five years as a sound engineer, but after 3½ years in a seven-foot-by-seven-foot cubicle mixing music for an American soap opera *(Guiding Light)* he decided that anything – anything – would be a step up.

In 1990 he took a job as a morning DJ at Warsaw's first privately owned radio station, Radio Zet, and soon afterwards did a stint as a creative director at a multinational advertising agency (a post from which he was unceremoniously sacked).

With another American expat, he set up a small publishing company in St Petersburg, Russia, and in 1992 he wrote *The Visitor's Guide to the New St Petersburg*. Since then, he's traveled throughout South-East Asia, all too little of Australia, written Lonely Planet's *St Petersburg city guide* and co-authored *Russia, Ukraine & Belarus – a travel survival kit*, as well as *Florida – a travel survival kit*.

Corinna Selby

Corinna Selby was born and raised in Munich, Germany. As soon as she could afford it, she set out traveling through Europe, and spent a year in Portugal. After making more money back home, she traveled to South-East Asia, where she spent the next two years traveling with a minuscule backpack. When she wasn't working as an English teacher in Tainan, Taiwan, or as an illegal art merchant in Japan, she spent her time perfecting a suntan, becoming familiar with the local flora and trying to do as little as possible.

Corinna returned to Germany to study English and Spanish translation, and to work in various departments of Munich's *Süddeutsche Zeitung*. After graduation she traveled to Eastern Europe, Russia, Cuba, back through Asia, down to Australia, and finally, to the USA.

Corinna is the co-author of Lonely Planet's *Florida – a travel survival kit*.

From the Authors

We're very grateful to the 'without whom . . . ' crowd in Miami: Melanie Morningstar, Eugene Patron, Scott Silverman, Michael Aller, the mysterious MT, Mitchell Kaplan, Les Standiford, Bonnie Clearwater, Rebecca Terrell, Burt Compton, Anna and Gonzalo at the Mermaid Guest House, Linda Polanski at the Clay Hostel and, at the Miami CVB, José Lima and Jeanne Sullivan. Thanks to Marlies Arnold and Maria (Mutti) Jungwirth, Amy Portnoy and Joe Bornstein, Bernie Goldstein for all the help and counsel, Carolyn Djanogly for making us look *so* good, Irwin Stein, Phil and Cathy in St Augustine, and Gaja. Thanks also to Lonely Planet's USA office, especially Beth 'got it right here' Eilers, Ann Neet, Greg Mills, David Stanley, Carolyn Hubbard and Laini Taylor. And thanks (again) to the Artilleriestraße. And Pirate.

Nick would especially like to thank his mother, Angela Wilson, for copy editing, grammar checks, cunning wordplay, general support and for taking him to Disney for the most important reason: his birthday.

From the Publisher

This 1st edition was created in Lonely Planet's US office by editor Laini Taylor, proofer Carolyn Hubbard, cartographers Beca Lafore and Cyndy Johnsen, and designer Hugh D'Andrade, with the guidance of Caroline Liou, Alex Guilbert and Scott Summers. Thanks, all.

Warning & Request

Things change – prices go up, schedules change, good places go bad and bad places go bankrupt – nothing stays the same. So if you find things better or worse, recently open or long-since closed, please write and tell us and help make the next edition better.

Your letters will be used to help update future editions and, where possible, important changes will also be included in a Stop Press section of reprints.

We greatly appreciate all information that is sent to us by travelers. Back at Lonely Planet we employ a hard-working readers' letters team to sort through the many letters we receive. The best ones will be rewarded with a free copy of the next edition or of another Lonely Planet guide. We give away lots of books, but, unfortunately, not every letter/postcard receives one.

Lonely Planet books provide independent advice. Accredited Lonely Planet writers do not accept discounts or payment in exchange for positive coverage.

Contents

Maps

Introduction

It used to be called 'God's Waiting Room'. And even today, if you mention Miami Beach to someone who hasn't been here or read about it lately, they might be able to conjure up a blurry memory of octogenarians mingling poolside while Aunt Sadie implored them to wait half an hour before going into the water. But to the arbiters of Fabulousness, SoBe (the inevitable contraction of 'South Beach') has been The Fabulous Spot in the USA since the early 1990s.

The current boom, which showed signs of stirring to life in the mid-1980s, marked the end of a long dead period that began just after James Bond first met Goldfinger as they sat poolside at the landmark Fontainebleau Hotel.

The big Boom brought renovation and the restoration of the city's Deco District, but overzealous developers were given a very short leash by local preservation groups who made certain that the Deco look wouldn't be demolished in favor of the high-rise monstrosities that line the beaches to the near north.

Trying to attract development money, while at the same time attempting to preserve the unique look of the community by severely limiting development, was a gamble that paid off entirely due to locals' activism and their determination to keep their neighborhood. And it is worth noting that the Miami Design Preservation League succeeded in having the entire Deco District placed on the National Register of Historic Places, cementing federal protection of the buildings.

Today, many of the beach's locals are imports from New York, people tired of sitting through five hours of snarled traffic on their way to the Hamptons, who decided that SoBe made a lot more sense. They brought with them a fledgling art and culture crowd whose numbers included many younger artists, their careers stunned by recession, who were looking for cheaper digs and a new audience that was easier to access.

This conglomeration of affluent and educated domestic transplants who knew a good thing when they saw it, mixed with the city's already organized immigrant communities from Cuba, Haiti and Latin America, resulting in as solid a neighborhood community as one could ever hope for.

That sense of neighborhood is precisely the reason that today, Miami Beach is what you make of it. Trendy or not, at the end of the day it's a great stretch of white sand beach lapped by clear blue water, on an island squarely between the Atlantic Ocean and downtown Miami, which sits only a causeway (and several lifestyle light years) to the west.

The Greater Miami Area, which includes Coral Gables, Miami, Aventura and other cities, as well as unique and distinctive neighborhoods like Little Havana and Little Haiti, is as much a melting pot as the USA's founding fathers could have envisioned.

Facts about Miami

HISTORY

Miami Beach and Miami are very new cities, even by American standards. They were developed mainly during the 20th century.

European Settlement

A full 50 years before the Pilgrims lurched up to Plymouth Rock, and 40 before even the establishment at Jamestown, Florida was settled by Spanish explorer Don Pedro Menéndez de Avilés. It would become to North America what Poland is to Europe: the flattest piece of land between battling superpowers. Before it was officially ceded to the US by Spain in 1821, the entire northeast section of the state was sacked, looted, burned and occupied by Spanish, English and US forces.

While the Spanish had claimed Florida after its European discovery in 1513 by Juan Ponce de León, the French had sailed in (as they tended to) and established Fort Caroline, on the St Johns River in 1564. In 1565, Menéndez arrived at Cape Canaveral with about 1500 soldiers and settlers, who made their way north and established St Augustine.

Menéndez headed north and was whupped but good by the French; Spaniards retreated south to St Augustine.

NICK SELBY

Soon after, the French, in an effort to fight *fuego* with *feu*, launched a fleet to head south and take on the pesky Spaniards. But the French fell victim to one of Florida's famous coastal storms, and their fleet was destroyed. Menéndez, no shirk when it came to opportunism, immediately forged north to the then relatively unpopulated French fort and destroyed it.

The Spanish retained control of the region despite repeated British attacks in 1586, 1668 and 1702.

The Brits

Beaten finally by fighting elsewhere, in the French & Indian (Seven Years) War, the Spanish ceded Florida in 1763 to Great Britain in a swap for Havana, Cuba. The British would hold the territory through the American Revolution, though as part of the Treaty of Paris ending that war, the fort was ceded back to Spain in 1783.

And the Spanish Again

With two rather significant interruptions, the Spanish ran the show from then until 1817, when the US moved in to hold the territory 'in trust' for Spain – rather in the same way shakedown artists 'protect' the merchandise of shopkeepers from potential 'damage' by 'bad guys'.

In 1812, a group of US-financed and -backed rebels took over Amelia Island, in far northeast Florida, and the next day turned over control to the US, but after the Spaniards expressed their rather understandable and considerable dismay over this, the US conceded that they really had no right to keep the place. The island's strategic location – that is, off the mainland – became key. In 1807, US President Jefferson established his Embargo Act and, in 1808, a prohibition on slavery importation, and Amelia Island became black market central: pirates, cut-throats and smugglers traded slaves and rum, and prostitutes roamed freely.

Then in 1817, Sir Gregor MacGregor, a Scottish mercenary with revolutionary experience in Venezuela, and the financial support of businessmen in Savannah and Charleston, hired on a force which again took over the island from the Spanish on June 29, 1817. When the money ran out, so did MacGregor, who left two lieutenants in command. But wait... there's more!

The US Moves In

The two left holding the bag, Lieutenants Ruggles Hubbard and Jared Irwin, formed a joint venture with a Mexico-based French pirate named Louis Aury (who was permitted to fly the Mexican flag anywhere he wanted, so long as he kicked back a percentage of his plunders to the Mexican government), and these three managed to turn the place into an even *more* scandalous town – it's said that there were more bars than street corners, and even more brothels.

Perhaps using moral outrage as an excuse to nab some nifty real estate, US troops moved in and took over in December. In a face-saving compromise, Spain officially turned Florida over to the US in 1821 in exchange for US promises to pay land claims of Spanish subjects (none of which, by the way, were ever paid).

In 1825, the US Army built the Cape Florida Lighthouse, the first permanent structure in South Florida, which was then marshy wetlands. In 1835, the Cape Florida Lighthouse was destroyed during the Seminole Wars. These would last seven years, resulting in the massive displacement of the Seminoles to reservations in the American West. (An interesting note is that the Seminoles are still technically at war with the USA – they say they never signed a valid peace treaty.)

In 1843, William F English settled in Miami, bringing investment, settlers and slaves. By 1850, a post office had been established, and a few dozen handfuls of people had moved into the area; by 1870, William B Brickel had established an Indian trading post at Miami.

In 1881, Henry B Lum bought up and cleared most of Miami Beach (for between 35¢ and $1.25 an acre) in an ill-conceived attempt to grow coconuts on the island. The plants he didn't lose to rabbits and deer he lost to poor soil, and by 1890 he admitted defeat. But the Lum family held on to much of the land.

Tuttle & Flagler

The first real shot at development of Miami Beach came with John S Collins, who bought the five-mile strip between the Atlantic and Biscayne Bay from what is now 14th to 67th Sts, and began selling parcels of beachfront property in 1896. But the two most significant arrivals were Julia Tuttle in 1875, and Henry Morrison Flagler in 1894.

Tuttle had stayed in the area earlier with her husband, who had tuberculosis, and after his death she returned to land she had inherited. Over the next 20 years, she also bought up quite a bit of property in the area.

Flagler, a developer and the business partner of John D Rockefeller in Standard Oil, had been developing the Florida coast at the northern end of the state, building resorts in St Augustine and Palm Beach. He built the

Florida East Coast Railroad, which extended down as far as Palm Beach, and Tuttle contacted Flagler with a proposition: if he would extend his railroad to Miami, Tuttle would split her property with him. Flagler wasn't interested.

Then in 1895, a record freeze enveloped most of the state of Florida, wiping out citrus crops and sending vacationers scurrying. Legend has it that Tuttle – said to be rather quick both on the uptake and with an 'I-told-you-so' – went into her garden at Fort Dallas, snipped off some flowers and sent them to Flagler, who hightailed it down to Miami to see for himself.

What he saw was a tropical paradise that was very warm indeed. Flagler and Tuttle came to terms, and Flagler announced the extension of the railroad. At that, thousands of people whose livelihoods had been wiped out by the big freeze, including citrus growers and workers and service industry workers like doctors and merchants, began to head down to Miami in anticipation of the boom that was to come.

Passenger train service to Miami began April 22, 1896, and in that year the city of Miami incorporated.

The Spanish-American War

The USA showed the world it was a power to be reckoned with during the 10-week-long Spanish-American War in 1898. As Cuba struggled for independence from Spanish rule, and as reports drifted back of Cuban farmers being gathered into prison camps, newspapers like William Randolph Hearst's *New York Journal* began a campaign of 'yellow journalism' which riled the American public. The stories ostensibly supported the 'humanitarian annexation' of Cuba, which perhaps not coincidentally would have been a culmination of the USA's Manifest Destiny and a darn happy windfall to US businessmen.

President William McKinley resisted intervention, but when the battleship *Maine* was destroyed in Havana's harbor, McKinley declared war on Spain; Congress ratified the Declaration on April 25.

The main fighting took place in two theaters: the South Pacific and Cuba. After handy victories in Manila and Guam, US army and volunteer regiments landed in Cuba in late June, including the Rough Riders (who actually had to leave all their horses in Florida), led by Leonard Wood and Theodore Roosevelt. Bully.

The Spanish surrendered on July 17.

20th-Century Miami

Flagler extended his railway into farming-rich sections in Homestead and Cutler, and in 1905 the Overseas Highway (a railroad causeway connecting the Keys to the mainland) for Flagler's railroad was begun, fueling another, bigger wave of settlement. Development of Miami and Miami Beach kicked off and in 1914, James Deering set to building the eye-popping Vizcaya mansion (see the Things to See & Do chapter).

The wave peaked during WWI, when the US military established an aviation training facility here. Many of the thousands who came to work and train settled here.

After the war, the first full-fledged Miami Boom (1923-25) was fueled not just by the area's idyllic beachfront location and perfect weather, but also by gambling and the fact that it never really took to the idea of prohibition – though it was illegal, liquor flowed freely throughout the entire Prohibition period.

But the Boom was cut short by a devastating hurricane, which was immediately followed by statewide recession and national depression.

After the Boom, though, Miami remained a favorite haunt of gangsters; Al Capone's mansion on Palm Island was a pleasure palace (it's now occupied by a Miami police officer), and he wasn't alone.

Through WWII

The Depression hit Miami quite badly, and the city and state were major supporters of Franklin Delano Roosevelt and his socialistic New Deal. When elected, Roosevelt made his way to Miami to thank South Florida for its support, and during that visit an attempt was made on his life.

In the mid-1930s, a mini-boom saw the construction of Miami Beach's famous Art Deco buildings, and this reasonably prosperous period continued until 1942, when a German U-Boat sank a US tanker off Florida's coast. The ensuing freak-out created a full-scale conversion of South Florida into a massive military base, training facility and staging area. The Army's central Anti-U-Boat Warfare School was based in Miami.

The Postwar Era

After the war, many of Miami's trainee soldiers returned and settled there; the city was maintaining its pre-war prosperity. In 1947, the Everglades (see the Excursions chapter), a sensitive marsh and swamp area, and home to thousands of indigenous wildlife species, was granted national park status by President Truman.

The 1950s

In the 1950s, Miami Beach had another boom, as the area became known as the 'Cuba of America': gamblers and gangsters, enticed by Miami's gambling, as well as its proximity to the fun, sun and fast times of Batista-run Cuba, moved in en masse. Even a hurricane didn't discourage people too badly. In 1954, Leroy Collins became the first southern governor to declare racial segregation 'morally wrong'. Oranges and cotton were becoming huge business in northern Florida, and as the aerospace

The Cuban Revolutions

While most people peg the influx of Cubans to the rise of Castro in 1959, Cubans have been flocking to Miami – and Florida – for over a century. The first large wave of immigration was in 1868, when socialist-minded cigar workers fleeing the Ten Year's war made Key West sort of an 'enlightened masses tobacco combine'.

Those enlightened masses, educated about the struggle in Cuba as they were, began demanding more and more money and benefits at a time when the economy was in a downturn. Cigar maker Vicente Martínez Ybor practically single-handedly squashed Key West's cigar industry by moving his factory to Tampa and steaming in Cuban laborers from Havana.

The move to Miami began during the Spanish-American War, but took off after Cuban independence and really soared after regular aviation between Miami and Havana was established in the late 1920s.

From then until Castro's Revolution – despite intrigue and the murderous Batista regime – were the swinging days of the Cuban-American relationship. Gamblers and hot shots poured into Cuba on hourly flights from Miami, and wealthy Cubans poured right back at Miami to buy clothes and American products.

What ended this reign has played a key role in US attitudes towards Cuba and Cubans to this very day.

Most people agree that Fulgencio Batista, whose regime controlled Cuba for almost 30 years before the rise of Fidel Castro, was a horrible gangster who terrorized a nation. And at the time, it seemed the best hope of losing him was to back his adversaries, a coalition headed by Fidel Castro that had been trying for years to oust Batista.

In late 1958 US President Eisenhower announced an arms embargo against the Batista government, which was interpreted by many to be tacit US support for Fidel Castro industry moved into Florida near the end of the decade, an entire 'Space Coast' was created around Cape Canaveral to support the development of the National Aeronautics & Space Administration (NASA)'s Mercury, Gemini and later, Apollo space programs.

Cuba & the Bay of Pigs

After the 1959 Cuban Revolution, Miami became flooded with anti-Castro immigrants, who in gathering to arrange a counterrevolutionary force managed to establish a permanent Cuban community in Miami.

A group of exiles formed the 2506th Brigade, sanctioned by the US Government, which provided help in the form of weapons and CIA training for the purpose of

Fidel Castro, fomenting revolutionary fervor

and his revolutionary coalition. Castro had made a formal promise to the coalition to hold free elections as soon as they took power.

Batista abdicated on January 1, 1959. There is some dispute as to just how forthcoming Castro was about his intentions, but over the next year and a half, Castro broke his promise of free elections, consolidated his power, and in a move that would set the tone of the next three decades, nationalized business – including major US-owned businesses – and property without compensation.

The US responded by canceling its Cuban sugar quota, and Castro, pressed for cash, turned to the Great Soviet Market. In the ultimate thumb-nose to the USA, which was reaching the height of its Cold War with the Soviets, Castro had allied himself with Moscow. ■

launching an attack on Cuba (memo to would-be Cuban dictators: enlist for your opponents the help of the CIA).

In April, 1961, the counterrevolutionaries (CRs) launched an attack against the beaches at Playa de Giron: the Bay of Pigs (actually the beach of pigs, but whatever). But the State Department had leaked warning to the Cubans – a *New York Times* correspondent says he heard about the impending attack weeks before it happened – and the pathetic, half-baked, poorly planned and badly executed attack was little more than an ambush.

And to add insult to injury, Kennedy, when the magnitude of the botch-up became clear, refused to send in air cover or naval support in the name of 'plausible deniability'; the first wave of CRs was left on the beach with their cheese in the wind – no reinforcements or supplies arrived. The CRs were all captured or killed (though all prisoners were released by Cuba about three months later).

Kennedy vs Krushchev

Kennedy and the CIA both looked rather silly after the fiasco, and that is probably why Kennedy stood his ground so firmly during the event that brought the world to the brink of nuclear war: the Cuban Missile Crisis.

Smelling blood after the Bay of Pigs fiasco, the USSR's General Secretary Nikita Krushchev began secretly installing missile bases in Cuba. By some stroke of luck – or perhaps by accident – the CIA managed to take photographs of the proceedings, which were shown to Kennedy on October 16, 1962.

The Kennedy administration debated what to do about it, and for almost a week after Kennedy was shown the photos, the Soviet embassy denied the existence of the bases.

On October 22, Kennedy went on national television and announced that the USSR was installing missiles on Cuba; that installing missiles in such close proximity to Florida was a direct threat to the safety and security of the country. He announced a naval 'quarantine' of Cuba (a nice euphemism for a naval blockade, which would have been an act of war) and further, that any attack on the USA from Cuba would be regarded as an attack by the USSR.

As tensions mounted, a flurry of letters passed between Washington and Moscow, beginning with 'Well, okay, we *do* have missiles but they're there as a deterrent not an offensive threat' and culminating in two offers from the Soviets on ending the stalemate.

CORINNA SELBY

Color coordination is everything.

CORINNA SELBY

Miami makeover in progress

The first, dated October 26, agreed to remove the missiles in exchange for a promise by the USA not to attack Cuba. The second, on the 27th, tied the removal to the USA's removal of similar sites it had in Turkey.

Publicly, Kennedy responded to the first offer; it was announced that the USA would not invade Cuba, and the Soviets began removing their missiles. Several months later, and with markedly less fanfare, the US removed its missiles from Turkey.

Miami's Cuban population swelled, as Cubans emigrated to the US. A special immigration center was established in Miami's Freedom Tower to handle the overflow – the Ellis Island of the South.

Racial Tensions

Miami's record of harmonious race relations was not altogether impressive. The Ku Klux Klan has been active in Florida since the 1920s, and bombings of black-owned housing were not unknown. Blacks were relegated to an area north of downtown known as Colored Town, later Overtown, but in the 1950s, as the city grew, many were displaced to the federal housing projects at Liberty City, a misnomer if ever there was one. See the Things to See & Do section for more information.

In 1965, the two 'freedom flights' that ran every day between Miami and Havana disgorged over 100,000 Cuban refugees. Sensing the tension that was building up between blacks and Cubans, Dr Martin Luther King, Jr pleaded with the two sides not to let animosity lead to bloodshed.

Riots broke out, skirmishes and acts of gang-style violence occurred. But not all were caused by simmering Cuban-black tensions: whites got in the fray as well. In 1968, a riot broke out after two white police officers arrested a 17-year-old black male, stripped him naked and hung him by his ankles from a bridge.

In 1970, the 'rotten meat' riot began when blacks picketed a white owned shop they had accused of selling spoiled meat. After three days of picketing, white officers attempted to disperse the crowds and fired on them with tear gas. Between 1970 and 1979, there were 13 other race-related violent confrontations.

The Mariel Boatlift

As Florida's economy began to recover in the late 1970s, after the oil crisis and recession, Fidel pulled a fast one and opened the floodgates, allowing anyone who wanted to leave Cuba access to the docks at Mariel.

Before the ink was dry on the proclamation, the largest flotilla ever launched for non-military purposes set sail (or paddle) from Florida in practically anything that would float to cover the 90 miles between there and Cuba. The Mariel Boatlift, as the largest of these would be called, brought 150,000 Cubans to Florida, including an estimated 25,000 prisoners and mental patients that Ol' Frisky Fidel had cleverly decided to foist off on the US Cuban population. The resulting economic, logistical and infrastructural strain on South Florida only added to still-simmering racial tensions.

The Liberty City Riot

These tensions would explode in Miami on May 17, 1980, when four white police officers, being tried on charges that they beat a black suspect to death while he was in custody, were acquitted by an all-white jury. When the verdict was announced, severe race riots broke out all over Miami, which lasted for three days.

The riots resulted in 18 deaths, $80 million in property damage, and 1100 arrests.

The 1980s

In the Roaring 1980s, the area gained prominence as the major East Coast entry port for drug dealers, their product, and the unbelievable sums of money that went along with them. As if to keep up, many Savings & Loans (S&Ls) opened here in newly built headquarters. While *Newsweek* called Miami America's Casablanca, locals dubbed it the City with the S&L Skyline.

CenTrust, a particularly heinous S&L, used a helicopter to load a marble staircase into its IM Pei-designed downtown headquarters, installed gold-plated faucets in the bathrooms and several million dollars worth of art on the walls before the company went down in flames (today the building is the NationsBank Tower, see the Things to See & Do chapter).

A plethora of businesses – both totally legitimate concerns as well as drug-financed fronts – and buildings sprung up all over Miami, and the downtown was completely remodeled. But it was still a city being reborn while in the grip of drug smugglers: shootouts were common, as were gangland slayings by cocaine cowboys.

The police, Coast Guard, Drug Enforcement Agency, Border Patrol and FBI were in a tizzy trying to keep track of it all. Roadblocks were set up blocking off the Overseas Highway to Key West. Police on I-95, the main

NBC-TV (COURTESY KOBAL)

Miami Vice – the show that made pink a cool color.

East Coast north-south highway, were given extraordinary powers to stop vehicles that matched a 'drug runner profile' – which, according to a public defender, amounted to the power to stop anyone.

And then it happened: *Miami Vice*.

The show, which starred Don Johnson and Philip Michael Thomas as two outrageously expensively – and yet pastel – clad narcotics detectives driving around in a Ferrari Testarossa and million dollar cigarette boats – was responsible for Miami Beach rising to international attention in the mid-1980s.

The show's unique look, its slick soundtrack and music video-style montages glamorized the rich life lived in South Florida, and before long people were coming down to see it.

Photographer Bruce Weber began to use South Beach as a grittily fashionable backdrop for modeling shoots in the early 1980s, which led to imitators and eventually to the situation that exists today: modeljam.

By the late 1980s, Miami Beach had risen to international Fabulousness. Celebrities were moving in, photo shoots from all over the world were being shot here, and the Art Deco District, having been granted federal protection, was going through a renovation that turned a city that had been filled with drug addicts into a showpiece of fashion and trendiness.

Hurricane Andrew

On August 24, 1992, Hurricane Andrew, with sustained 140 mph winds and gusts of up to 170 mph, slammed down over Homestead. By the time the hurricane had passed, it was the costliest disaster to ever hit the USA.

It wasn't worse because a) people had had time to prepare and evacuate, and b) the hurricane – while a Category 4 storm – was obliging enough to keep on moving and not sit on the area. But had the storm been 20 miles farther north when it hit land (as was expected), the storm surge surely would have destroyed Miami Beach. See the Dangers & Annoyances section in the Facts for the Visitor chapter for complete hurricane information.

The effects of Hurricane Andrew are still evident in many areas to the south of Miami. Throughout the book you'll read again and again of things that were either closed or significantly changed by the storm. From the loss of all Bill Baggs State Recreation Area's exotic plants – including about half a million Australian pines – to the extensive damage at Metrozoo, Andrew is pretty much a dirty word in South Florida.

Hurricane Andrew Stats

Deaths:	52
Industry destroyed:	tropical fruit, lime and nursery industries
Businesses destroyed:	8000
Jobs affected:	300,000
Property damage:	$30 billion
Evacuees:	300,000
Displacement:	250,000
Residents who permanently left the area:	100,000
Homes with minor damage:	40,000
Homes with major damage:	37,000
Homes destroyed:	8000
Mobile homes damaged:	10,500
Mobile homes destroyed:	8900
Apartments with minor damage:	3800
Apartments with major damage:	14,000
Apartments destroyed:	10,700
People left homeless:	175,000
Top wind speed:	clocked at 163 mph before the meter at the National Hurricane Center broke.

(Sources: Florida Department of Community Affairs, Division of Emergency Management and *Wire*.)

The Area Today

The area is riding the peak of a boom that's been going on for the past several years. Andrew barely affected the tourist industry, which is the city's economic backbone. And despite highly publicized crimes against tourists in 1993, Miami is now the third most popular city for international tourists after Los Angeles and New York. In 1993 11.6 million visitors came to Greater Miami.

But as the 1990s progress, drug smuggling has once again become fashionable. Smaller traffickers, who make runs between the Florida coast and 'mother' ships and air-drops in the Bahamas, are becoming common once again: during the opening ceremonies for the Brickell Ave Bridge, news cameras panned away from the speaking dignitaries to get a shot of a speedboat chase right beneath them on the Miami River, a route that a bridge tender said is like a hospital gown – wide open at the back. And in a truly 1990s twist, one drug smuggler was also charged with bringing 30 boxes of black market Cuban Cohiba cigars.

How long the Boom will last is debatable. On the one hand, more people than ever are coming. On the other, there are distinct murmurs amongst the European and supermodel crowd that South Beach is in danger of imploding and getting – gasp – passé.

Locals are not worried. After the film, TV and European fashion shoots; the Stallones and Schwarzeneggers, Sharon Stones and Madonnas, Versaces, and the thousands of oh-so-trendy people who swarm the chic neon-emblazoned cafés and boutiques of SoBe leave, South Beach will still be here, and better than ever.

CLIMATE

The area's warm weather may have been the only reason anyone would have dreamed of inhabiting the place at all. Call ☎ 229-4522 for a weather report.

Ideal conditions in Miami Beach exist between December and May, when temperatures average between around 60°F and 85° (16°C and 30°), and average rainfall is a scant 2.14 inches.

Summer can be summed up as very hot and humid with thunderstorms at 3 pm – June is the rainiest month (with an average of 7.14 inches), and temperatures average between 75°F and 88° (24°C and 32°). August is probably the hottest month, with average temperatures between 78°F and 87° (26°C and 31°), but you have to take the heat index – a product of heat and humidity – into account. It feels a *lot* hotter than 89°F when there's 90% humidity! See the Climate Chart appendix.

GOVERNMENT

Metropolitan Dade County, which includes the City of Miami and environs, has a two-tiered government system including a large unincorporated area and 27 separate municipalities. The Metro-Dade Board of County Commissioners consists of 13 commissioners elected by districts.

Metro-Dade provides services such as police and fire, zoning, garbage and trash collection and other services to the unincorporated areas, which make up about 60% of the county. In some cases, as in police and fire coverage, Metro-Dade may overlap with another municipality: Metro-Dade Police respond to certain calls made in, say, the city of North Miami Beach.

Buses and other public transport to the entire county fall under the domain of Metro-Dade.

Each municipality within Metro-Dade has its own city government, police force, fire department, etc.

ECONOMY

Miami's economy relies heavily on tourism, but its position as gateway to Latin America has given it powerhouse status as an international business city: over 400 multinational companies have operations in Miami, and 150 have their Latin American headquarters here, including AT&T, Sony, Toshiba, Apple, American Airlines, UPS, Eastman Kodak and Texaco. Miami customs processes 40% of all US exports to Latin America and the Caribbean. The city is also establishing itself as an international banking center: over 100 international banks call it home.

The Beacon Council (☎ 579-1300, fax 375-0271, see the Online Services appendix) is a nonprofit organization that provides business introductions, research studies and many business services at no charge.

POPULATION & PEOPLE

There are 93,000 residents in Miami Beach. Population figures for the City of Miami are misleading, as there are only 373,000 people living in the city limits, but 1.9 million in Metropolitan Dade County (See Government, above). An astounding 45.1% of the population is foreign born: Cubans are the largest group, followed by Canadians, Haitians, Germans and Jamaicans.

ARTS

Over the past decade, Miami's gentrification and redevelopment has resulted in an explosion of artistic and

NICK SELBY

NICK SELBY

NICK SELBY

Native Miamians, transplants and tourists:

NICK SELBY

NICK SELBY

Miami is a mosaic of ages, ethnicities and sexual persuasions.

cultural activity, and it's coming from all demographic sectors. Many artists who were formerly based in other areas of the country, notably the northeast, headed down here to take advantage of the lower real estate prices and the increase in quirky and affluent visitors.

The influx of foreigners to the area has resulted in a boom in Caribbean and South American art as well.

Literature

While inroads are being made in poetry and experimental fiction, the Miami literature scene remains primarily a hotbed of mystery, scandal and detective novels.

Of the poets emerging, most notable are Jeffrey Knapp and Adrian Castro (mainly spoken word performances), Campbell McGrath *(American Noise* and *Capitalism)*, Michael Hettich *(Small Boat* and *Immaculate Bright Rooms)*, John Balaban *(Blue Mountain* and *Words for My Daughter)* and Ricardo Pau-Llosa *(Cuba)*.

Pick up *Probable Cause, Latino Stuff Review* or *Mangrove*, all free journals of local poetry and literature available at Books & Books.

The area has over a dozen major suspense/thriller writers, and more are coming up every day. The local heavy hitters include Carl Hiaasen whose books *(Stormy Weather, Skin Tight, Native Tongue* and *Strip Tease)* offer snarling satire of South Florida and especially its tourists and developers; Pulitzer Prize-winning *Miami Herald* columnist Edna Buchanan *(Miami, It's Murder, Suitable for Framing, Nobody Lives Forever)*; Paul Levine, whose attorney Jake Lassiter and ex-coroner-sidekick traipse through intricate psychological suspense in books like *Mortal Sin, To Speak for The Dead* and *Night Vision*; Les Standiford, whose eco-thriller *Spill* is being made into a movie, and whose other novels star building contractor John Deal in *Deal to Die for, Done Deal* and the new *Book Deal*; the quintessential grizzled Miami author Charles Willeford, best known for *Miami Blues* and author of almost two dozen other titles including *The Way We Die Now* and *Sideswipe*; James W Hall, whose Florida Keys-based mysteries include *Mean Hightide, Beginning Algebra, Buzz Cut* and *Hard Aground*; and Dan Wakefield, who wrote *Going All the Way* and *Starting Over* in addition to *New York in the '50s*. Not to be forgotten, of course, is Elmore Leonard, author of dozens of books including *Swag, The Moonshine War, Get Shorty, Gold Coast, The Switch* and *Maximum Bob*.

Fred D'Aguiar, a poet who teaches at the University of Miami, has just seen two new novels published, and brothers Robert and Brian Antony are novelists, very well known around the Miami literature scene.

Keep one eye on Lynn Barrett, whose collection of short stories is entitled *The Land of Go*, and the other eye on Cuban-born mystery writer Carolina Garcia-Aguilera, whose first book, *Bloody Waters*, has been very successful.

Also incredibly well known is Dave Barry, the humorist whose columns are syndicated throughout the world. He's the author of books including *Dave Barry Is Not Making This Up, Dave Barry Turns 40, Dave Barry's Only Travel Guide You'll Ever Need* and *Dave Barry's Greatest Hits*.

The biggest news to come out of the Miami literature scene in recent days is *Naked Came the Manatee*, which began as a series by 13 of Miami's best known writers in *Tropic* magazine in the Sunday *Miami Herald*. The story involves the discovery (by a character much like Marjory Stoneman Douglas) of two metallic canisters that had landed in Biscayne Bay after a skiff crashed into a manatee. Both canisters turn out to contain what appears to be the head of Fidel Castro. The book, by authors including Les Standiford, Carl Hiaasen, Dave Barry, Paul Levine, Edna Buchanan, James W Hall, Vicky Hendricks, John Dufresne and Elmore Leonard, is published by Putnam; the payment is being donated to charity.

The last Friday of every month is Open Poetry Night at Books & Books (see the Shopping chapter) and every November, the Miami Book Fair is among the finest in the USA (see the Facts for the Visitor chapter).

The Butterfly Reading Series is held during the winter season upstairs at Tobacco Road (see the Things to See & Do chapter) on Tuesday evenings at 8 pm.

Florida International University (FIU) publishes *Gulf Stream*, a national magazine of poetry and literature. The FIU Creative Writing Program, with Standiford as current director, has spawned several new literary up-and-comers, most notably Vicky Hendricks *(Miami Purity)* and Barbara Parker *(Suspicion of Innocence)*.

Music & Theater

While classical music has a local hero in the innovative New World Symphony, and some local bands are gaining recognition, the biggest story in Miami is Latin and Caribbean music, including salsa, reggae, merengue, mambo, rhumba, cha-cha-cha and calypso. The big stars are Gloria Estefan, Celia Cruz, the androgynous Albita, Giolberto Santa Rosa, Willy Chirino and Jerry Rivera, and dance bands like Los Van Van, who perform in all-night *bailable* dance concerts. See the Entertainment chapter for venues.

The best times to see ensemble Cuban bands – with up to 20 musicians and singers – is during special celebrations, like the Calle Ocho Festival (see the Facts for the Visitor chapter).

And then there's classical. Every once in a while you hear of an idea so absolutely sensible and so totally reasonable that you kick yourself for not having thought it up yourself: the New World Symphony is one of those. Established in 1987, the NWS is described as a 'learning and performing experience for gifted graduates of the most prestigious music schools' – it is a collection of the best and the brightest young (usually in their twenties) musicians in the country spending about three years of post-graduate time performing with the NWS in concerts around the country and the world.

The members live in absolutely tiny rooms in a renovated Deco hotel near the Bass Museum, and spend pretty much all their waking hours either talking about, rehearsing, jamming or otherwise being involved with the performance of music. The energy level in the dorms is enough to guarantee a good concert, so by the time these people get into the fantastically renovated Lincoln Theatre for a concert – whoa, Nelly, hold onto your hat. See the Entertainment chapter for more information.

The best bets for new and independent theater productions are those at the smaller houses, like Florida Shakespeare Theatre, Ring Theatre and the Edge Area Stage; see the Entertainment chapter for full details.

Dance

There are 46 nonprofit dance organizations registered with the Metro-Dade cultural affairs council, and hundreds of dance-related businesses like studios, schools and production companies, and the mix of American, African, Cuban, Haitian, European and Latin American cultures is obvious in the productions you'll see here. The two biggest players are the Miami City Ballet and the Florida Dance Association; see the Dance section in the Entertainment chapter for more information on both of these and on other dance venues.

Art

In the mid-1980s, artists began to discover that South Beach was a place where they could get much more space, and live far more cheaply, than in other art centers, notably New York and Los Angeles.

The SoBe Boom was almost single-handedly responsible for the injections of cash that have fueled the art boom in South Beach. As recently as the early 1980s, Miami's art scene was virtually non-existent, and today – while the lack of many major galleries or a truly world-class museum is still an issue – the arts market can definitely be described as fledgling.

Real estate developers encouraged the arts by incorporating local artists' projects in the designs of private and public spaces, like the Margulies sculpture garden which includes works by Richard Serra, Isama Noguchi, Mark di Suivero and Jonathan Borofsky, all now on long-term loan to the campus of Florida International University (FIU). The South Florida Art Center (an artist-run organization) bought and leased buildings to provide affordable studios and exhibition space in the mid-'80s, which significantly helped to revitalize Lincoln Road. The Museum of Contemporary Art, designed by Charles Gwathmey, is an excellent example of a fusion of urban and cultural planning, placing a civic and cultural center within a residential and commercial area.

Established Miami artists today include Susan Banks, Carol Brown, Robert Thiele, Marilyn Gottlieb-Roberts, Sheila Friedman and Salvatore La Rosa. Transplants, artists well known in other markets who have now made their homes in Miami, include Jack Pierson, Felix Gonzalez-Torres, Robert Juarez and Kenny Scharf.

Another major impact on Miami's art community has been the influence of Cuban and Latin American artists like Felix Gonzalez-Torres, Jac Leirner, Ernesto Nero, Gabriel Orozco, Jorge Pardo, Jose Bedia (perhaps best known), Tomas Sanchez, Consuelo Castaneda, Teresita Fernandez, Maria Martinez-Canas and Wilfredo Lam.

The art galleries along Lincoln Road are the most accessible in the area, though tonier ones can be found in Coral Gables, and the Miami Design District is set to be home to many new galleries. See the Things to See & Do chapter for information on all these as well as the area's museums.

Film

At the turn of the century, before Hollywood, California was the shoe-in for world film central, places like Jacksonville and even Hollywood, Florida, were cranking out films. These days, with Miami being as hot as it is, filmmakers are flocking back to the area: in the last few years the Beach was featured in staggeringly successful films including *The Bodyguard*, *The Specialist*, *Ace Ventura: Pet Detective*, *True Lies*, *Get Shorty* and *Bird Cage*.

But from the beginnings of film the area has been featured in some of America's most beloved classics, like

The Cocoanuts (the Marx Brothers' first feature); *Where the Sidewalk Ends*, filmed entirely at Miami Studios; *Citizen Kane*, which used the south-Florida coastline as the setting for Xanadu, the largest pleasure palace in the world; *Key Largo* with Bogie and Bacall, *The Barefoot Mailman*; and three Bond films: *Dr No*, *Live & Let Die* and *Goldfinger*.

For a wonderful glimpse of Miami Beach in the worst of its recent troubles, rent a copy of *Black Sunday*, which features a car and foot chase through South Beach of the early 1980s – as witnessed by thousands of octogenarians in beach chairs.

Alec Baldwin played a total sicko in *Miami Blues*, based on the book by Charles Willeford, but by that time everyone in the world knew where Miami is, due to a television phenomenon: *Miami Vice*.

If you watch the show today (it's available in many of the larger video rental shops) you'll see the Beach at the turning point from Scuz-ball Alley to Fabulous beach spot. The series was filmed mainly in Miami Beach, but it's hilarious to see the way the action would jump to spots throughout the city that no film could possibly get away with today, now that the layout of the place is so universally recognizable.

The annual Miami International Film Festival, the Miami Beach Film Festival and the Miami Beach Film Society (see the Special Events section in Facts for the Visitor, and the Entertainment chapter) showcase the works of some of the area's rising talent as well as classics.

Independent filmmaking is slowly making inroads, and foreign productions are streaming into the area so quickly that the local Film Commission has placed an 'express permit application' form on the internet (see the Online Services appendix) to handle the overflow.

Architecture

While famous for three distinct architectural styles – Mediterranean Revival, towering skyscrapers and Art Deco – Miami is made up mainly of Boom-era construction with concessions to styles here and there.

Miami Beach is best known for its collection of Art Deco buildings. In the course of researching this book we became convinced of only one thing: a group of architects discussing Art Deco will undoubtedly behave in the same manner as would a group of economists discussing . . . anything. Few agree on anything except the derivation of the term, a contraction of the title of the 1925 Parisian *Exposition Internationale des Arts Décoratifs et Industriels Modernes*, in which a strong emphasis was placed upon *Arts Décoratifs*, decorative arts.

The Exposition wasn't the starting point, but rather was the dawn of a style that combined many existent forms – predominantly turn of the century and pre-WWI European movements such as Art Nouveau, Arts & Crafts, the Vienna Secession and Italian Futurism, and the more geometric Modernism.

Today the term loosely refers to the product of the morphing of many styles in decorative and applied arts as well as architecture that occurred *essentially* between the 19-teens and 1940s.

Deco can be broken into three distinct categories, European Art Deco, Northeast/WPA and 'Tropical' Art Deco.

European Art Deco Art Deco in Europe, which was fairly short-lived, had a lot to do with the Exposition itself, and was a play on classical Greek, Roman and Egyptian decorations using more modern materials like sandstone, steel and frosted glass in an almost cubist manner – plain lines as opposed to the froufrou associated with architecture of the time. Good examples are the Palais Chaillot, at the Trocadero in Paris, and the main post office at 13th St and Washington Ave. It maintains the austerity of a government building while achieving a modern look.

Northeast/WPA This is a category that's almost absent on the Beach but is seen mainly in the northeastern USA as well as in any project associated with FD Roosevelt's Works Projects Administration (WPA). It is characterized by heavy overtones of socialist ideals in concrete and granite, with lots of stainless steel and socialist frescos and big relief sculptures of workers – a perfect example is New York's (Japan's, actually) Rockefeller Center. This never caught on down here: there's no place for socialism in this bourgeois vacationland.

'Tropical' Art Deco The Deco of Miami Beach relied less on the implied meaning of decoration and more on simple geometric forms and colors, which worked well with the harsh sunlight to create interesting façades. It's important to note that the colors you now see are more garish than they originally were – earlier, many of the buildings were white with only a color trim, and more pastels were used as opposed to the neon coloring of today, which look very pretty but are essentially island color.

This branch of Deco – thrown up in Boom-era construction – is often asymmetrical and inexpensively constructed of masonry and stucco with applied color. This is unlike the other two, richer styles of Deco, which relied on the color of the materials like the pinkish hue of sandstone or the pink, brown or gray of granite.

It's also interesting to note that the value of these buildings on Miami Beach is based more on the sheer number of protected historic buildings: individually, the inexpensively constructed houses would be worth far less.

RELIGION

The area's residents are predominantly Christians, but there are significant numbers of Jews here as well: many are transplants from the northeastern USA but there are also a healthy number of Russian-Jewish and Cuban-Jewish immigrants. Many of the area's Jews are Reform, who do not adhere as strictly to the religious and social teachings of the Torah, as opposed to Orthodox. The area is also the home of the Florida branch of the Chabad Lubovitchers, a faction of Judaism that proselytizes within the Jewish faith: if a long-haired, bearded man

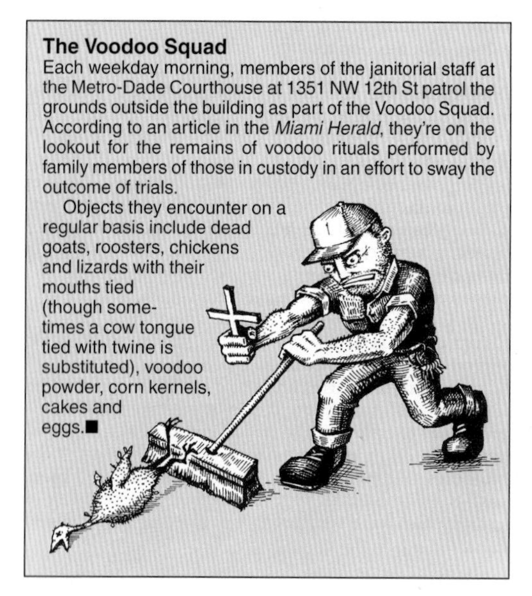

The Voodoo Squad

Each weekday morning, members of the janitorial staff at the Metro-Dade Courthouse at 1351 NW 12th St patrol the grounds outside the building as part of the Voodoo Squad. According to an article in the *Miami Herald*, they're on the lookout for the remains of voodoo rituals performed by family members of those in custody in an effort to sway the outcome of trials.

Objects they encounter on a regular basis include dead goats, roosters, chickens and lizards with their mouths tied (though sometimes a cow tongue tied with twine is substituted), voodoo powder, corn kernels, cakes and eggs. ■

dressed in a black suit and white shirt and wearing a hat or *yarmulke* asks you a) if you're Jewish and b) to step inside a recreational vehicle, you've just met a Lubovitcher.

Afro-Caribbean area religions include *Santeria* a synchronism of the west African *Yoruba* religion with Catholicism. It was brought to Cuba by slaves who settled there, and is primarily practiced in Cuba. Voodoo is Yoruba as practiced by Haitians. Both of these religions practice animal sacrifice as a token of fidelity to the gods and spirits, and it's not uncommon to come upon animal remains at various places around the city, like along the Miami River, in parks and, strangely, near the Bass Museum.

Candomblé is an African religion as brought to northeast Brazil.

LANGUAGE

'One of the nicest things about Miami,' goes an old joke, 'is how close it is to the USA.' Indeed, while English is the predominant language in the USA, Miami's proximity to countries that have tended to generate mass refugee migrations has resulted in an above-average number of non-English speaking, and some may say intentionally unassimilated, foreigners.

It's a somewhat unique situation in the USA. While pockets of foreigners have gravitated to other large cities, notably New York, Chicago and Los Angeles, there seems to be a higher degree of linguistic assimilation there than here, where as some put it, 'Them Cubans just won't talk English like everybody else.'

Visitors can get away with English only, but to do that is to essentially write off experiencing a huge chunk of Miami culture and life. While we've never had cause to speak Creole, we found that our Spanish was indispensable when we lived here.

Spanish is the main language in almost every shop, café, coin laundry and restaurant in Little Havana, and in a surprising number of businesses elsewhere in the city.

Spanish

Books When you go, take along Lonely Planet's *Latin American Spanish Phrasebook* by Anna Cody, which is comprehensive and compact. If you're planning on romancing some Latin types, the absolute finest resource for you is *Hot Spanish for Guys and Girls* and *Hot Spanish for Guys and Guys*, both published by BabelCom Books (New York), and both containing an amazing number of useful phrases from 'I'd like to hold your hand' to 'lick around the edges'.

Pronunciation Spanish has five vowels: **a**, **e**, **i**, **o** and **u**. They are pronounced something like the highlighted letters of the following English words: f**a**ther, **e**nd, mar**i**ne, **o**r and p**u**ll. The stress is placed on the syllable with an accent over it (México=MEH-hiko) or the second to last syllable (hasta luego=AH-sta loo-EH-go).

Greetings & Civilities

hello/hi	*hola*
good morning/good day	*buenos días*
good evening/good night	*buenas noches*
see you later	*hasta luego*
goodbye	*adiós*
pleased to meet you	*mucho gusto*
please	*por favor*
thank you	*gracias*
you're welcome	*de nada*
excuse me	*perdóneme*

Useful Words & Phrases

yes	*sí*
no	*no*
good/OK	*bueno*
bad	*malo*
best	*mejor*
more	*más*
less	*menos*
very little	*poco* or *poquito*

Buying

How much does it cost?	*¿Cuanto cuesta?*
I want . . .	*Quiero . . .*
What do you want?	*¿Qué quiere?*
Do you have . . . ?	*¿Tiene . . . ?*
Is/are there . . . ?	*¿Hay . . . ?*
I understand.	*Entiendo.*
I do not understand.	*No entiendo.*
Do you understand?	*¿Entiende usted?*
Please speak slowly.	*Por favor hable despacio.*

Getting Around

street	*calle*
avenue	*avenida*
corner (of)	*esquina (de)*
block	*cuadra*
to the left	*a la izquierda*
to the right	*a la derecha*

straight ahead	*adelante*
Where is . . . ?	*¿Donde está . . . ?*
the bus station	*el terminal de gua gua*
the train station	*la estación del ferrocarril*
bus	*gua gua* or *autobús*
train	*tren*
taxi	*taxi*
toilet	*sanitario*

Numbers

0	*cero*	13	*trece*
1	*un, uno* (m), *una* (f)	14	*catorce*
		15	*quince*
2	*dos*	16	*dieciséis*
3	*tres*	17	*diecisiete*
4	*cuatro*	18	*dieciocho*
5	*cinco*	19	*diecinueve*
6	*seis*	20	*veinte*
7	*siete*	30	*treinta*
8	*ocho*	40	*cuarenta*
9	*nueve*	50	*cincuenta*
10	*diez*	100	*cien*
11	*once*	500	*quinientos*
12	*doce*	1000	*mil*

Facts for the Visitor

WHEN TO GO

See the Climate section in Facts about Miami for specifics on temperature and rainfall. The boundaries of the 'season' down here – which used to be limited to winter – have been blurred by the stampede of models, photo and film shoots and a huge number of people moving to the area, both from the US and abroad. But the most popular time to come here is still between December and May.

The advantage of coming during the early summer, despite the higher temperatures and increased rainfall, is that you get more of the place to yourself.

The hurricane season – from June 1 to November 30 – can be a perfectly pleasant time to visit, but you've got to be aware that one little hurricane can ruin a holiday. See the Dangers & Annoyances section for more information.

WHAT TO BRING

Miami and the Beaches are very casual places, until they're not. Minimal requirement for Miami Beach is a pair of cut-off jeans and a bathing suit, with an optional set of in-line skates, but people wear just about anything they want. But that casualness is a tricky bugger: Cubans dress very fashionably for a night out, and for South Beach nightlife you're really going to want to dress to the nines – see the Entertainment chapter for more.

NICK SELBY

You'd do well to bring along some rain gear and a sturdy umbrella (rain storms here tend to get very windy).

Key on the list is suntan lotion. Bring lots of this stuff (see the Dangers & Annoyances section for more information), as well as good sunglasses. Toiletries, hygiene and first aid products are readily available, so if you forget something you can get it here. The area is a very inexpensive place to buy clothes, so plan on leaving with more than you brought.

ORIENTATION

The City of Miami covers an enormous, sprawling area that's subdivided into neighborhoods and sections, and is adjacent to several cities – city lines are so indistinct that you may not even realize you've left Miami and entered, say, Coral Gables or Hialeah. Neighborhoods and cities are detailed below.

Miami is on the mainland, while the city of Miami Beach is on a thin barrier island about four miles east, across Biscayne Bay – locals call it the Billion Dollar Sandbar.

On the mainland the street numbering system is based on north-south and east-west dividers. With the exception of Coral Gables and Hialeah (whose founding fathers should be arrested for making their street systems so stupid – see below) getting around the area is a snap – despite how intimidating it looks on a map.

The north-south divider is Flagler St; the east-west divider is Miami Ave; prefixes are given to streets – N, W, S, E, NW, NE, SW, SE – based on that street's position relative to the intersection of Flagler St and Miami Ave.

Most avenues and streets are numbered: avenues begin at 1 and count upwards the farther east and west they are from Miami Ave, so E 1st Ave would be one block east of Miami Ave, while W 42nd Ave would be 42 blocks west of Miami Ave. Streets are numbered similarly, increasing in number progressively the farther north or south of Flagler St, so N 1st St would be one block north of Flagler, etc.

With the exception of Coral Gables and Hialeah, most streets, terraces, lanes and drives run east-west and most avenues, places, courts and roads run north-south.

Addresses

Most of Miami operates on the 'hundred-block' system, or the first digits of the address is a product of its lower-number cross-street. So a specific address is based on the streets it's between: 7012 NW blah-blah-blah is on blah-blah-blah between 70th and 71st Sts, northwest of Flagler St and Miami Ave.

Miami Beach

Most visitors aren't here for the City of Miami itself, but rather to visit the City of Miami Beach, an entirely separate municipality built on a barrier island four miles east of Miami across Biscayne Bay. In this book, despite common practice, we break the Beach up into two distinct regions: South Beach (SoBe) and Northern Miami Beach.

South Beach's grid closely follows Miami's – streets run east-west and avenues run north-south, but the avenues are named, not numbered, and there are no directional sectors like NW or SE. Note there are major differences between Northern Miami Beach and South Beach, which is far more than the trendiness of the latter and the stodginess of the former.

South Beach South Beach, on the widest section of the island, has a grid which mostly runs due north-south and east-west, except for curving bits of Alton Rd and the fact that Washington and Collins Aves and Ocean Drive run at a 20° angle northeast to the main grid system.

Washington Ave is the bustling main drag; Collins Ave the famous Deco hotel-lined thoroughfare; and the chic and pretentious outdoor cafés and restaurants of Ocean Drive overlook the wide Miami Beach Atlantic shorefront.

Alton Rd is the utilitarian main drag on the west end of town, gaining in popularity quickly as the sexier eastern end of town becomes more and more crowded.

Lincoln Road is pedestrian-only between Washington Ave at the east and Alton Rd at the west; the strip is called Lincoln Road Mall and would seem to be perpetually under construction.

South Pointe is below 5th St at the southern tip of Miami Beach, directly across Government Cut from Fisher Island.

Northern Miami Beach Northern Miami Beach (which we have arbitrarily decided as being north of 43rd St and which should not be confused with an entirely different city on the mainland called, funnily enough, North Miami Beach) is divided by narrow Indian Creek, which separates Collins Ave on the thin strip of land at the east – almost exclusively lined with high-rise condominiums and luxury hotels – from the residential districts at the west. South of La Gorce Island is the La Gorce Country Club. Alton Rd heads straight through this exclusive neighborhood and connects with Collins Ave at 63rd St.

The northern border of Miami Beach is 96th St. If you're up this far and need to get west to Miami, take the Broad Causeway (50¢ toll) from the City of Surfside at 96th St.

Downtown Miami

Downtown Miami is a fairly straightforward grid, with Flagler Ave as much the main drag as any. The downtown area is divided by the Miami River, crossed by the newly-renovated Brickell Ave Bridge – which sports a statue of a Tequesta warrior and his family – and continues on the south side of the river.

The Greyhound station is at the corner of NE 7th St and Biscayne. The Port of Miami is on Dodge Island, diagonally opposite the now-abandoned downtown trademark, the Freedom Tower. The Miami Arena is between NW 7th and NW 8th Sts just west of N Miami Ave. A new Miami Arena complex is said to be under construction between Bayside Marketplace and the Port of Miami.

Coral Gables

The lovely Mediterranean-style City of Coral Gables is essentially bordered by Calle Ocho at the north, Sunset Drive (SW 72nd St/Hwy 986) at the south, Le Jeune Rd (SW 42nd Ave/Hwy 953) at the east and Red Rd (SW 57th Ave/Hwy 959) at the west. US Hwy 1 slashes through at a 45° angle from northeast to southwest.

Now here's the fun part: the address system in Coral Gables is bass-ackwards when compared to Miami: avenues here run east-west, while streets run north-south.

The main campus of the University of Miami is located just south of the enormous Coral Gables Biltmore Golf Course, north of US Hwy 1.

Maps

All rental car companies are required by law to hand out decent city and area maps when you rent a car – Alamo's isn't bad at all. Rand McNally, AAA and Dolph Map Company all make area maps of Miami. Freebies are usually not very good as they're simplified to the point of being totally inaccurate. You can get somewhat usable free maps from the Greater Miami & the Beaches Convention & Visitor's Bureau (see below).

TOURIST OFFICES

Local Tourist Offices

There are several tourist offices in the Greater Miami Area, all of which hand out visitor guides, pamphlets, advice of varying usefulness and, especially, discount tickets and flyers to many area attractions.

Miami Beach The Art Deco Welcome Center (☎ 531-3484) at 1001 Ocean Drive, run by the Miami Design Preservation League, has tons of Deco District information. The MDPL also organizes walking tours and bicycle tours of the District (see Organized Tours in the Miami Beach section of the Things to See & Do chapter). The Miami Beach Chamber of Commerce (☎ 672-1270) has an office at 1920 Meridian Ave; it's open Monday to Friday 8.30 am to 6 pm, Saturday 10 am to 4 pm, closed Sunday.

Downtown Miami The Greater Miami & the Beaches Convention & Visitor's Bureau (☎ 539-3063, 800-933-8448, 800-283-2702) has their fantabulously luxurious headquarters on the 27th floor at 791 Brickell Ave, about a five-minute walk south of the Miami River. They also operate a tourist information center at Bayside Marketplace (☎ 539-2980), 401 Biscayne Blvd.

The Black Archives Historical & Research Foundation of South Florida (☎ 636-2390) in Liberty City at 5400 NW 22nd Ave, Building B, has information about black culture and can arrange tours of Liberty City and other areas of the city.

Coral Gables The Coral Gables Chamber of Commerce (☎ 446-1557) at 50 Aragon Ave has that city's absolutely excellent tourist maps and other information.

Advance Tourist Information

For information on Florida from the UK, contact the Florida Division of Tourism (☎ (0171) 727-1661), 18/24 West Bourne Grove, 4th floor, London W25 RH. Call them to order their Florida Information Pack, or the 24-hour hotline at ☎ (0891) 600-555 for information on Florida tours. To get their information pack by mail, send a £2 cheque made out to ABC Florida to PO Box 35 Oxton OX14 4XF.

The Latin American office is in Miami (!), run by JHJ & Associates (☎ 670-0231), 9200 S Dadeland Blvd, 603, Miami, FL 33156.

DOCUMENTS

With the exception of Canadians, who need only proper proof of Canadian citizenship, all foreign visitors to the USA must have a valid passport and many also require a US visa. It's a good idea to keep photocopies of these documents; in case of theft, they'll be a lot easier to replace.

If you could, on the best of days, be mistaken as being under 30, carry a photo ID card with your age on it – a major ID like your national identity card or your driver's license. Anyone who appears to be under 30 is asked for ID at bars and nightclubs.

You'll also want to have an International Student ID Card (ISIC), which can get you substantial discounts at museums and tourist attractions and some airfares.

Visas

A reciprocal visa-waiver program applies to citizens of certain countries who may enter the USA for stays of 90 days or less without having to obtain a visa. Currently these countries are: Andorra, Austria, Belgium, Brunei, Denmark, Finland, France, Germany, Iceland, Italy, Japan, Liechtenstein, Luxembourg, Monaco, the Netherlands, New Zealand, Norway, San Marino, Spain, Sweden, Switzerland, and the UK. Under this program you must have a roundtrip ticket on an airline that participates in the visa-waiver program; you must have proof of financial solvency; sign a form waiving the right to a hearing of deportation; and you will not be allowed to extend your stay beyond the 90 days. Consult with your travel agent or contact the airlines directly for more information.

Other travelers (except Canadians) will need to obtain a visa from a US consulate or embassy. In most countries the process can be done by mail, but in others, notably Turkey, Poland and Russia, you'll need to go in person to the nearest US consulate or embassy.

Your passport should be valid for at least six months longer than your intended stay in the USA and you'll need to submit a recent photo with the application. Documents of financial stability and/or guarantees from a

US resident are sometimes required, particularly for those from third world countries.

Visa applicants may be required to 'demonstrate binding obligations' that will insure their return back home. Because of this requirement, those planning to travel through other countries before arriving in the USA are generally better off applying for their US visa while they are still in their home country, rather than while on the road.

The validity period for US visitor visas depends on what country you're from. The length of time you'll be allowed to stay in the USA is ultimately determined by US immigration authorities at the port of entry.

Visa Extensions

Tourist visitors are usually granted a six-month stay on first arrival. If you try to extend that time the first assumption will be that you are working illegally, so come prepared with concrete evidence that you've been traveling extensively and will continue to be a model tourist. Extensions are manhandled by the US Government Justice Department's Immigration & Naturalization Service (INS; ☎ 536-5741) at 7880 N Biscayne Blvd. Get there early, bring along a good, long book and pack a lunch.

Other Documents

Bring your driver's license if you intend to rent a car; visitors from some countries may find it wise to back up their national license with an International Driving Permit, available from their local auto club. A comprehensive travel or health insurance policy is very important for overseas visitors and they should bring a membership card or documentation.

EMBASSIES & CONSULATES

US Embassies Abroad

US diplomatic offices abroad include the following:

Australia
21 Moonah Place,
Yarralumla ACT 2600
(☎ (6) 270 5900)

Austria
Boltzmanngasse 16, A-1091,
Vienna (☎ (1) 313-39)

Belgium
Blvd du Régent 27, B-1000,
Brussels (☎ (2) 513 38 30)

Canada
100 Wellington St, Ottawa,
Ontario 1P 5T1
(☎ 613-238-5335)

Denmark
Dag Hammarskjolds Allé 24, Copenhagen
(☎ 31 42 31 44)

France
2 rue Saint Florentin, 75001 Paris (☎ (1) 42 96 12 02)

Germany
Deichmanns Au 29, 53179 Bonn (☎ (228) 33 91)

Greece
91 Vasilissis Sophias Blvd, 10160 Athens
(☎ (1) 721-2951)

India
Shanti Path, Chanakyapuri 110021, New Delhi
(☎ (11) 60-0651)

Ireland
42 Elgin Rd, Ballsbridge, Dublin (☎ (1) 687 122)

Israel
71 Hayarkon St, Tel Aviv
(☎ (3) 517-4338)

Italy
Via Vittorio Veneto 119a-121, Rome (☎ (6) 46 741)

Japan
1-10-5 Akasaka Chome, Minato-ku, Tokyo
(☎ (3) 224-5000)

Korea
82 Sejong-Ro, Chongro-ku, Seoul (☎ (2) 397-4114)

Mexico
Paseo de la Reforma 305, Cuauhtémoc, 06500 Mexico City (☎ (5) 211-00-42)

Netherlands
Lange Voorhout 102, 2514 EJ, The Hague
(☎ (70) 310 92 09)

New Zealand
29 Fitzherbert Terrace, Thorndon, Wellington
(☎ (4) 722 068)

Norway
Drammensvein 18, Oslo
(☎ (22) 44 85 50)

Russia
Novinskiy Bulvar 19/23, Moscow (☎ (095) 252-2451)

Singapore
30 Hill St, Singapore 0617
(☎ 338-0251)

South Africa
877 Pretorius St, Box 9536, Pretoria 0001
(☎ (12) 342-1048)

Spain
Calle Serrano 75, 28006 Madrid (☎ (1) 577 4000)

Sweden
Strandvagen 101, S-115 89 Stockholm (☎ (8) 783 5300)

Switzerland
Jubilaumsstrasse 93, 3005 Berne (☎ (31) 357 70 11)

Thailand
95 Wireless Rd, Bangkok
(☎ (2) 252-5040)

UK
5 Upper Grosvenor St, London W1
(☎ (0171) 499 9000)

Foreign Consulates in Miami

Check under Consulates in the white pages of the telephone book for diplomatic representation in Miami. Embassies are located in Washington, DC, the US capital. Be patient: Miami is considered a cushy post by the always-hardworking diplomatic set, and some consular offices have ridiculously limited hours and act as if you're really interfering with their day if you ask for things. Most consulates are in Miami, but a few are in Coral Gables.

Consulates include:

Argentina
800 Brickell Ave, Penthouse 1 (☎ 373-7794)

Austria
1454 NW 17th Ave, Suite 200 (☎ 325-1561)

Bahamas
25 SE 2nd Ave, Suite 818 (☎ 373-6295)

Bolivia
25 SE 2nd Ave, Suite 545 (☎ 358-3450)

Brazil
2601 S Bayshore Drive, Suite 800 (☎ 285-6200)

Canada
200 S Biscayne Blvd, Suite 1600 (☎ 579-1600)

Chile
1110 Brickell Ave, Suite 616 (☎ 373-8623)

Colombia
280 Aragon Ave, Coral Gables (☎ 448-5558)

Costa Rica
1600 NW 42nd Ave, Suite 300 (☎ 871-7485)

Dominican Republic
1038 Brickell Ave (☎ 358-3220)

Ecuador
1101 Brickell Ave, M 102 (☎ 539-8214)

El Salvador
300 Biscayne Blvd Way (☎ 371-8850)

France
2S Biscayne Blvd, Suite 1710 (☎ 372-9798)

Germany
100 N Biscayne Blvd (☎ 358-0290)

Guatemala
300 Sevilla Ave, Suite 210, Coral Gables (☎ 443-4828)

Honduras
300 Sevilla Ave, Suite 201, Coral Gables (☎ 447-8927)

Israel
100 N Biscayne Blvd, Suite 1800 (☎ 358-8111)

Italy
1200 Brickell Ave (☎ 374-6322)

Jamaica
25 SE 2nd Ave, Suite 842 (☎ 374-8431)

Mexico
1200 NW 78th Ave, Suite 200 (☎ 716-4979)

Netherlands
801 Brickell Ave, Suite 918 (☎ 789-6646)

Nicaragua
8370 W Flagler St, Suite 220 (☎ 220-6900)

Paraguay
2800 Biscayne Blvd, Suite 700 (☎ 573-5588)

Peru
444 Brickell Ave, Suite 135 (☎ 374-1305)

Portugal
1901 Ponce de León Blvd, Coral Gables (☎ 444-6311)

South Korea
201 S Biscayne Blvd (☎ 372-1555)

Spain
2655 Le Jeune Rd, Suite 203, Coral Gables (☎ 446-5511)

UK
1001 S Bayshore Drive, Suite 2110 (☎ 374-1522)

Uruguay
1077 Ponce de León Blvd, Suite B, Coral Gables (☎ 443-9764)

Venezuela
1101 Brickell Ave, Suite 901 (☎ 577-3834)

Australian and New Zealand citizens may contact the British or Canadian consulates for emergency assistance, as neither country maintains consular offices in Miami.

CUSTOMS & IMMIGRATION

You'll pass first through Immigration – which checks your passport and visa – and if they're happy they'll pass you through to the next section, where you clear customs. US customs allows each person over the age of 21 to bring one liter of liquor and 200 cigarettes duty free into the USA. US citizens are allowed to import, duty free, $400 worth of gifts from abroad while non-US citizens are allowed to bring in $100 worth. See Currency below for information on bringing in money.

Due to Miami's infamous popularity as a drug-smuggling gateway, customs officers in Miami are known to be . . . let's call them *thorough* in their examination of backpackers and other travelers who may fit a profile they have of a 'mule', or someone ferrying narcotics. They may also not be very polite – but you should be, and you should dress neatly and carry a large wad of cash or travellers cheques and credit cards – or show signs of prosperity lest they think you're here to work illegally.

HIV & Entering the USA

Anyone entering the USA who is not a US citizen is subject to the authority of the Immigration & Naturalization Service (INS), who can keep someone from entering or staying in the USA by excluding or deporting them, meaning they have the power to prevent entrance or to return a visitor from whence they came. Being HIV-positive is not a grounds of deportation, but it is a grounds of exclusion, and the INS can refuse to admit HIV-positive visitors to the country.

Although the INS does not test people for HIV when they try to enter the USA, the form for the non-immigrant visa asks: 'Have you ever been afflicted with a communicable disease of public health significance?' The INS will try to exclude anyone who answers 'yes' to this question.

If you do have HIV but can prove to the consular officials you are the spouse, parent or child of a US citizen or legal resident (green-card holder), you are exempt from the exclusionary rule.

For legal immigration information and referrals to immigration advocates, visitors may contact the National Immigration Project of the National Lawyers Guild (☎ 617-227-9727), 14 Bacon St, Suite 506, Boston, MA 02108, and the Immigrant HIV Assistance Project, Bar Association of San Francisco (☎ 415-267-0795), 685 Market St, Suite 700, San Francisco, CA 94105. ■

Both Customs and Immigration officers have the right to drag you into a room for questioning, or worse; Corinna's even been hauled into the back room here in Miami, and she's got a green card! Her tip:

> Be as polite as you can. I was detained, it turned out, to verify my resident visa was still current, but no one told me that – they just said, 'Follow me.' The Immigration officer in the holding area told me to 'sit down and shutup', and when I asked why I was being detained he told me that if I wanted to make things difficult for myself I could keep asking questions. I left four hours later.

If you are taken back there, one thing to make certain of is that a representative of your airline (who can call your relatives and get you information) knows you're there and who you want told of your predicament.

MONEY

Currency

The US dollar (US$ or just $) is divided into 100 cents with coins of one cent (penny), five cents (nickel), 10 cents (dime), 25 cents (quarter), and relatively rare 50 cents (half dollar). There are even rarer $1 coins in circulation; they're unpopular and used almost exclusively at post office stamp machines and toll booths as change.

Banknotes are called bills. Be sure to check the corners for amounts, as they're all the same size and color! Circulated bills come in denominations of $1, $2 (rare), $5, $10, $20, $50 and $100.

In March, 1996, the US Treasury introduced a new $100 bill, featuring a larger, off-center portrait of Benjamin Franklin. The older $100s will stay in circulation for the foreseeable future.

There are three straightforward ways to handle money in the US: cash, US dollar travellers cheques and credit cards, with the proliferation of ATMs (Automated Teller Machines, see below) facilitating the process.

Regulations US law permits you to bring in, or take out, as much as US$10,000 in American or foreign currency, travellers cheques or letters of credit without formality. Larger amounts of any or all of the above – there are no limits – must be declared to customs.

Travellers Cheques

Travellers cheques are virtually as good as cash in the USA; most establishments (not just banks) will accept them just like cash. The major advantage of travellers cheques over cash is that they can be replaced if lost or stolen. But changing travellers cheques denominated in a foreign currency (while much easier than it used to be) is rarely convenient or economical.

Get larger denomination US$100 cheques, as you may be charged service fees when cashing them at banks.

Automated Teller Machines (ATMs)

You can often withdraw money straight from your bank account at home. Most ATMs in the area accept bank cards from the Plus and Cirrus systems, the two largest ATM networks in the USA. Honor is another popular network.

You can also easily obtain cash from bank ATMs all over the area with a Visa or MasterCard and a PIN (personal identification number).

The disadvantage of credit card cash advances is that you are charged interest on the withdrawal beginning immediately until you pay it back.

Credit Cards

Major credit cards are widely accepted by car rental agencies and most hotels, restaurants, gas stations, shops, and larger grocery stores. The most commonly accepted cards are Visa, MasterCard (Eurocard) and American Express.

In fact, you'll find it hard to perform certain transactions without a credit card – it's virtually impossible to rent a car without one. Even if you loathe them and prefer to rely on travellers cheques and ATMs, it's a good idea to carry one (Visa or MasterCard are your best bets) for emergencies.

Changing Money

The best advice for people who need to exchange a foreign currency for US$ is to do so at home, before you arrive. Exchange rates are generally poorer in the US than at home. For example, when banks in Munich were routinely charging DM1.41 for $1, banks in the US were charging as much as DM1.53 for $1.

If you must change money in the states, you're probably best off at a real bank, as opposed to an exchange office. Barnett Bank (☎ 800-553-9026) offers foreign exchange services in all its branches, and has branches all through the city and the state. Worse rates are available at some branches of NationsBank (☎ 800-367-6262) and SunBank (☎ 591-6000). Shop around if you have time.

Private exchange offices generally offer the least competitive rates and charge the highest commissions. There are private exchange offices around town, such as in places like drugstores and record shops.

Some exchange offices:

American Express
330 Biscayne Blvd, Suite 100 (☎ 358-7350)
Thomas Cook
155 SE 3rd Ave (☎ 374-0655)
SunTrust
777 Brickell Ave, ☎ 591-6000,
also at Lincoln Road at Alton Rd
Chequepoint
865 Collins Ave (☎ 538-5348)

Exchange Rates These are particularly volatile, but *at press time* exchange rates were:

Australia	A$1	=	US$0.78
Canada	C$1	=	US$0.73
Germany	DM1	=	US$0.66
France	FF1	=	US$0.19
Hong Kong	HK$10	=	US$1.30
Japan	¥100	=	US$0.93
New Zealand	NZ$1	=	US$0.68
Singapore	S$1	=	US$0.71
UK	£1	=	US$1.51

CORINNA SELBY

Traveler's Palm

Costs

You can really get away with the amount of luxury or penury you're striving to hit: youth hostels and cheap hotels abound, and there are good choices for every price range from backpacker to business traveler.

Getting here is sometimes stunningly cheap, especially from the UK or Germany which are rife with package deals. It's also cheap from the US, especially if you take a Greyhound or drive here. See the Getting There & Away chapter for more information.

Florida rental cars tend to run cheaper than in most other states; rates start at around $20 a day (or $1.99 per hour with no minimum at Value; see Getting Around for more information) or $100 a week, but you have to seek those out; an average rate can be figured at $25/140.

If you're staying in Miami Beach for most of or the whole time, a car can be hell for the parking situation (See Getting Around) and you're better off on foot or bicycle (rentals run around $10 to 15 a day or $40 to 50 a week; see the Activities section under Things to See & Do).

Tipping

Tipping is a US institution which can, initially, be a little confusing for foreign visitors. Waitstaff at restaurants, bartenders, taxi drivers, bellhops, hotel maids and others are paid a mere stipend. Owners and indeed American culture expect that customers compensate these people directly: the tips are actually part of their salary.

So tipping is not really an option; the service has to be absolutely *appalling* before you should consider not tipping. In a bar or restaurant a tip is customarily 15% (for a standard tip, double the tax and add a smidge) of the bill; a tip for outstanding service in a restaurant is 20%. You needn't tip at fast-food restaurants or self-serve cafeterias. Hotel maids should be tipped about $1.50 a day, unless they don't deserve it. Tip daily, as maids rotate shifts.

Just Say 'No! No!' to Tipping Twice

There's an insidious plot afoot in many Miami-area restaurants: a 15% tip is included in the bill. Of course, the staff may not go to heroic lengths in order to point this out to you – if you forget to check, and leave a cash tip as well, staff gets tipped twice. Unless you're feeling inordinately philanthropic, are a show-off or were *really* happy with the service, make absolutely certain that you're not tipping twice by examining the bill before you pay. ■

Add about 10% to taxi fares even if you think your driver should be institutionalized. Hotel porters who carry bags a long way expect $3 to $5 or add it up at $1 per bag; smaller services (holding the taxi door open for you) might justify $1 but we don't think so. Valet parking is worth about $2, to be given when your car is returned to you.

Consumer Taxes

In this book, we list base prices, onto which you must add tax, unless otherwise indicated. In Miami the consumer (value added) tax is 6.5% (6% state and .5% local) on goods and services, with additional taxes of 5% on hotel accommodations (11.5% total tax on hotels). Area rental cars carry the 6.5% sales tax and a Florida state road surcharge of $2.05 a day.

POST & COMMUNICATIONS

Mail

Mail within the USA takes generally two to three days, to destinations within Florida from one to two days. To Europe, allow at least a week, two weeks at peak times of the year like Christmas. If you have the correct postage, you can drop your mail into any blue official mail box, found at places like shopping centers and street corners. The times of the next mail pickup are written on the inside of the lid of the mail box.

Postal Rates Currently, rates for 1st-class mail within the USA are 32¢ for letters up to one ounce (28 grams; 23¢ for each additional ounce) and 20¢ for postcards.

International airmail rates (except Canada and Mexico, which are slightly cheaper) are 60¢ for a half-ounce letter, 95¢ for a one-ounce letter and 39¢ for each additional half ounce. International postcard rates are 40¢. Aerogrammes are 45¢.

Parcels airmailed anywhere within the USA are $3 for two pounds or less, increasing by $1 per pound up to $6 for five pounds. For heavier items, rates differ according to the distance mailed. Books, periodicals and computer disks can be sent by a cheaper 4th-class rate.

Receiving Mail You can have mail sent to you care of General Delivery at any post office that has its own zip (postal) code. It's best to have your intended date of arrival (if the sender knows it) clearly marked on the envelope. Mail is usually held for 30 days before it's returned to the sender. Alternatively, have mail sent to the local representative of American Express or Thomas Cook, which provide mail service for their clients.

Miami Beach South
13th St at Washington Ave
General Delivery, Miami Beach, FL 33139
Miami Beach North
71st St at Versailles
General Delivery, Miami Beach, FL 33141

Telephone

Area Codes The ☎ 305 area code covers the Metropolitan Miami area and the Florida Keys. Fort Lauderdale's area code is ☎ 954.

Dialing All phone numbers within the USA consist of a three-digit area code followed by a seven-digit local number. If you are calling locally, just dial the seven-digit number. If you are calling long distance, dial 1 + the three-digit area code + the seven-digit number.

If you're calling from abroad, the international country code for the USA is '1'.

The 800 and new 888 area codes are designated for toll-free numbers within the USA and sometimes from Canada as well.

The 900 area code is designated for calls for which the caller pays at a premium rate, usually only available from private phone. They have a reputation for being sleazy operations – a smorgasbord of phone sex at $2.99 a minute is one of many offerings.

Directory assistance can be reached locally by dialing ☎ 411; this is free from most pay phones but costs as much as 50¢ from a private phone. For directory assistance outside your area code, dial 1 + the three-digit area code + 555-1212.

Pay Phones Local calls cost 25¢ at pay phones. Almost all hotels (especially the more expensive ones) add a service charge of 50¢ to $1 for each local – and sometimes even toll free – call made from a room phone, and they also have hefty surcharges for long-distance calls, like 50% on top of their carrier's rates. Public pay phones, which can be found in most lobbies, are always cheaper.

Long-distance rates vary depending on the destination and which telephone company you use. There are literally hundreds of long-distance companies in the US, and rates vary by several hundred percent – call the operator (☎ 0 or 00) for rate information. Don't ask the operator to put your call through, however, because operator-assisted calls are much more expensive than direct-dial calls. Generally, nights (11 pm to 8 am), all day Saturday and from 8 am to 5 pm Sunday are the cheapest times to call. Discounts also apply in the evenings from 5 to 11 pm daily. Daytime calls (Monday to Friday 8 am to 5 pm) are full-price calls within the USA.

You can receive calls at almost all pay phones in the area – the phone's number should be typed on the rate sheet.

Debit Cards A new long-distance alternative is phone debit cards, which allow purchasers to pay in advance, with access through an 800 number. In amounts of $5, $10, $20 and $50, these are available in airports, post offices, some youth hostels and from Western Union and some other sources. Shop around.

International Calls To place an international call direct, dial 011 + country code + area code (dropping the leading 0) + number. From a pay phone, dial all those numbers before inserting coins; a voice will come on telling you how much to put in the phone after you dial the number. For international operator assistance and rates dial ☎ 00. Treat Canada as a domestic call.

As a general rule it's cheaper to make international calls at night, but this varies with the country you're calling. The exact cost for making an overseas call from a pay phone will depend on the long-distance company and the country in question. For calls from a private phone to Australia or Europe, typically the cost should be about $1.50 for the first minute and $1 for each subsequent minute. Other continents usually cost about twice that.

Collect & Country Direct You can call collect (reverse charge) from any phone. There is an increasing number of providers, but beware that there really is a difference in price, so check before you dial. The main players at the time of writing were AT&T (☎ 800-225-5288, or 800-CALL ATT) and MCI (☎ 800-365-5328, or 800-COLLECT). During our research, MCI was always more expensive than AT&T. You can also just dial 0 + the area code and number, eg, 0+212+123-4567, but local telephone carriers are generally the most expensive option of all.

Fax Fax machines are easy to find in the USA, at shipping outlets like Mail Boxes, Etc, photocopy services, and hotel business service centers, but be prepared to pay high prices (over $1 a page to the US, $4 or more to Europe and elsewhere). Prices for incoming faxes are usually half the outgoing domestic rate – about 50¢ a page.

E-mail & Internet Access

SoBeNET (☎ 674-7007, e-mail riley@sobenet.net, website http://www.sobenet.net) is a social project, not an economic enterprise, that offers internet access to registered voters, businesses with occupational licenses and property owners in the zip code area 33139 for $10 a month.

Non-members of SoBeNET visiting South Beach can rent a computer station for e-mail transfer at a nominal printing cost.

CyberGate (☎ 954-428-4283, 800-638-4283, e-mail sales@gate.net, website http://www.gate.net), is Florida's largest commercial provider. They offer PPP accounts for $20 including 50 hours of access time. See the Online Services appendix in the back of the book for websites and e-mail addresses of businesses and services listed in this book.

Hotel business service centers may provide connections, and trendy restaurants and cafes sometimes offer internet service as well, though the latter hasn't caught on in Miami as much as in other parts of the country.

Note that many hotels are using digital PBX systems that do not provide a dial tone that standard modems can't 'hear', so if you're going to be staying in a few places, it's worth checking out a converter, available from techno-geek outlets like Radio Shack.

BOOKS

Most of the books listed here are available locally, some nationally and internationally. For literature set in the area, check the Literature section in the Facts about Miami chapter. If you'll be traveling around the state, a key resource is Lonely Planet's *Florida – a travel survival kit*. Other good books on the area include Nixon Smiley's *Yesterday's Miami* (EA Seeman Publishing, Miami, probably only available in the library), a fascinating photo history book; and Donald C Gaby's *The Miami River* (The Historical Association of Southern Florida). *Miami: City of the Future* by TD Allman is a solid, general interest read, though also somewhat dated.

If you're coming with kids, Lonely Planet's *Travel with Children* is a must-read for strategy, and don't miss the excellent *Places to Go with Children in Miami & South Florida* by Cheryl Lani Juárez and Deborah Ann Johnson (Chronicle Books), which is indispensable in keeping the little darlings calm and entertained.

For getting out in nature, Marjory Stoneman Douglas's classic *The Everglades: River of Grass* (Pineapple Press), should be required reading for those heading out into the Glades. Also check out Susan D Jewell's excellent *Exploring Wild South Florida* (Pineapple Press); Allen de Hart's *Adventuring in Florida* (The Sierra Club); and one of our favorites, Frank Zoretich's *Cheap Thrills Florida – The Bottom Half* (Pineapple Press) written by an admittedly very stingy man, containing lots of real cheap things to do around here.

Deco Delights by Barbara Capitman, and *Miami: Architecture of the Tropics*, edited by Maurice Coulot and Jean François Legune are two excellent books on Art Deco architecture.

MEDIA

Newspapers & Magazines

The *Miami Herald* is the city's only major daily. While local coverage tends to draw fire from all sides, it's a good source of international and national news. And it simultaneously publishes and distributes *el Nuevo Herald* (see below).

Wire is the paper of record to find out where to play on the beach. Their weekly *Nights Out with Morningstar* section features the clubbing diary of one of the beach's most outlandish partiers, Aussie-expat Melanie Morningstar, and their Calendar section has lists of everything Fabulous on South Beach.

Great coverage of local issues, along with superb listings of restaurants, a club/pub/bar/theater/cinema/special events calendar and reviews is in the *New Times*, available free around town. On Fridays the Herald features a pullout section called *Weekend*, which has movie and music reviews and listings, gallery information for Miami and surrounding areas, comedy and a whole lot of other stuff.

Other locally available newspapers include Florida editions of *The New York Times* and the *Wall Street Journal*, sold at vending boxes around town. For excellent, unbiased and thoughtful international news, pick up a copy of the *Christian Science Monitor*.

Spanish & Overseas Papers The *Miami Herald* publishes *el Nuevo Herald*, an excellent Spanish daily (in fact, if you speak Spanish, you should look here first for coverage of Latin America). *El Diario Américas* is another Spanish language daily. To get your revolutionary fervor whipped up, pick up *Libre* at boxes all over Little Havana.

Most major Western European newspapers are available at good newsstands. See the Shopping chapter for more information.

Television

With the exception of the local public access cable television station Channel 3, which runs some . . . *eccentric* . . . programming, like Steve Cohen's *Open to the Public*, there are few surprises. Alas, even the vilified smutty talk shows, which brought American television out of the gutter and down to the sewer pipes, themselves are under fire, and may not survive: when Geraldo talks ethics, we're all in trouble.

But gore springs eternal in Miami, where the local news motto is 'If it bleeds, it leads.' They are cleaning up, but most of the local news stuff is as sensationalistic as a British daily newspaper.

The local stations are:

WPBT	PBS	Channel 2
WFOR	CBS	Channel 4
WTVJ	NBC	Channel 6
WSVN	FOX	Channel 7
WPLG	ABC	Channel 10

On Gold Coast Cablevision, CNN is at Channel 13, Headline News at Channel 47; Comedy Central at Channel 49, Nickelodeon on Channel 48. The Weather Channel is at Channel 59. For Spanish-language broadcasting, there's Telemundo (Channel 22), Univision (Channel 51) and over on Channel 46 there are rebroadcasts of Mexican news programs via ECCO.

Radio

Miami radio is a colorful place, with lots of Spanish- and Creole-language programming, salsa and oldies in addition to the standard American offerings of talk shows featuring vulgar blabbermouths and convicted felons, and a smattering of musical styles. For balanced coverage and an international take on the news, there's National Public Radio (NPR)'s *Morning Edition* from 7 to 9 am and *All Things Considered* from 5 to 7 pm on WLRN,

91.3 FM. WLRN also offers Creole-language news at 10 am daily and, of course, the Radio Reader weekday mornings at 11 am.

Some other stations are:

WINZ	940 AM	news, sports, traffic
WLQY	1320 AM	French & Creole-language news and information
WPOW	96 FM; WKIS 99.9 FM	top 40 or 100 dance music
WSHE	103.2 FM	adult contemporary

TOILETS

There are public toilets at several spots on South Beach, but generally speaking, the area doesn't offer much in the way of public facilities. Usually restaurants will allow you to use theirs if you're reasonably presentable and ask politely. In fact, even the ones that have signs saying that their rest rooms are for customers only will often let you as long as you ask very nicely. Bars are also a good bet, and usually in crowded ones you just need to walk back and to the right or left, as if you're a customer.

NICK SELBY

Powder rooms

Toilets

For a country with a worldwide reputation for its outspoken, sometimes coarse and even foul-mouthed citizenry, it's an amazing phenomenon that very few of them can bring themselves to utter the word for the porcelain appliance into which they empty their bowels and bladders.

For ladies and gentlemen to refer to anything vaguely personal was to open themselves to scorn and embarrassment – even today, American television commercials hawk 'bathroom tissue', not toilet paper.

So Americans don't have toilets. They have (and these are just a few of the euphemisms you will come across in your travels) the: rest room, facilities, comfort station (?!?), commode, john, latrine, head, powder room, little girl's/boy's room, bathroom, way station and potty. ■

WEIGHTS & MEASURES

The US continues to resist the imposition of the metric system. Distances are in feet, yards, and miles; weights are in ounces, pounds, and tons. Gasoline is measured in US gallons, about 20% smaller than the Imperial gallon and equivalent to 3.79 liters. Temperatures are given in degrees Fahrenheit.

METRIC CONVERSION

Temperature
To convert °C to °F multiply by 1.8 and add 32.
To convert °F to °C subtract 32 and divide by 1.8.

Length, Distance & Area	*multiply by*
inches to centimeters	2.54
centimeters to inches	0.39
feet to meters	0.30
meters to feet	3.28
yards to meters	0.91
meters to yards	1.09
miles to kilometers	1.61
kilometers to miles	0.62
acres to hectares	0.40
hectares to acres	2.47
sq miles to sq kilometers	2.59
sq kilometers to sq miles	0.39

Weight	*multiply by*
ounces to grams	28.35
grams to ounces	0.035
pounds to kilograms	0.45
kilograms to pounds	2.20
British tons to kilograms	1016
US tons to kilograms	907

A British ton is 2240 pounds, a US ton is 2000 pounds.

Volume	*multiply by*
imperial gallons to liters	4.55
liters to imperial gallons	0.22
US gallons to liters	3.79
liters to US gallons	0.26

Five imperial gallons equal just over six US gallons.
A liter is slightly more than a US quart, slightly less than a British one.

TIME

Call ☎ 324-8811 for accurate time. Miami is in the US Eastern standard time zone, three hours ahead of San Francisco and Los Angeles, and five hours behind GMT/UTC. When it's noon in Miami it's:

5 pm in London
6 pm in Munich
1 am in Beijing, midnight in summer Beijing
4 am in summer Sydney, 2 am in winter Sydney
6 am in summer Auckland, 4 am in winter Auckland

ELECTRICITY

Electric current in the USA is 110-115 volts, 60 Hz AC. Outlets may be suited for flat two- or three-prong plugs. If your appliance is made for another electrical system, you will need a transformer or adapter; if you didn't bring one along, check Radio Shack or another consumer electronics store.

LAUNDRY

Coin laundries are scattered throughout the area. Generally the cost is $1.25 to wash and either a flat rate (like $1.25) to dry or dryers that cost 25¢ for between five and 10 minutes. On the Beach, the folks at the coin laundry at 510 Washington Ave (☎ 534-4298) are very friendly, they're open daily 6 to 2 am.

Mark's Dry Cleaning (☎ 538-6275) is, as the impossibly thick New York-accented announcer on their TV commercials says, 'at the breezy corner of Alton Rd and 20th St'.

PHOTOGRAPHY & VIDEO

Overseas visitors who are thinking of purchasing videos should remember that the USA uses NTSC color TV standard, which is not compatible with other standards like PAL. See the Shopping chapter for places to buy cameras and to buy and develop film.

HEALTH

Miami is a typical first world destination when it comes to health. For most foreign visitors no immunizations are required for entry, though cholera and yellow fever vaccinations may be required of travelers from areas with a history of those diseases. There are no unexpected health dangers, excellent medical attention is readily available, and the only real health concern is that, as elsewhere in the USA, a collision with the medical system can cause severe injuries to your financial state.

Health Insurance

No sensible visitor will arrive in the USA without the security of a good travel insurance policy. When looking for a policy, what you're really after is coverage against a true catastrophe. Your travel agent will have suggestions about travel insurance and many policies offer higher levels of coverage for the USA. Check the fine print as some policies may exclude coverage for 'dangerous' occupations that can include scuba diving, motorcycling, surfing and the like. Policies issued through student travel-oriented organizations like STA, Travel Cuts, Campus Travel or Council Travel are usually a good value.

If you do require medical attention be sure to save all invoices and documentation and put in a claim to your insurance company as soon as possible.

Medical Attention

The Stanley C Myers Community Health Center (☎ 538-8835) is a public clinic that charges based on your income. You'll need to get there early (they're open Monday to Friday from 7.30 am to 4.30 pm, closed Saturday and Sunday) as lines to this walk-in clinic are usually very long. You'll need to bring ID. If you're foreign born, bring your passport and I-94 card; US citizens should bring proof of residence and income. They're at 710 Alton Rd.

We've used Burgos Medical Center (☎ 534-5627) at 840 5th St in Miami Beach. A visit is $75; they're open Monday to Saturday 9 am to 5 pm, closed Sunday. Check in the yellow pages under Physicians or Clinics to find a doctor, or call the Dade County Medical Association (☎ 324-8717) Monday to Friday 9 am to 5 pm. Look in the white pages under Dentists to find one of those, or try ☎ 800-DENTIST (☎ 800-336-8478), a free referral service.

In a serious emergency, call ☎ 911 for an ambulance to take you to the nearest hospital's emergency room. Mount Sinai Medical Center (☎ 674-2121) at 4300 Alton Rd is considered to be the best in the area. But note that ER charges in the USA are stellar: Mount Sinai charges a *minimum* ER fee of $276, and that's just the flagfall. There are additional charges for x-rays, casting, medicines, analysis . . . *everything*, so the cost of a visit can easily top $1000. The moral: don't get sick or hurt in the USA without insurance!

WOMEN TRAVELERS

Women often face different situations when traveling than do men. If you are a woman traveler, especially a woman traveling alone, it's not a bad idea to get in the habit of traveling with a little extra awareness of your surroundings.

Men may interpret a woman drinking alone in a bar as a bid for male company, whether you intended it that way or not. If you don't want the company, most men will respect a firm but polite 'no thank you'.

Women must recognize the extra threat of rape, which is a problem not only in urban but also in rural areas. The best way to deal with the threat of rape is to avoid putting yourself in vulnerable situations. Conducting yourself in a common-sense manner will help you to avoid most problems. It's said that shouting 'Fire!' may draw assistance more effectively than yelling 'Help!'

If despite all precautions you are assaulted, call the police; in any emergency, telephoning ☎ 911 will connect you with the emergency operator for police, fire and ambulance services. The Miami Rape Crisis Hotline (☎ 585-7273, which spells out as 585-RAPE) is a 24-hour, seven-day resource for women who have been raped or assaulted. The service, which is free, offers comprehensive medical and psychological treatment. Using the service does *not* necessarily mean filing a police report (except in cases involving children). The center is at the University of Miami/Jackson Memorial Hospital at 1611 NW 12th Ave. Call for directions.

GAY & LESBIAN TRAVELERS

Miami Beach is a key spot for gay and lesbian tourism in the USA: over $83 million of the $17 billion gay travel market was spent in Miami in 1995. The two big circuit parties (parties around which weekends or even weeks are built) are the White Party and the Winter Party. The White Party (known as the Jewel of the Circuit Parties), held annually on the Sunday after Thanksgiving at Vizcaya (see the Things to See & Do chapter). Everyone dresses in white, and anywhere from 2500 to 3000 people pour in: proceeds benefit the Health Crisis Network. It's a very sophisticated event, people arrive in yachts, and there's jazz and other live music.

During the Winter Party, in March, a dance floor is constructed on the sand at South Beach. Well, just imagine pink palm trees and about 4000 nearly naked men dancing on the beach and you get the idea.

The club scene is ever changing (during the research

for this book, four closed) so newspapers that give absolutely up-to-date information during your trip.

On the internet, check out the Queer Resources Directory (see the Online Services appendix) for hundreds of links to gay and lesbian travel and other information resources.

Online, America Online (AOL) hosts the Gay & Lesbian Community Forum, National Gay/Lesbian Task Force, Gay and Lesbian Alliance Against Defamation and other regional, state and national organizations.

Information In an emergency, call the Switchboard of Miami (☎ 358-4357). The Lesbian, Gay & Bisexual Community Center (☎ 531-0366) is an excellent (if underfunded) resource for information and referrals. They hold a wide variety of meetings including a monthly bisexual support group the first Friday of the month at 8 pm. They're at 1335 Alton Rd in Miami Beach. The South Beach Business Guild (☎ 234-7224) represents businesses that are owned by or friendly to gay men, lesbians and bisexuals.

Books *The Out Pages*, an excellent book filled with listings of gay-owned or gay-friendly businesses in Miami and South Florida, is available at many local bookshops and gay/lesbian-owned businesses. For information on those, contact the SoBe Business Guild (☎ 234-7224). National guidebooks with sections on South Florida are *The Womens' Traveler*, providing listings for lesbians, and *Damron's Address Book* for men, both published by the Damron Company (☎ 415-255-0404, 800-462-6654) PO Box 422458, San Francisco, CA 94142-2458, and the Gay Yellow Pages (☎ 212-674-0120), PO Box 533, Village Station, NY 10014-0533, which has a Southern Edition, covering areas from Washington, DC south to the US Carribean ($5).

Newspapers A local weekly newspaper focusing on gay and lesbian community issues is *twn*. In the *Miami Herald*, Eugene J Patron writes the weekly *Out and Around* column, which covers happenings and events of social or political significance in the metropolitan area.

Lips is a lesbian-oriented monthly newspaper with a very good calendar section featuring club and special event listings; *Pride* is a biweekly gay listings magazine with some features; *Hotspots* is a much flashier weekly packed with ads from discos to straightforward classifieds for prostitutes. *Scoop* is Hotspots' main competitor. *She Times* is another monthly lesbian-oriented paper with a hodgepodge of self-help, beginner poetry, useful listings and personals (from a mix of men, women, drag queens and others).

DISABLED TRAVELERS

Miami is mainly wheelchair friendly, though in certain places in the Deco District doorways may be too tight. Many buses, all Tri-Rail trains and stations and Metromovers are wheelchair accessible, though travelers with special needs can contact the Metro-Dade Transit Agency Special Transportation Service (STS; ☎ 263-5406) which provides door-to-door transport for disabled (physically or mentally) people who are unable to use regular transport options. The application process takes three weeks, so contact them before your visit.

The Deaf Services Bureau (☎ 668-4407, TDD 668-3323) at 1320 S Dixie Hwy, suite 760, has interpreters and an information and referral service. They're open Monday to Thursday 8 am to 5 pm, Friday 8 am to noon, closed Saturday and Sunday. The Florida Relay Service (☎ relay 579-8644, TDD 800-955-8771, voice 800-955-8770, customer service 800-955-8013) is a very cool thing: 24-hour operators to connect TDD users to people without TDDs.

For information for the blind, contact the Lighthouse for the Blind (☎ 856-2288) at 601 SW 8th Ave.

Organizations

There are a number of organizations and tour providers around the world that specialize in the needs of disabled travelers. In Australia, try *Independent Travellers* (☎ (08) 232 2555, fax (08) 232 6877) at 167 Gilles St, Adelaide, SA 5000; and in the UK, *RADAR* (☎ (0171) 250-3222) 250 City Rd, London, or *Mobility International* (☎ (0171) 403-5688). The following is a list of organizations within the USA:

Twin Peaks Press
: publishes several useful handbooks for disabled travelers, including *Travel for the Disabled* and the *Directory of Travel Agencies for the Disabled*; PO Box 129, Vancouver, WA 98666 (☎ 202-694-2462, 800-637-2256)

Access
: The Foundation for Accessibility by the Disabled; PO Box 356, Malverne, NY 11565 (☎ 516-887-5798)

Information Center for Individuals with Disabilities
: Fort Point Place, 1st Floor, 27-43 Wormwood St, Boston, MA 02210 (☎ 617-727-5540, TTY 345-9743, 800-248-3737)

Mobility International USA
: program that advises disabled travelers on mobility issues, and runs an exchange program; PO Box 3551,

Eugene, OR 97403 (☎/TDD 503-343-1284, fax 503-343-6812; see the Online Services appendix)

SATH

Society for the Advancement of Travel for the Handicapped; 347 5th Ave No 610, New York, NY 10016 (☎ 212-447-7284)

SENIOR TRAVELERS

Though the age at which senior benefits begin varies, travelers from 50 years and up (though more commonly 65 and up) can expect to receive cut rates at such places as hotels, museums and restaurants. Some national advocacy groups that can help seniors in planning their travels are the American Association of Retired Persons (AARP; ☎ 202-434-2277, 800-424-3410), 601 E St NW, Washington, DC 20049 (for Americans 50 years or older); Elderhostel (☎ 617-426-8056), 75 Federal St, Boston, MA 02110-1941 (for people 55 and older, and their companions); and the National Council of Senior Citizens (☎ 202-347-8800), 1331 F St NW, Washington, DC 20004.

MIAMI FOR CHILDREN

Miami is very kid-friendly – it's hard not to be with all that beach. Watch out for the topless spots if that sort of thing bothers you and you'll have a great time. There are playgrounds along Ocean Drive in a couple of spots; our favorite is the one between 2nd and 3rd Sts, though watch out: those slides get pretty hot in summer! There are public toilets and water fountains at most playgrounds. And then, of course, there are the old standbys:

Whose Ami?

Kids love Miami: it's brightly colored, the buildings look like something out of *The Jetsons*, there are all these weird-looking people ('Mom! I saw a man in a dress and a lady without a shirt!') and, above all, beach as far as you can see! Kids even love the name Miami. Sounds cool, I guess.

We were speaking with Ben, the child (then six) of some close friends. We had lived (perhaps even *over*-stayed, according to the friends) with them in New Jersey for a while and had become close to Ben, so when we left for Miami we had to explain where we'd be going and why we wouldn't see him for quite a while.

'Well where are you going?' asked Ben, fidgeting.

'Down to Miami,' Corinna said.

He considered this for a moment, and then said, 'Well, okay, but call me when you get back from your Ami.' ■

the Miami Museum of Science & Space Transit Planetarium, the Venetian Pool, Seaquarium, Metrozoo, the National Hurricane Center.

The Lincoln Road Partnership has arranged kids' activities during the Farmer's Markets, and kids get discounts on almost all museums and attractions. See the Things to See & Do chapter for more information, and pick up Lonely Planet's excellent *Travel with Children* by Maureen Wheeler (1995) for general information and encouragement.

Ask for baby sitter recommendations at your hotel.

NICK SELBY

LIBRARIES

With almost 4,000,000 books and a surprisingly helpful staff, the Miami Public Library (☎ 375-2665, 375-5184) is an excellent resource for locals and visitors alike. They have an enormous Florida room containing thousands of books on all aspects of Florida life, history and travel, as well as a large video and audio-tape library. The library is open Monday to Wednesday and Friday and Saturday from 9 am to 6 pm, Thursday from 9 am to 9 pm, Sunday from 1 to 5 pm.

A good branch of the library is on Miami Beach (☎ 535-4219) at 2100 Collins Ave, open Monday and Wednesday 10 am to 8 pm, Tuesday and Thursday to Saturday 10 am to 5.30 pm, closed Sunday.

CAMPUSES

The two major players in the area are the state-run Florida International University (FIU) and the University of Miami (UM).

FIU, with a liberal arts core curriculum, is the larger of the two, with enrollment of over 26,000 students. Their University Park campus is located on US Hwy 41 (west of Calle Ocho) between SW 107th Ave and Florida's Turnpike. The North Campus is located off US Hwy 1 at NE 151st Street.

Founded in 1925, UM's Coral Gables campus (made up of two colleges and 10 schools) occupies 260 acres within the City of Coral Gables. The university has a total enrollment of about 13,000 full- and part-time students.

DANGERS & ANNOYANCES

Unsafe Areas

There are a few areas considered by locals to be dangerous, and racism – overt or implied – may be responsible for some, like Liberty City, a predominantly black neighborhood in northwest Miami, or Little Haiti. We've never had any problems in either, but in these and other reputedly 'bad' areas, you should avoid walking around alone late at night, use common sense and travel in groups.

Any deserted area, like below 5th St in Miami Beach or the area near the Greyhound station in downtown Miami, is more dangerous at night, as are areas under causeways and bridges from Miami, where homeless people and some refugees have set up shantytowns.

If you're considering sex on the beach, consider that it's not a very original idea: police patrol as do muggers.

Use caution when changing money – muggers have been known to hang around at exchange offices looking for victims.

Highway Robbery & Carjacking

In 1992 and 1993, several highly publicized incidents of attacks on tourists in Miami made headlines all over the world. Since then, attacks against tourists have been considerably reduced. In fact, of the 8.7 million tourists who stayed in unincorporated Dade County in 1995, there were 134 reported robberies; in 1993, the 'really bad year', there were 391 robberies.

You'd still do well to use caution. Official police cars have flashing blue *and* red lights; if any other vehicle attempts to pull you over, using any other means, keep driving and get to a well-lighted area, like a gas station, and call the police. And that's what you should do if someone rams your car from behind – forget about stopping to exchange insurance information, just get to someplace safe and call the police. Don't stop for 'stranded' motorists.

Carjacking is a relatively new activity, in which a crazed lunatic approaches you at a stop light, points a gun at you and orders you out of the vehicle, which they then drive off in. Police say that resisting a gun-wielding person is not wise; just follow instructions and hope for the best.

Panhandlers & the Homeless

The waves of refugees from poor countries, in addition to waves of refugees from the northeastern US, has resulted in a high percentage of homeless people and panhandlers. This is a very touchy issue, and all we'll do is tow the official Lonely Planet line: don't encourage them – it only helps to make visitors an easy mark. If you're really concerned, you can volunteer at a homeless shelter, or donate to homeless relief programs at local churches and synagogues.

Credit Card Scams

When using phone credit cards of any sort, be aware of people watching you, especially in public places like airports. Thieves will memorize numbers and use them to make lots of international calls. Shield the telephone with your body when punching in your credit card number. Use touch tone key pads to avoid having to actually say aloud your credit card number in a public place – the walls do have ears.

Don't give your credit card number out over the phone – people can charge anything they want if they have your name, card number and expiration date. Destroy any carbons generated by a credit card sale.

Never ever ever give out personal information over the phone to someone who has called you. No legitimate company representative would ever call and ask for your social security number, credit card number or expiration number or anything else.

Hotels customarily ask for a credit card imprint when you check in to cover incidental expenses. Make certain that this is destroyed if not used.

Enter a '$' sign before, and make certain there's a decimal point in, numbers written in the 'total' box on a credit card slip – we've heard reports of Japanese tourists being charged $1500 for a T-shirt instead of $15.

Sunburn

Use a good sunscreen and take your time – don't try to become a bronzed god or goddess on the first day (or for that matter for the first week). Most doctors recommend sunscreen with a protection factor of 40 for easily burned areas like your shoulders and, if you'll be on nude beaches, areas not normally exposed to sun like breasts and genitals.

If all that isn't enough to convince you, think about this: *no one* wants to have sex with someone with bright pink, festering skin who says 'Ouch!' when hugged.

Sharks

Shark attacks off Miami Beach happen a couple of times a year, and there are more sharks out there than you would like to think. But other than staying out of the water there's not much one can do about it, so, like, don't go see *Jaws* right before you come, OK?

Alligators

It's pretty unlikely that you'll even see an alligator in the city, but it's been known to happen. Alligators generally only eat when they're hungry – not as a punitive measure – unless they think they're being attacked. Things alligators like: small animals or things that look like them, such as small children or people crouching down real small to snap a photo. Things alligators don't like: you.

Bad Service

Service in some Miami Beach restaurants can be atrocious. Many waitstaff and others in the 'service' industry are really here (they think) to be discovered by a talent agent. When they decide that you're not one, you are of no value to them – and they'll probably get angry at you for impersonating one in the first place. Petulant and pouty wanna-be models of both sexes can be seen at practically every Ocean Drive restaurant acting as 'hosts'. There's nothing much you can do about it except keep your dignity and remember: real models don't have to hand you a menu.

If you encounter any problems with hotels, restaurants or businesses during your stay, you aren't powerless; you have a couple of options other than the police. For incidents that occur anywhere in Miami Beach, contact Michael Aller (☎ 673-7010, emergency beeper 886-4795), the City of Miami Beach's lovable Tourism & Convention coordinator. The Better Business Bureau of South Florida (☎ 625-0307) is a consumer advocacy group.

Plotting a Hurricane

Scientists and National Weather Center (NWC) meteorologists closely observe as tropical depressions over the ocean and gulf become tropical storms and are finally upgraded to hurricanes. But plotting a hurricane's path is tricky business – in fact, it can't really be done.

NICK SELBY

In 1995, Miami television and NWC meteorologists predicted that Hurricane Erin was headed for a touchdown right in the center of the city. Miami and Miami Beach neighborhoods were evacuated and shelters sent out pleas for volunteers and supplies. Local television news teams ran gleefully around looking for driving rain ('Well, Patricia, it isn't coming down quite yet, but it's looking *very* ominous indeed . . . .') and waiting for something awful to happen, and a mild degree of panic set in among local residents who had not evacuated. And then . . .

Nothing. At least, nothing in Miami, where it rained a little. That evening a startlingly clear, star-filled sky, combined with a gentle breeze across the bay, made conditions lovely for a stroll on the beach.

The storm had suddenly veered due north, catching northern Florida residents totally by surprise – in fact, many South Florida residents who had listened to news reports and evacuated their homes drove into the eye of the storm!

Hurricanes

A hurricane is a concentrated system of very strong thunderstorms with high circulation. The 74- to 160-mph winds created by a hurricane can extend for hundreds of miles around the eye (center) of a hurricane system. Floods and flash floods caused by the torrential rains it produces cause additional property damage, and perhaps most dangerous of all, hurricanes can cause a storm surge, forcing the level of the ocean to rise between four and 18 feet above normal: the 13- to 18-foot storm surge caused by a category four hurricane like Andrew would have easily destroyed the entire city of Miami Beach. And after a hurricane, as if to add insult to injury, conditions become just ducky for a tornado.

Every year during hurricane season, which is from June 1 to November 30, storms form over the Atlantic Ocean and the Gulf of Mexico and gather strength – and some roll right through the area. Some years are worse than others: in 1992, Hurricane Andrew flattened the

As Erin continued over land, it socked the Florida Panhandle with a wallop that knocked out power, destroyed houses as if they were built of matchsticks and caused millions of dollars in damage.

About a month later, the second half of the one-two punch slammed the Panhandle as Hurricane Opal came through and flattened almost all of Panama City Beach, ripping down condominiums, actually tearing up highways, houses and hotels. The city of Pensacola Beach was still under several feet of sand months later.

What this illustrates is the danger of becoming lulled into a false sense of security (or of panic) by mustachioed television personalities with complicated Doppler Radar charts and satellite imagery. Hurricanes are much like the proverbial 800-pound gorilla: they set down wherever, and whenever, they want. ■

NICK SELBY

area, decimating the city of Homestead just south of Miami, but 1994 had no major hurricane activity at all.

Hurricanes are generally sighted well in advance and there's time to prepare. When a hurricane threatens listen to radio and television news reports. Give credence only to forecasts attributed to the National Weather Center (shortwave radio listeners can tune to 162.55 MHz), and dismiss anything else as a rumor.

There are two distinct stages of alert: Hurricane Watch is given when a hurricane *may* strike in the area within the next 36 to 48 hours; Hurricane Warning is given when a hurricane is likely to strike the area.

If a Hurricane Warning is issued during your stay, you may be placed under an evacuation order. Hotels generally follow these orders and ask guests to leave. The Red Cross operates hurricane shelters, but they're just that – shelter: they do not provide food.

For a full list of tips on preparedness, check on page 29 in the Miami white pages telephone directory.

LEGAL MATTERS

Florida law tends to be tougher than in most non-southern states when it comes to drug possession or use, though in Miami the police are more tolerant than in, say, St Augustine, where someone arrested for carrying a pot pipe makes the newspaper. But 1995 and 1996 saw an increase in police raids on nightclubs, and dozens of people were arrested on minor drug charges. It's illegal to walk with an open alcoholic drink – including beer – on the street. If you're driving, all liquor has to be unopened (not just sealed, but new and untouched) and, technically anyway, stored in the trunk of the car.

Driving under the influence of alcohol or drugs in Florida carries a whopping $5000 fine and possibly some imprisonment in addition to a license suspension.

BUSINESS HOURS & HOLIDAYS

Office hours in the Miami area are generally 9 am to 5 pm, though there can be a variance of half an hour or so. Many shops are open longer hours and through the weekends while many food shops and supermarkets are open 24 hours. Banks are generally open from about 9 am to about 4 pm; some have extended hours one day a week and limited hours on Saturday.

Whether holidays fall on a weekday or weekend they are often celebrated on the nearest Friday or Monday, to create a three-day weekend. Banks, offices and many businesses close on these days.

New Year's Day	January 1
Martin Luther King, Jr Day	3rd Monday in January
Presidents' Day	3rd Monday in February
Easter	a Sunday in April
Memorial Day	last Monday in May
Independence Day	July 4
Labor Day	1st Monday in September
Columbus Day	2nd Monday in October
Veterans Day	November 11
Thanksgiving	4th Thursday in November
Christmas Day	December 25

SPECIAL EVENTS

There are special events all the time in Miami, a city known for its partying, though during the summer months the pickings are slim; the Greater Miami & The Beaches Convention & Visitor's Bureau's *Destination: Miami* and *Greater Miami & The Beaches Meeting Planner* has a complete list, updated annually.

January

FedEx Orange Bowl See December, below, for information on the New Year's Eve Orange Bowl Parade, a Miami tradition. The Orange Bowl football classic is a major college football game at the Orange Bowl Stadium.

Art Deco Weekend Festival Second week in January, and 1996 became the first year in recent memory when it didn't rain on this parade – arts & crafts stalls on the east side of Ocean Drive, food stalls and the usual block party types. When it doesn't rain, it's great.

Martin Luther King, Jr Parade & Festival January 16 in Liberty City. Call ☎ 636-1920 for more information.

South Florida Food & Wine Fest Probably worth a visit if you're in town; it's held at the Doral Beach Ocean Resort (☎ 532-3600).

February, March & April

Miami Film Festival International film festival, held the first two weeks of February at the Gusman Center for the Performing Arts (☎ 374-2444).

Jazz under the Stars This annual jazz festival on the Concert Meadow at the Miami Metrozoo (☎ 238-1811) has seen performances by some of the greatest of the greats, like Dizzy Gillespie and Nestor Torres; it's held in the second week of February.

AIDS Walk Miami A 5 K run and walk in South Beach held the last week in February. Proceeds go to the Health Crisis Network's counseling, information and education hotline.

Miami International Boat Show Late February at the Miami Beach Convention Center (☎ 666-8515): South Florida takes its boating quite seriously and this is *the* show to hit.

Marlboro Grand Prix of Miami The PPG Indy Car World Series opener is held each year during this race, in the beginning of March at the new Homestead Motorsports Complex, in the city of Homestead.

Annual Miami Orchid Show Second week of March at the Coconut Grove Convention Center, the annual show shows off flowers from growers all over Florida.

Taste of the Beach In mid-March; culinary and music festival at South Pointe Park. Local restaurants give out samples and about 30,000 people come to hear live jazz. Call ☎ 672-1270 for more information.

Carnaval Miami There are festivals and parties throughout the nine-day event at the beginning of March; including a Miss Carnaval contest, Carnaval Night concerts at the Orange Bowl, an in-line skating contest and jazz concerts at South Beach, a Latin drag queen show, and a Calle Ocho cooking contest. Call ☎ 644-8888.

Calle Ocho Festival The culmination of Carnaval Miami, the Calle Ocho Festival is a great time in Little Havana, with lots of concerts, giveaways, Cuban food and more.

Italian Renaissance Festival Held in March at Vizcaya (see the Things to See & Do chapter) with plays, people in traditional Italian costume and concerts.

South Beach Film Festival Held in April at the Colony Theater on Lincoln Road (☎ 448-9133), the festival showcases small, independently made American films and videos.

Baynanza The last week in April; cleanup of Biscayne Bay and a host of activities to coerce people to come: if you're here it's a great thing to do. Call ☎ 372-6770 for more information.

May & June

Miami Summer Boat Show The largest summer boat show in the USA, held at Miami Beach Convention Center (☎ 666-8515) in the first week of May.

Coconut Grove Bed Race This race is held in the middle of the month, benefiting the Muscular Dystrophy Association. Contact ☎ 624-3714.

Great Sunrise Balloon Race Fifty hot-air balloons participate in a race down at Homestead Air Reserve Base in May, benefiting Sunrise Community Inc, which benefits people with disabilities. Call ☎ 273-3051.

International Hispanic Theater Festival From late May to mid-June, this celebration at El Carrusel

NICK SELBY

Art Deco Weekend

Theater (☎ 446-7144) in Coral Gables is one of the largest Hispanic theater events in the USA, featuring US, Latin America, Caribbean and European theater companies.

World's Largest Flea Market Third week of June at the Miami Beach Convention Center; a collection of 1200 vendors selling . . . well, *stuff*.

July, August & September

America's Birthday Bash Excellent fireworks and laser show with live music and celebrations that draws crowds of over 100,000. It's held July 4 at Bayfront Park; call ☎ 358-7550 for more information.

Annual Miami Reggae Festival One of the largest reggae events in the country, this is held in the first week of August at Bayfront Park.

Festival Miami An annual concert series at the Gusman Concert Hall at the University of Miami Campus in Coral Gables (☎ 284-3941), running from mid-September to mid-October.

October & November

Key Biscayne Lighthouse Run A 5 K and 10 K run and 5 K walk in the Bill Baggs Recreation Area and throughout Key Biscayne, on the second Saturday in November.

South Miami Art Festival Held for the last 26 years in the first week in November at the corner of SW 72nd St and SW 57th Ave.

Miami Book Fair Second week in November; this international book fair (☎ 237-3258) is among the most important and well-attended in the USA, with hundreds of nationally known writers joining hundreds of publishers and hundreds of thousands of visitors. The last three days of the eight-day fair is a Street Fair. If you're in town it is absolutely mandatory.

Coral Gables Int'l Arts & Crafts Festival Second week in November, in downtown Coral Gables; call ☎ 445-9973.

December

Annual King Mango Strut This parade in Coconut Grove is sort of a spoof on Mardi Gras; call ☎ 444-7270 for more information.

Miracle Mile Holiday Stroll Block party on Miracle Mile, Coral Gables; call ☎ 446-1657.

Orange Bowl Parade The annual New Year's Eve blowout, with an enormous Orange Bowl Parade: floats, clowns (professional and unintentional), a Folkloric Dance competition, a Queen and a whole lot of other stuff. It would seem that all of Miami turns out for it at the Orange Bowl Stadium, and afterwards, the AT&T Big Orange celebration at Bayfront Park has a fireworks salute.

WORK

Foreigners are not allowed to work legally in the USA without the appropriate working visa, and recent legislative changes specifically target illegal immigrants, which is what you will be if you try to work while on a tourist visa.

Miami has been ground zero for large numbers of refugees from the Caribbean area, notably Haiti and Cuba, so INS checks are frequent. Local businesses are probably more concerned here than anywhere outside Southern California and Texas when it comes to verifying your legal status. See Visa Extensions under Documents for warnings on longer stays.

EMERGENCIES

Dial ☎ 911 for police, fire and ambulance emergencies – it's a free call from any phone. Check the inside front cover of the Miami white pages for a slew of emergency numbers. Some useful ones include:

Coast Guard Search & Rescue	
Air:	☎ 536-5611
Water:	☎ 535-4314
Crisis Intervention	☎ 358-4337
Metro-Dade Police (non-emergency)	☎ 595-6263
Miami Beach Police (non-emergency)	☎ 673-7900
Miami Police (General Investigation Unit)	☎ 579-6545
Poison Information Center	☎ 800-282-3171
Rape Hotline	☎ 585-7273
Suicide Intervention	☎ 358-4357

If you're robbed, report the theft to the police on the above non-emergency numbers. You'll need a police report in order to make an insurance claim back home.

If your credit cards, cash cards or travellers cheques have been stolen, notify your bank or the relevant company as soon as possible. For refunds on lost or stolen travellers cheques (not cards) call American Express (☎ 800-221-7282), MasterCard (☎ 800-223-9920), Thomas Cook (☎ 800-223-7373) or Visa (☎ 800-227-6811).

To report lost or stolen credit cards, call American Express (☎ 800-528-4800), Visa (☎ 800-336-8472), MasterCard (☎ 800-826-2181), Diners Club (☎ 800-234-6377) and Discover (☎ 347-2683).

Foreign visitors who have lost their passports should contact their consulate. Having a photocopy of the important pages of your passport will make replacement much easier.

Getting There & Away

AIR

Miami is served by two main airports: Miami International Airport (MIA) and the Fort Lauderdale/Hollywood International Airport (FLL). See the Getting Around chapter for information about getting from the airports to downtown and the Beach.

Miami International Airport

MIA (☎ 876-7000, flight information 876-7770), is now the USA's busiest international airport in terms of aircraft, and the second busiest in terms of passengers. It is also one of the most poorly laid out and badly signed airports in the country. Parking lots are a good hike from the terminals, which are spread out in an open horseshoe design that makes all areas inconvenient. The main airport terminal building is in Concourse E. Concourses D, C and B are to the north of it, and F, G and H to the south.

There is a ridiculous number of tiny airlines that call MIA home, including Copa Airlines (☎ 871-6331), Paradise Island Airlines (☎ 895-1223) and Zuliana Airlines (☎ 597-8780). The result is a swirling, swarming and swamped place the only saving graces of which are the frequency of flights and the excellent coffee stand in front of the drugstore in Concourse D.

Information The airport is open 24 hours a day, and there are information booths throughout. The central information booth is in Concourse E, in the main lobby on the 2nd floor – check here for lost & found. There are other booths in B, on the 3rd floor in the International Arrivals area; D on the 1st floor in the American Airlines baggage claim area; and in G on the 1st floor in the baggage claim area. To page someone, or to answer any page, pick up any white courtesy phone, which will automatically connect you to paging central. There could be a very, very, very long wait on some days to actually speak with an operator. There's a foreign exchange office in the international arrivals areas that gives awful rates on any currency: see the Changing Money section in the Facts for the Visitor chapter for more information.

There are several ATMs throughout the terminal.

Smoking is prohibited anywhere inside the terminal except in the members-only airline lounges.

Fort Lauderdale/Hollywood International Airport

FLL (☎ 359-1200) is about 30 miles north of Miami, just off I-95. It's a much smaller and friendlier airport than MIA, but obviously there are fewer services. There are three terminals and surprisingly, they're named 1, 2 and 3. International flights arrive at Terminal 3. There are no information booths in the airport, but there are several airline counters, which are also the place to go to page someone, as the airport has no courtesy phone system.

There are ATMs in the business centers in each terminal.

Within North America

Scan the ads in the *New Times* and the *Miami Herald* for travel ads and news of discounted fares out of Miami. Good travel agents include Travel by Design (☎ 673-6336, 800-358-7125) at 1436 Washington Ave, just around the corner from the Clay Hotel & International Hostel; Pilar Tours (☎ 538-7026), at 1655 James St, specializing in cruises and some discount flights; Council Travel (☎ 670-9261, 800-226-8624), south of Coral Gables at 9100 S Dadeland Blvd; and Travel Now at 1600 Collins Ave, Miami Beach (☎ 532-7243) and at 14374 Biscayne Blvd, Miami (☎ 919-9000).

The New York Times, *Los Angeles Times*, *Chicago Tribune*, *San Francisco Examiner*, *San Jose Mercury News*, *Boston Herald* and other major newspapers all produce weekly travel sections with numerous travel agents' ads. Council Travel and STA Travel (☎ 602-596-5151, 800-777-0112) have offices in major cities nationwide.

The magazine *Travel Unlimited*, PO Box 1058, Allston, MA 02134, publishes details of the cheapest air fares and courier possibilities.

The best deals to Miami by air are from New York metropolitan area airports, but the New York-Miami route is the most crowded: reserve early as planes sell out well in advance of the date of departure. In addition to the big carriers, there are also some itty-bitty airlines that compete on these routes. Of these, SunJet International Airlines (☎ 800-479-6538) is perhaps the best known and the one we like the least (we have an aversion to emergency landings, of which we've had two on SunJet – 'now folks, we're just getting indication that our wheels aren't quite down yet . . . .') which sells only one-way tickets with no advance purchase requirements that can be as low as $59 between New York and Miami. Kiwi Airlines (☎ 201-645-5494, 800-538-5494) has similar fares, a lot more planes and better service. On Scheduled Airlines, the lowest you can expect is $150 advance purchase between New York and Miami; $300 from Los Angeles, $350 to 450 from San Francisco.

From Toronto you could expect a high-season/low-season roundtrip ticket price of C$220/340, from Vancouver C$420/675.

To/From Overseas

Visit USA Passes Almost all domestic carriers offer Visit USA passes to non-US citizens. The passes are a book of coupons redeemable for flights; high-season prices average $479 for three coupons and $769 for eight. Often the coupons can only be used in conjunction with an international flight (Canada and Mexico excluded). Delta, American and Continental all have good programs; call them and other airlines for information.

Round-the-World Tickets If you're coming from overseas you may want to consider including Miami in a Round-the-World (RTW) itinerary. Travel agents in London can put together an itinerary using several airlines for as little as £800 either via the northern hemisphere or dipping down to Australia. Add in South Africa as well and you're looking at around £1000. Two or three airlines also group together to offer their own combination deals, typically from £1400 to 1600 via the north Pacific and £1800 to 2200 when including Australia and/or South Africa.

In Australia fares are around A$1800, or Africa can be added to the itinerary starting from A$2200. Qantas, British Airways and USAir offer RTW possibilities utilizing their combined routes for less than A$3000.

A variety of combinations are offered from Asia using, for example, an Asian or US airline to fly to the USA, the US airline to fly on to Europe, and the Asian airline to take you back to the starting point. Typically, these tickets cost around S$4800 from Singapore, HK$18,000 from Hong Kong.

Bargain Tickets & Flights Airlines are not the places to buy cheap tickets from, but their best deals – usually advance-purchase tickets – will give you a point of reference. In this chapter we list prices quoted by airlines; cheaper and more convenient are agencies that specialize in finding low fares, like STA Travel and Trailfinders in the UK, Kilroy Travel in Finland, Travel Overland in Germany, Council Travel in the USA, Travel Cuts in Canada and the UK and STA Travel in Australia and New Zealand. See below for more information.

To/From the UK & Continental Europe Most major European airlines, including Air France, British Air, Finnair and Lufthansa, as well as others, like Aeroflot, have service to Miami. Note that in the UK some incredible deals can be had; for example, in January you can get a roundtrip air ticket from London for as low as £209; while in June and July, the price goes as high as £465. From Paris, the highest scheduled airfare price hovers at about FF3000. In June/January, other scheduled prices are: Dfl 1650/1289 from Amsterdam; FIM4600/4000 from Helsinki; ESP99,000/93,000 from Madrid; and DM1550/1175 from Munich or Frankfurt.

Good travel agents in London include:

Campus Travel
- 174 Kensington High St, London W8 (☎ 0171-938-2188)
- 28A Poland St, London W1 (☎ 0171-437-7767)

STA Travel
- 86 Old Brompton Rd, London SW7
- 117 Euston Rd, London NW1 (☎ 0171-937-9962)

Trailfinders
- 42-50 Earl's Court Rd, London W8 6TF
- 194 Kensington High St, London W8 (☎ 0171-937-5400)

Travel Cuts
- 95A Regent St, London W1 (☎ 0171-637-3161)

In continental Europe, contact:

NBBS Travels
- The Dutch Student Travel Service (☎ 020 638 17 38)

Travel Overland
- Munich (☎ 089 272 760)
- Bremen (☎ 0421 320 477)

Die Neue Reisewelle
- Berlin (☎ 030 323 1078)

To/From Australasia There is no direct service from Australia or New Zealand to Miami; you'll have to change planes and/or carriers in Los Angeles, the US hub for Qantas and Air New Zealand. With long-range 747-400 aircraft most services now overfly Hawaii, so at least the Pacific is covered in one mighty leap. From Auckland to Los Angeles it takes 12 to 13 hours; from Sydney to Los Angeles 13½ to 14½ hours. Typical APEX roundtrip fares vary from A$2000/2400 from the Australian east coast and NZ$2500 from Auckland.

Some good travel agents in Australia and New Zealand include:

Flight Centres International
 19 Bourke St, Melbourne (☎ 03-9650-2899)
 317 Swanson St, Melbourne (☎ 03-9663-1304)
 82 Elizabeth St, Sydney (☎ 02-235-3522)
STA Travel
 224 Faraday St, Carlton, Victoria (☎ 03-9347-6911)
 855 George St, Sydney (☎ 02-281-9866)
 10 High St, Auckland (☎ 09-309-0458)

To/From Latin America Miami is the main US/Latin American gateway, and MIA is served by everyone and his brother's airlines. Deals are sometimes incredible – like the $199 roundtrip to/from Caracas which has been offered several times in the last couple of years; check with discount brokers in Latin America while you're there for the best deals, which come and go quickly. By scheduled air, the highest roundtrip tickets are: $300 to 450 from San Jose, Costa Rica; $450 from Managua, Nicaragua and Guatemala City, Guatemala; $950 to 1100 from Rio de Janeiro, Brazil; and from Caracas, Venezuela $180 to 280 in June, $250 to 300 in January.

Airline Offices

Airlines serving Miami include the following. Those with local telephone numbers have local offices.

Aero Costa Rica	☎ 888-2727, 800-237-6274
Aero Mexico	☎ 441-0090, 800-237-6639
Aero Peru	☎ 448-1947, 800-777-7717
Aeroflot	☎ 577-8500, 800-867-8774
Aerolinas Argentinas	☎ 261-0100, 800-333-0276
Air Canada	☎ 871-2828, 800-776-3000
Air France	☎ 374-2626, 800-237-2747
Air Jamaica	☎ 358-3222, 800-523-5585
Air New Zealand	☎ 800-262-1234
Air South	☎ 869-1200, 800-247-7688
Alitalia	☎ 539-0593, 800-223-5730
American Airlines	☎ 800-433-7300
British Airways	☎ 526-7800, 800-247-9297
Carnival Airlines	☎ 891-0199, 800-437-2110
Chalk's Int'l Airlines	☎ 371-8628/9
Continental Airlines	☎ 871-1400, 800-525-0280
Delta Air Lines	☎ 351-4700, 800-221-1212
Gulfstream Int'l Airlines	☎ 871-1200, 800-992-8532
Haiti Trans Air	☎ 590-1200, 800-394-5313
Iberia Airlines	☎ 526-2010, 800-772-4642
Japan Air Lines	☎ 379-3823, 800-525-3663
Ladeco Chilean Airlines	☎ 670-3066, 800-825-2332
LAN Chile	☎ 670-1961, 800-735-5526
LAPSA-Air Paraguay	☎ 477-2104, 477-3947, 800-795-2772

The Price of Terrorism
Due to security crackdowns after the Oklahoma City bombing in 1995, there are no luggage lockers or stands in the airport or bus and train stations. The only place we know of that has a left luggage service is the Clay Hotel & International Hostel (see the Places to Stay chapter). Other hotels will probably allow guests to store luggage for limited amounts of time. ■

Lufthansa	☎ 536-8936, in state 800-645-4361, out of state 800-645-3880
Martinair Holland	☎ 800-627-8462
Mexicana Airlines	☎ 526-6214, 800-531-7921
Nicaraguense De Avacion	☎ 223-0312, 800-831-6422
Northwest Airlines	☎ 441-1096, 800-225-2525 domestic, 800-447-4747 int'l
Qantas Airways	☎ 800-227-4500
Tower Air	☎ 871-6431, 800-348-6937
Transbrazil Airlines	☎ 597-8322, 800-872-3153
TWA	☎ 371-7471, 800-221-2000
United Airlines	☎ 800-241-6522
USAir	☎ 800-428-4322
ValuJet	☎ 869-1385, 800-825-8538
Varig Brazilian Airlines	☎ 262-1440, 800-468-2744
Viasa-Venezualean Airways	☎ 358-3900, 374-5000, 800-468-4272
Virgin Atlantic Airways	☎ 445-9940, in state 800-877-2537, out of state 800-862-8621

See the Online Services appendix for airlines' websites.

BUS

Greyhound (☎ 800-231-2222) has three main terminals in Miami. The sleazy main downtown terminal is Bayside Station (☎ 379-7403) at 700 Biscayne Blvd. Greyhound's Airport Station (☎ 871-1810) is at 4111 NW 27th St, about a $5 cab or $1.25 bus ride away from the airport terminals; see the Getting Around chapter for specific information. The last is the North Miami Station (☎ 945-0801) at 16560 NE 6th Ave.

See the Key West section in the Excursions chapter for information on buses between Miami and the Florida Keys.

To Tampa-St Petersburg (weekday $29/39, weekend $30/41) via Fort Lauderdale ($5) takes between seven and eight hours, so we beg you to rent a car. There are buses at 7.50, 10.30, and 10.40 am, and 12.35, 2.55 and 9.55 pm.

Other Greyhound service includes:

Orlando
: 10 buses a day, trip time between five and 11 hours depending on the route, weekend fare is $33 one-way, $66 roundtrip.

New Orleans
: Six per day, 20 hours, $79/129

Atlanta
: Eight per day, 16 to 18 hours, $69/129

Washington, DC
: Five per day, 23 to 24 hours, $130/260

New York City
: Five per day, 28 hours, $130/260

TRAIN

Amtrak (☎ 800-872-7245) connects the Miami Terminal (☎ 835-1222) at 8303 NW 37th Ave with cities all over the continental USA and Canada. If you're coming here by train from anywhere, you will at some point have to connect with Amtrak's *SilverMeteor* or *SilverStar* trains, which run between New York City and Miami and Tampa. The *SilverMeteor* runs directly to Miami via Orlando; the *SilverStar* breaks up after Orlando: half the train's cars head to Miami and the other half to Tampa. Travel time between Miami and Orlando is about five hours.

Prices are highly complex and change often, though it's generally a bit more than Greyhound at its cheapest and a lot more than even flying (sometimes even flying business class) at peak times; call Amtrak to sort them out. Bus Nos L and 42 connect the Amtrak station with downtown Miami.

CAR & MOTORCYCLE

One particularly rewarding way to get here from west of Florida is to take I-10, which passes near the gorgeous beaches of Pensacola and across the Florida Panhandle, connecting with I-95 down the coast to Miami. From New York, expect a 19-hour trip without stopping. Speed limits are in the process of being changed along the way, and note that some states along the way ban radar detectors.

See the Getting Around chapter for regional highway information and rental car agencies.

HITCHHIKING

Hitchhiking in the USA is dangerous, and it's therefore less common than in other countries. That said, if you

A Free Car
Want a free car? Try Auto Driveaway of San Francisco (☎ 415-777-3740) or New York (☎ 212-967-2344). People who want their car moved from city A to city B leave the car with this organization and so long as you're willing to drive there at an average speed of 400 miles per day and pay for the gas (the first tank's free) the car's yours. To qualify, drivers (not passengers) must be 21 years old, have a valid driver's license and one other form of ID. Non-US citizens can use an international driver's license, but must show a valid entry visa and passport as well. They require a $300 to 350 refundable cash or travellers cheque deposit, and a $10 non-refundable registration fee. ■

do choose to hitch, the advice that follows should help to make your journey as fast, if not as safe, as possible. Officially, hitching is not illegal, except on interstate highways, but it *is* frowned upon by law enforcement and you can expect to be hassled by them if they see you. As signs at the on-ramps will tell you, pedestrians are not allowed on major highways, so keep off the on-ramps and away from these signs. It helps to look neat and carry a neatly printed sign with your destination. Lots of baggage, two or more men or groups of three of any sex slow you down substantially. Women should think very carefully about hitching, especially if alone but even in groups.

WARNING

This chapter is particularly vulnerable to change – prices for international travel are volatile, routes are introduced and canceled, schedules change, rules are amended, special deals come and go. Airlines and governments seem to take a perverse pleasure in making price structures and regulations as complicated as possible and you should check directly with the airline or travel agent to make sure you understand how a fare (and ticket you may buy) works.

In addition, the travel industry is highly competitive and there are many lurks and perks. The upshot of this is that you should get opinions, quotes and advice from as many airlines and travel agents as possible before you part with your hard-earned cash. The details given in this chapter should only be regarded as pointers and cannot be any substitute for you own careful, up-to-date research.

Getting Around

THE AIRPORTS

Miami International Airport

MIA is about 12 miles west of downtown, sandwiched between the Airport Expressway (Hwy 112) and the Dolphin Expressway (Hwy 836). Before you decide between a taxi or a shuttle, consider that one of the most civilized and cheapest methods of getting out of MIA is through Value Rent-A-Car's hourly rentals – this is an exceptional deal, and Value says it will continue for some time. See the entries for Car under the airports below, as well as Car Rental.

Bus Public transport from MIA to Miami and Miami Beach is tricky. There is Metrobus service between MIA and downtown Miami's Government Center station, but it always seems to get fouled up when we try to use it. Indeed, in three years of going in and out of MIA constantly, neither of us – nor any of our friends – has ever seen a Metrobus in the airport. We, along with other backpackers, have waited and waited on several occasions, and in the end always opted for a taxi or the SuperShuttle (see below), but your luck may be better than ours: Metrobus No 7 to Government Center (where you can catch a connecting bus to your final destination) leaves from the lower level of Concourse E, ostensibly every 40 minutes. The ride takes 35 minutes and costs

NICK SELBY

Miami's Water Taxi is a scenic transportation alternative.

$1.25. They run from 5.25 am to 9.06 pm. The J bus leaves from the same place ostensibly every 30 minutes and takes a circuitous route ending up in Miami Beach about an hour and some later, with service starting and ending about the same time.

Greyhound from the airport is also a pain in the ass; you can take a J or No 37 bus (every 30 minutes) or No 42 (one an hour) to the stop at NW 42nd Ave and NW 27th St and walk one block east to the Greyhound Airport Station (☎ 871-1810) or a taxi for about $5. From there, Greyhound makes the 20-minute journey to the sleazy downtown Bayside Station (☎ 379-7403) between 13 and 15 times a day; the first bus leaves at 7.10 am, the last at 9.45 pm, the cost is $5 – that SuperShuttle is still looking better. For more on Greyhound, see the Getting There & Away chapter.

Shuttle Consider your options carefully: it is sometimes cheaper for two people (and always cheaper for three) to take a taxi from MIA to Miami and Miami Beach. From MIA, blue SuperShuttle (☎ 871-2000) vans prowl the lower level outside the baggage claim area frequently – just wave one down. Costs vary depending on destination, calculated by the zip code of where you're going. But another major factor is whether your destination is a hotel or a private residence: the cost from the airport to the Clay Hotel & International Hostel is $10, but to a private residence in the same area (zip code 33139) it's $13, so if you're staying with a friend in South Beach you can save yourself $3 by walking there from the Clay. MIA to/from a private residence in the 33141 zip code is $14.

Car If you have your own liability and collision damage waiver insurance, are over 25 and have a major credit card, the cheapest way to get from MIA to Miami Beach (South or Northern), Coral Gables or the Port of Miami is to drive in a car from Value Rent-A-Car, which offers an hourly rate on its cars with no minimum charges. So a one-hour rental (plenty of time to get to, say, the Value office at 24th St and Collins Ave in South Beach) of a full-size car including Florida road charges ($2.05) and sales tax (6.5%) would clock in at a whopping $4.30. That's right, $4.30.

All the major car rental companies, as well as some little ones, have offices at MIA as well – see Car Rental below. The most direct route from MIA to Miami is to take Hwy 112 to I-95 south (25¢ toll) and follow the signs for downtown. To South Beach, take 37th Ave to

Hwy 836 east to I-395, which leads into the MacArthur Causeway. For Northern Miami Beach, take Hwy 112 to I-195, the Julia Tuttle Causeway. There's always a traffic jam in front of the terminals.

Taxi There is a flat fee scheme in place between MIA and five zones: generally the flat fee to anywhere in Miami Beach between Government Cut and 63rd St (Zone 4, which includes all of South Beach) from MIA is $22; north of 63rd St to 87th Terrace (Zone 3) is $27; between 87th Terrace and Haulover Beach (Zone 2) is $32, and from Haulover Beach to the Broward County Line (Zone 1) is $38. Zone 5 is the village of Key Biscayne, which is $29. There's also a flat rate between MIA and the Port of Miami of $15.75. These rates are per carload, not per person. Taxis swarm the lower level roadway.

Fort Lauderdale/Hollywood International Airport

Many deeply discounted tickets from the USA and Europe plop you down in Fort Lauderdale's shimmering new terminal. While it's about 30 miles north of Miami, it's a great airport: fewer crowds, a slower pace and newer, cleaner and easier-to-use terminals speed you through.

Bus & Train Tri-Rail (☎ 800-874-7245) has a shuttle bus from the airport to the Fort Lauderdale Airport Tri-Rail station (you can also take Broward County Transit (BCt) bus Nos 3 or 6), with trains heading down to the Tri-Rail/Metrorail Transfer Station ($3) about once an hour at rush hours, once every two hours in midday, starting at about 5.50 am to 11.30 pm on weekdays and less frequent service on weekends. From the Transfer Station, take Metrorail to Government Center, where you can change for a bus to your destination. To Miami Beach, this journey will take about two to 2½ hours, and cost about $4.25.

Shuttle Gray Line (☎ 954-561-8886) runs private limos and shuttles. A shared shuttle bus from the airport to South Beach is $12 per person. A private limo (more of a car, really) is $48. Catch the shuttle outside the terminal baggage area. They run from 8 am to 2 am.

SuperShuttle can take you to, but not from, Fort Lauderdale. From the Clay Hotel the cost is $21; from a residence anywhere in the 33139 and 33141 zip codes it's $28.

Car Value has an office in Fort Lauderdale, and hourly rentals are available for the same price of $1.99 per hour or less, with no minimum. The price differs slightly from Miami, though: the sales tax here is 6%, but there's a one-time Airport Fee of $3.10, so a one-hour rental (which you could also make if you hustled right to South Beach) here would be $7.26.

There are almost as many car rental companies here as there are in MIA – see Car Rental below. Driving is really straightforward: I-95 south (there's an airport on-ramp) to I-195 east for Northern Miami Beach; I-395 for South Beach; and straight through to downtown Miami.

Taxi Yellow Cab Company (☎ 954-565-5400, 954-565-8400) is the official airport taxi in Fort Lauderdale; their cabs are metered and charge $2.45 flagfall for the first mile, and $1.75 for each additional mile. A trip from Fort Lauderdale Airport to South Beach would run about $40 to 45.

METROBUS

Metro-Dade Transit's buses cover a healthy amount of the city. They're not the fastest things on wheels, and in many cases they're nowhere near as convenient as a car, but they'll get you there.

Each bus route has a different schedule. Buses generally run from about 5.30 am to about 11 pm, some earlier, some later; call ☎ 638-6700 (TDD 638-7456) Monday to Friday from 6 am to 10 pm (though hold time in the evening can be exasperatingly long), Saturday and Sunday 9 am to 5 pm for specific route information, or for travel planning assistance. For information by fax, submit your request to fax 654-6587.

For transit maps by mail call ☎ 654-6586 Monday to Friday 9 am to 5 pm. See the Disabled Travelers section in the Facts for the Visitor chapter for Special Transportation Services (STS) information. For lost & found, call ☎ 375-3366 Monday to Friday from 8.30 am to 4.30 pm.

Transit Booths & Routes

Transit booths, where you can get maps, scheduling information and tokens, are at Government Center (☎ 375-5771), NW 1st St between NW 1st and 2nd Aves; a second booth is at the corner of E Flagler and E 1st Aves (no ☎), and a third at the Omni Metromover Terminal (no ☎) at the Omni Mall at Biscayne Blvd just south of NE 15th St.

The Omni Metromover and Government Center Terminals are main junction points for buses downtown.
Some major routes are:

C, K Between Miami Beach and Government Center

S, M Between Miami Beach and Omni Mall

S From the Omni Mall, to South Beach, north on Alton Rd then east on 17th St and north on Collins Ave past the South Beach Library and Bass Museum, and up to the Aventura Mall

8 Between the downtown transit booth and Calle Ocho

17, 6, 22 Between Government Center and Vizcaya/Museum of Science & Space Transit Planetarium and Coconut Grove

B Between the downtown transit booth and Seaquarium and Key Biscayne on the Rickenbacker Causeway.

24 Between the downtown transit booth and Miracle Mile, Coral Gables

Fares & Passes

You pay as your board. Bus fare is $1.25; meters accept dollar bills, all coins including 50¢ pieces and Susan B's, or tokens, available from the transit booths. A transfer from bus-to-Metrorail or bus-to-bus is 25¢; ask your driver for the transfer slip. A monthly pass is $60, and a monthly rail parking permit bought with the pass is an additional $2.

METROMOVER

One-third bus, one-third monorail, one-third train, Metromover is a neat solution to downtown congestion: it is made up of one- to two-car, rubber-wheeled, computer-controlled vehicles (there's usually no driver on board), running on an elevated track. It's also a great way to get a cheap orientation tour of the entire downtown area.

There are three lines on two 'loops'. The Outer Loop's two lines, the Omni and Brickell Loops, run between the School Board Station west of the Omni Mall, and the Brickell Financial Center Station at SE 14th St and Brickell Ave. The Omni Loop starts at School Board Station, through the Omni, around downtown and Government Center then back north. The Brickell Loop starts at the Brickell Financial Center Station, north to Government Center and around downtown then back south. The Outer Loop runs from about 5 am to 10.30 pm, and shuttle buses run on the Brickell Loop between 10.30 pm and midnight.

The Inner Loop starts and ends at Government Center and loops around downtown. It runs from about 5 am to midnight.

The fare is 25¢; turnstiles accept quarters, dimes and nickels; some (not all) stations have dollar-bill change machines.

You can change between Metrorail and Metromover at Government Center. Metromover information is available at the transit booths or call the telephone numbers above for Metrobus information.

METRORAIL

This is a 21-mile-long heavy rail system with one line, running from Hialeah, through downtown Miami and then south to Kendall, connecting with Tri-Rail (at the Tri-Rail/Metrorail Transfer Center at 2567 E 11th Ave, Hialeah), and Metromover and Metrobus (at Government Center).

The fare is $1.25, or $1 with a Metromover transfer. Transfers to Tri-Rail or Metromover are free; transfers from Metrorail to Metrobus are 25¢. The trains run every day from 6 am to midnight.

TRI-RAIL

Tri-Rail (☎ 800-874-7245, TDD 800-273-7545) is a commuter rail system that runs between three counties: Dade, Broward and Palm Beach. The double-decker trains are a marvel of cleanliness and, at least for the time being, they're very cheap. For longer trips, like to Palm Beach, however, it takes about four times longer to take Tri-Rail than to drive.

Fares are calculated on a zone basis, and the route spans six zones. The costs for a one-way ticket are: one zone $2; two zones $3; three zones $4: four zones $4.50; five zones $5; and six zones $5.50. So the most you'll ever pay is for the ride between Miami International Airport and West Palm Beach, which is $5.50 one way, $9.25 roundtrip.

A transfer from Tri-Rail to Metrorail is free. From Metrobus, you buy a 25¢ Tri-Rail transfer from the bus driver, and then trade the transfer at the Tri-Rail ticket booth for a $1.50 discount on your Tri-Rail ticket.

The new Tri-Rail station at MIA is expected to open in early 1997, but as we went to press, no further information was available on it.

The main connection between Miami city transportation and Tri-Rail is at the Tri-Rail/Metrorail Transfer

Station, northwest of downtown at 2567 E 11th Ave, Hialeah.

Tri-Rail does some very neat marketing tricks; as we went to press, they were offering 'guided' tours from Miami to (on Monday) Lake Worth, and (on Thursday) to Worth Ave in Palm Beach. The roundtrip cost is $3 including all bus transfers. A 'guide' rides with the group on the train, which leaves the Tri-Rail/Metrorail Transfer Station at 9.03 am, and answers questions about the destination. You get on a shuttle bus at the far end, which takes you to the destination and brings you back to the train about 2½ to three hours later.

They also run a *Murder on the Sunshine Express* murder mystery 'drama' on board a train – you know, actors perform, passengers get involved, yadda yadda yadda – then you have dinner at West Palm Beach's Kravis Center before returning to Miami. The cost is $49.95 per person, the shows run periodically, about once every three weeks. There are Tri-Rail stations at the following locations: Miami Airport, Tri-Rail/Metrorail Transfer, Golden Glades, Hollywood, Fort Lauderdale Airport, Fort Lauderdale, Cypress Creek, Pompano Beach, Deerfield Beach, Boca Raton, Delray Beach, Boynton Beach, Lake Worth, Palm Beach Airport (actually West Palm International), West Palm Beach.

JITNEY

These are shuttle vans, once illegal, that take up slack in areas where public transit coverage is poor, generally in low-income inner city areas. Over the last few years, Metro Dade County has allowed jitneys to operate under limited circumstances on certain routes. They're operated by companies like Liberty City Jitney, Conchita's Express and Sun Jitney, and fares are usually $1.

WATER TAXI

The Water Taxi (☎ 467-6677) is a fleet of cute little boats that tootle around the local waterways. They have two major routes, both of which run from 10 am to about 11 pm every day. The first, between Bayside Marketplace and the 5th St Marina at the southwestern end of South Beach or the western end of Lincoln Road (you need to phone in advance to be picked up) costs $7 one way, $12 roundtrip and $15 for an all-day pass.

The second line is a downtown water shuttle service between Bayside Marketplace and the following locations: Biscayne Marriot, Crown Plaza, Plaza Venetian, Omni, Watson Island (Chalk's Airlines), Port of Miami,

Hard Rock Cafe, Hotel InterContinental, DuPont Plaza, Sheraton Biscayne, Barnett Plaza, Brickell Key, Hyatt Regency, Holiday Inn Downtown, José Martí Park, East Coast Fisheries, Fisher Island (with resident or guest ID).

The cost is $3.50/6/7 one-way/roundtrip/all day. They ask that you tip the driver; if they're nice, $1 for the shuttle or $2 for the Beach/Bayside trip is plenty, and if they're not, nothing is perfectly appropriate. Water Taxi also operates a much more comprehensive network of routes in Fort Lauderdale.

CAR & MOTORCYCLE

Driving

The sprawl of the Miami area is such that driving is something most visitors will end up doing. Miami drivers are generally civil, though see the Dangers & Annoyances section in Facts for the Visitor under Crime for tips on when they are not.

After the spate of carjackings in the early 1990s, the city formulated a method of letting tourists know they were on a major tourist route. They devised a Sun symbol: the idea is that if you follow the Sun you're going in the right direction. The problem is, they put Suns on every major route a tourist may take – including routes to Coral Gables and downtown Miami – and since a 'Sun' reminds most people of 'Beach', having six signs, all sporting Suns, next to each other at a highway interchange gets confusing.

We're not saying there is a better symbol (*we* certainly couldn't come up with one), but rather that you should not just mindlessly follow Sun symbols: Miami's highway interchanges can be very confusing, so read the signs (Sun or no Sun) carefully.

One word of caution: the venerable practice of cruising along Ocean Drive in South Beach has been illegal for the last couple of years.

Fuel Overseas visitors: unless you're coming here from Saudi Arabia or Indonesia, US gasoline prices are a gift from Heaven: they average $1.15 a gallon (a bit less than four liters) in Miami. Always use self-service islands, as full service ones cost 25 to 50¢ more per gallon.

Rules & Regulations Americans drive on the right (and yes, that also means *correct)* side of the road and pass on the left. Right turns on a red light are permitted after a full stop. Speed limits in the city are between 15 and 45 miles per hour. Be especially careful in school zones, which are limited to 15 mph when the lights are flashing, and on causeways, which – no matter how fast cars actually travel – are limited to no more than 45 mph. Speeding tickets are outrageous: for example, if you're clocked at 50 in a 40 mph zone, the fine is over $127. Radar detectors are legal in Florida (hint, nudge, wink).

All passengers in a car must wear seat belts, all children under three must be in a child safety seat (the rental car companies will rent you one for about $5 a day). The fine for not wearing a seat belt can be as high as $150.

Major Arteries

Miami Beach Miami Beach is connected to the mainland by four causeways built on Biscayne Bay. They are, from south to north (which is pretty much from most to least used) the MacArthur (which is also the extension of Hwys 41 and A1A), Venetian (50¢ toll), Julia Tuttle and John F Kennedy Causeways.

North-South The most important highway in the area is I-95, which runs almost straight north-south until it ends at US Hwy 1 south of downtown. US Hwy 1, which runs from Key West all the way north to Maine, hugs the coastline and is called Dixie Hwy south of downtown and Biscayne Blvd from there north to (and somewhat past) the city limits.

Florida's Turnpike takes a westerly curve north of the city and becomes the Homestead Extension.

You'll hear a lot about the Palmetto Expressway; see Weird Things below for the scoop on that.

Le Jeune Rd (42nd Ave) is a biggie, too, connecting Opa-Locka and the Amtrak station at the north, and Coral Gables and the University of Miami at the south, and Miami International Airport about midpoint.

Hwy A1A is mainly Collins Ave in Miami Beach.

East-West Besides the causeways to Miami Beach, the major east roads are Calle Ocho (see Weird Things); Hwy 112, which is the Airport Expressway; and Hwy 836, which connects to I-395, both called the Dolphin Expressway, which runs from the Homestead Extension through northern downtown and connects to the MacArthur Causeway.

Weird Things The Palmetto Expressway (Hwy 826) runs both north-south *and* east-west! It meets US Hwy 1 at the south and goes north straight as an arrow to 167th St then turns right and goes due east to the junction with I-95. In the same spirit of jocundity, US Hwy 27

(Okeechobee Rd) slashes across the city *diagonally* from northwest to southeast.

Calle Ocho has five (count 'em) names: it's called at various points along its stretch (officially): SW 8th St, US Hwy 41, the Tamiami Trail, Calle Ocho and Olga Guillot Way. Don't even attempt to get it – just call it Calle Ocho (KAH-yeh AW-cho) like everyone else around here, and as we do in this book.

Parking

Except in Coral Gables, South Beach and downtown, parking is pretty straightforward: regulations are well-signed and meters usually tell when you need to use them.

Parking in downtown can be a nightmare, or at least expensive. A good way to do it is to park in the Cultural Center Garage at 50 NW 2nd Ave, just west of the Metro-Dade Cultural Center. If you visit one of the museums in that complex, or take a book out of the library, you can have your parking ticket validated and parking is $2. Otherwise, you're at the mercy of private lots or un-discounted public ones.

Miami Beach has decided, it would seem, to save for a rainy day by filling up the town coffers with money raised through parking violations and meters. Meter parking is in effect along Washington and Collins Aves and Ocean Drive, and in any place convenient to them. Resident-only parking stickers are required in most areas that are not metered. And many choice parking spots in the heart of the Deco District have been leased by the restaurants and hotels they're in front of, and are used for *brief* loading and unloading or to wait for valet parking attendants (usually about $10) to take them to a private lot.

There is municipal parking at 13th St and Collins Ave, 12th St between Collins Ave and Ocean Drive, on the corners of Washington below 10th St, and just north of Lincoln Road Mall.

Parking fines are generally less than $20, but a tow could cost you up to $75. Meter-watchers make frequent rounds, never cut someone a break and don't take no guff from nobody. If you find your car gone, your first call should be to Beach Towing (☎ 534-2128) to ask them if they have it. They'll either tell you that they have it, the number of another company that may have taken it, or to call the police.

If Miami Beach is tough on enforcement, Coral Gables is positively Orwellian: meter parking is everywhere that valet parking is not, and if you're a second late the meter-watcher's there and you're hit with varyingly outrageous fines – we got hit with three tickets in two days, once because we were two hours late (and they put the second ticket right on top of the first one!).

Car Rental

All the big rent-a-car operators can be found in the Miami Area, particularly at the airports, along with a host of smaller or local operators. Rates go up and down like the stock market and it's always worth phoning around to see what's available. Booking ahead usually ensures the best rates – and that can mean from the pay phone in the rental office to the company's 800 number. Sometimes the head office can get you a better price than the branch office, so always check.

Many of the following companies have several locations around town; check in the Yellow Pages under Automobile Rental for others. Car rental companies in the Miami/Fort Lauderdale Area include:

Alamo	☎ 800-327-9633
Avis	☎ 800-831-2847
Budget	☎ 800-527-0700
Continental	☎ 871-4663
Dollar	☎ 800-800-4000
Enterprise	☎ 800-325-8007
Hertz	☎ 800-654-3131
Pass	☎ 871-6262
Sears	☎ 800-527-0770
Thrifty	☎ 800-367-2277
U-Haul	☎ 673-1400
Value	☎ 800-468-2583

Rates Rates in Florida for some reason tend to be lower than in most of the rest of the country; typically a small car might cost $23 to 45 a day or $129 to 179 a week. On top of that there will be 6.5% sales tax, $2.05 a day Florida road surcharge and $9 or 10 a day for each insurance option you take.

Generally speaking, the best deals come on weekly or weekend rental periods. At the time of writing, the consistently lowest rates seem to come from companies like Alamo, Budget, Enterprise and Value, and the highest from Avis and Hertz, though there are always specials and the best bet is to shop around carefully. The same car can vary in price from operator to operator by as much as $20 a day or $75 a week.

Insurance Note that in Florida, liability insurance is not included in rental costs. Some credit cards cover loss/damage waiver or LDW (sometimes also called CDW, or collision/damage waiver), which means that you won't have to pay if you damage the car itself, but liability insurance means that you won't have to pay if you hit someone and they sue you. If you own a car and have insurance at home, your liability insurance may extend to coverage of rental cars, but be *absolutely* certain before driving on the roads in the litigious USA. Also, if you opt out of the LDW, be certain that your card will really cover you for it.

Mileage Charges Most car rental companies here include unlimited mileage at no extra cost – be sure to check this point, as you can rack up hundreds of miles even just in the city, and at 25¢ per mile, this could be an unhappy surprise.

Age & Credit Requirements Most operators require that you be at least 25 years of age and have a major credit card in your own name. Some will let you get away with the age thing by paying varyingly outrageous surcharges, but renting without a credit card – if you can even accomplish it – will require a large cash deposit, and you'll have to work things out well in advance with the company. It's hard to do, and even if they let you, you will be treated with great suspicion!

Fuel Costs The amount of gas in the tank when you return the car is a crucial profit center for car rental companies. When you rent the car, you'll probably be offered an opportunity to buy the full tank from the operator at a slightly discounted rate. Unless you're the kind of person who can calculate exactly how far a tank will get you, and run on fumes all the way back to the airport, this is a bad idea, as there are no refunds on unused fuel: if you bring it back half full, you've just paid twice the going street rate for the gas. If you don't buy it from them, be certain to return the car with a full tank of fuel; if you let the operator refill the car for you the price is outrageous – generally $2.99 but sometimes as much as $3.99 a gallon.

Motorcycle Rental

Rolling Thunder (☎ 668-4600, 800-851-7420, fax 441-0519) at 4537 Ponce de León Blvd in Coral Gables rents late model Harley Davidson motorcycles including Low Riders, Heritage Softtails and a Fat Boy. The cost is $135 for a full day and $850 a week including 100 free miles (20¢ each additional mile or an extra $25 charge for unlimited mileage) and two helmets, rain suits and night glasses. You need a motorcycle license (from any state or country) and must be 25 or older. You'll need to put down a cash deposit or a credit card draft (which they don't put through) for a $1500 damage and theft deposit.

Buying a Car or Motorcycle

One way to possibly beat the high cost of renting a car is to buy a used vehicle on arrival and sell it when you leave. If you go this route, it helps to either have a bit of the auto mechanic in you, or find a mechanic you can trust; you won't get much return value on a 'lemon' or a gas guzzler. Don't ask yourself: 'Do I feel lucky?' because even minor repairs could cost well over $100.

Any owner who won't bring or let you take the car to a mechanic is hiding something. While you're there, tell the mechanic how much the seller wants for it, and if things look good, ask them to run an emissions test – it's no good finding out after you've bought it that the car won't pass state emissions levels. We have only heard good things about Shorty & Fred's Garage (☎ 672-1047), which has been at 1520 Alton Rd since 1956. They'll check out a car for $48, and run an emissions test for $39.95.

Once you've bought the car, you must buy a rather costly auto insurance policy (generally $500 to 800 a year depending on your age and driving record) and take the smog certificate and proof of insurance, along with the ownership title and bill of sale, to any office of the Department of Motor Vehicles (DMV). The main Miami office is at ☎ 673-7405, but check in the blue pages government section of the white pages under Florida State Department of Highway & Motor Vehicles for full listings.

It normally takes a full morning or afternoon to get your auto registration (waiting to speak with, as one comedian put it, people who 'look as if they grew up in the trunk of a Buick'), which will cost anywhere from 7 to 12% of the cost of the car.

As your departure from the USA approaches, you must set aside time to sell the car, perhaps also laying out additional money to place a classified ad in a newspaper.

If you don't object to a little wind, you might consider buying a motorcycle, which is cheaper than a car and tends to be easier to sell. But note that motorcycle insurance costs more, that my mother says it's too dangerous, and be sure to buy a helmet for yourself and any passengers: helmets are required by Florida law, which is strictly enforced.

See the Shopping chapter for a Harley Davidson dealer in South Beach.

TAXI

Taxis in Miami are metered, the fare is $1.25 for the first seventh of a mile, 25¢ for each additional seventh of a mile.

As with taxis in many large, racially integrated cities, Miami taxis are generally driven by recent immigrants. The radios will be blaringly loud, of poor quality, and feature garbled mish-mashes of Russian, Polish, Creole, Spanglish and other languages. Taxis here are in generally bad shape, but they'll get you where you're going. If they don't or if you have a bad experience, make sure you get the driver's chauffeur license number, his name and, if you can, the car's license plate number and contact the Taxi Complaints Line at ☎ 375-2460. These folks really do chase down offensive drivers.

There are taxi stands here and there, but the usual way of catching one – outside MIA and the Port of Miami – is to phone. See the Taxicab listing in the Yellow Pages for a complete list of companies, but in the past we've used:

AAA Cab	☎ 999-9990
All Dade Cab	☎ 638-4444
Central Cab	☎ 532-5555
Eights Cab	☎ 888-8888
Sunshine Cab Co	☎ 445-3333

BICYCLE

Miami is as flat as a pancake and as smooth as a baby's butt, so biking around the Beach makes a lot of sense. In fact it makes so much sense that people who don't have bikes will try to steal yours so they, too, can enjoy it: bring along a sturdy, U-type bike lock, or, better, two. Chains and padlocks do not deter people in Miami Beach, where bike theft rates rival those of Amsterdam. Everyone we know in Miami Beach has had a bike stolen, so be careful.

Bicycles are not allowed on buses, Metrorail or Tri-Rail, but you can bike across the causeways.

ORGANIZED TOURS

See the Organized Tours section in the Things to See & Do chapter for Art Deco walking tours. Between September and late June every year Dr Paul George (☎ 858-6021) does about 70 different walking tours and boat and train tours of Dade County, in conjunction with the

Historical Museum of South Florida. They're $10 for museum members, $15 for non-members. Dr George also offers private tours by appointment, though unless you're with a group it's going to be very expensive: two hour tours start at about $100. Write to him at 1345 SW 14th St, Miami, FL 33145.

For an interesting – if somewhat expensive – view of the city, you can take a spin over the city with an air tour from Chalk's International Airlines (☎ 371-8628/9). The half-hour tours fly all around Miami, Miami Beach, Key Biscayne and the surrounding areas for $39.50 per person. Tours depart their Watson Island airport on Saturday at 1.45 pm.

For tours outside the city, including the Everglades, the Keys, Orlando and other areas, Miami Nice Excursions (☎ 949-9180) does shuttle bus and guided excursions. They offer a wide range of tours and services.

Things to See & Do

As we've mentioned, Greater Miami is a huge, sprawling area. Below we've broken the attractions and activities into rough geographically determined sections.

Top 10 Attractions

Based on a totally unscientific assessment of a number of qualities, which can be summed up as uniqueness, bang-for-the-buck fun and redeeming value, we offer this totally subjective list of the top 10 attractions in the Greater Miami area:

- Gallery Walk, Ocean Drive and the Beaches
- Venetian Pool
- Preston B Bird & Mary Heinlein Fruit & Spice Park
- The New World Symphony
- Holocaust Memorial
- Metrozoo
- Miami Seaquarium
- Museum of Science & Space Transit Planetarium
- Museum of Contemporary Art
- Máximo Gómez Park and Calle Ocho

MIAMI BEACH

Most people come here for the beaches and the clubs and bars, but there are other compelling attractions within the City of Miami Beach that you should really try and see during your stay. And happily the attractions within the City of Miami Beach are easy to get to and between, so a day spent seeing what the Beach has to offer is one very well spent.

The Beach is filled with Jewish culture because of the large numbers of Jews who have settled here over the last 50 years, but there's also a decidedly Latin flair. In fact, there's even a **Cuban-Jewish Congregation** (☎ 534-7213), in a building that looks just like something out of Bedrock, at 1700 Michigan Ave.

The Deco District

The Art Deco Historic District, one of the largest areas in the USA on the National Register of Historic Places, is in the very heart of South Beach. Its protection and

KENNETH DREYFUSS

KENNETH DREYFUSS

KENNETH DREYFUSS

CORINNA SELBY

KENNETH DREYFUSS

KENNETH DREYFUSS

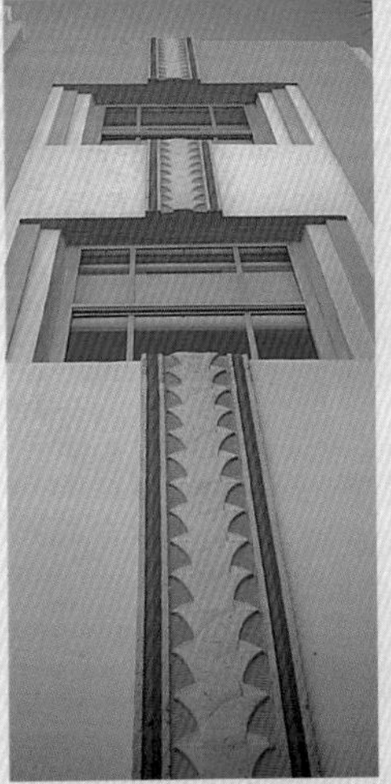

CORINNA SELBY

CORINNA SELBY

CORINNA SELBY

Art Deco detail in colorful South Beach

renovation has been one of the major forces in the rejuvenation of the entire area and the rebirth of it as a major tourist destination.

The Deco District's unique hotels and apartment buildings have been renovated with a decidedly colorful flair, the façades painted with pastel pinks, blues and greens that make for a walk into the roaring '20s or an unguided tour of the very best in American kitsch, depending on your views.

The listing on the Register is what protected the area from attempts by the city and developers to raze significant portions of what was in the 1980s a crime-ridden collection of crumbling eyesores populated by drug-crazed lunatics, Cuban refugees and elderly residents.

The listing was fought for and pushed through by the Miami Design Preservation League (MDPL; ☎ 672-2014), founded by Barbara Baer Capitman in 1976 after she heard plans by the City of Miami to raze several historic buildings in what is now the Omni Mall.

But Leonard Horowitz, a co-founder of the MDPL played a pivotal role in putting South Beach back on the map, by painting the then drably painted Deco buildings in shocking colors like pink, lavender and turquoise. When his restoration of Friedman's Pharmacy made the cover of *Progressive Architecture* in 1982, South Beach managed to find itself at the business end of a Hollywood lens: the would-be producers of *Miami Vice* saw something they liked, and the rest . . . .

The MDPL is still ferociously active with protection and restoration of South Beach and offers some first-rate walking and bicycle tours of the District that explain the architecture in excellent detail (see the Organized Tours section below for more information and see the Architecture section in the Facts about Miami chapter for a discussion on Art Deco in general). Stop in at the **Art Deco Welcome Center** (☎ 531-3484) at 1001 Ocean Drive for more information.

The Deco District is bounded by Dade Blvd at the north, 6th St at the south; the Atlantic Ocean at the east and Lenox Court (half a block east of Alton Rd) at the west. It contains an estimated 800 buildings, and the best thing about them is scale: most are no taller than the palm trees. And while the architecture is by no means uniform – you'll see examples of Streamline, Moderne and Mediterranean Revival as well as Art Deco – it all works well together, giving the entire district the feel of a small village.

Highlights in the Deco District include examples of Streamline, like the Avalon, Essex, Chesterfield, Carlyle, Leslie, The Tides, Cardozo and Breakwater Hotels;

Mediterranean including most buildings along Española Way but especially the Clay Hotel & International Hostel, the Old City Hall at 1130 Washington Ave, the Wolfsonian Foundation building, Edison Hotel, Casa Casaurina (Versace's house), the Fernwood at 935 Pennsylvania Ave, the Regal at the corner of 11th and Pennsylvania Ave; Parc Vendome at 736 13th St; Depression Moderne (the post office); and the Neo-Classical Revival Betsy Ross Hotel. Other highlights are the Coral House at the corner of 9th and Collins, and the lovely courtyard inside the Mermaid Guest House.

Organized Tours With over 400 registered historic landmark buildings and 800 buildings, it's very hard not to have an interesting walk through the Deco District.

NICK SELBY

The Miami Design Preservation League (☎ 672-2014) runs 1½-hour walking tours of the Art Deco District every Saturday at 10.30 am. Reservations are not required, but you should show up about 15 minutes early. The tours leave from the Oceanfront Auditorium at 1001 Ocean Drive and the cost is $6, no discounts for nobody. During February and March the tours can get crowded, but during the rest of the year there are usually crowds of 15 to 20 people.

On the first and third Sunday of each month, the MDPL offers two-hour bicycle tours (☎ 674-0150) in conjunction with the bike shop at 601 5th St, at the corner of Washington Ave. They leave at 10.30 am and the cost is $10 including a bicycle rental or $5 if you have your own.

Donna Zemo's Deco Tours Miami Beach (☎ 531-4465) does walking tours Monday to Friday at 10.30 am for $15. The 1½-hour tours cover most of South Beach. They usually leave from the Miami Beach Chamber of Commerce information kiosk in the middle of Lincoln Road Mall at Washington Ave, but that kiosk was under construction when we researched, so call to see where the tours are leaving from. Reservations are required, and the tours are canceled if there's a lack of interest.

Note that an interesting aspect of walking through the District is that you can follow the boom phases of the beach: beginning at 5th St in the 1930s through mid-beach, the late '30s and early '40s, to the area north of

27th St, which begins the new era of '50s resort and luxury hotels, dotted with condominiums.

Ocean Beach Historic District & South Pointe

Talk about closing the barn door after the cows have run off with your Chevy: because the boundaries of the Deco District only extended as far south as 6th St, the area from there to South Pointe at the island's southern tip was, as the developers like to say, 'in play'.

According to people like German-born developer Thomas Kramer – Miami Beach's Donald Trump – 'in play' meant ripping down everything in sight – including some streets – and putting up monstrously tall high-rise condominium towers with casinos in their basements. Thankfully, Miami Beach voters put the kibosh on the casino bill, and in February 1996, activists finally got the city to designate most of the area a historic district, but not before the developers managed to get many of their projects grandfathered in, meaning that they're given a variance due to the fact that they were in the process of building when the regulations were passed.

Note that the Ocean Beach Historic District does not cover all the area south of 6th St – its boundaries zig zag around, from 6th St at the northern end to 1st St at the south, but exclude a number of blocks, and, notably, some clearly historic structures, like the one housing Joe's Stone Crab Restaurant (see the Places to Eat chapter).

Still, while construction will continue in the area, **South Pointe Park** is a wonderful place to spend a sunny afternoon. It's got a nice little playground, a fishing pier from which kids (illegally) dive into Government Cut, a short boardwalk and an excellent stretch of beach that's less crowded during the week than the beaches to the near north (though on weekends it's positively overrun by Latin American families, see Beaches, below).

There is also an **observation tower**, a great place to watch the cruise ships chugging out to sea on most afternoons (of course, you may want to wash down that view with some suds –

NICK SELBY

see the Places to Eat chapter for the South Pointe Seafood House & Brewing Company, which brews some darn fine beers on the premises).

At the southwest corner of 5th St and Collins Ave, the bronze sculpture, ***The Paper Boy***, is a work by artist Glenna Goodacre, who's probably best known for her Vietnam Women's Memorial near the Vietnam Veterans Memorial in Washington, DC.

The graffiti-ed Miami Beach logo on the pastel pink **water tower** at the intersection of Jefferson Ave and Alton Rd is classic 1980s Miami Beach.

Washington Ave

Washington Ave is sort of the Beach's engine room: be as trendy as you like elsewhere, but when you need a quart of milk or a lug wrench, this is where you'll come. Over the past few years the nightclubs, bars and restaurants that have opened along this stretch of road have gotten decidedly trendier, but a good measure of the shops (at least for the time being) are still small, family- and often Cuban-run businesses.

Other than the Wolfsonian Foundation (see below) and the clubs and restaurants, there's not much to see on Washington Ave. An exception, believe it or not, is the 1937 **post office** (☎ 531-3763) at 1300 Washington Ave, a Depression Moderne building with an enormous dome on the south corner. Inside the dome is a mural – a really nice sun and stars – and post-office boxes. Ask staff (if

CORINNA SELBY

Washington Ave street life

the crowds ever die down) for a history of the building – some of them know a lot about it.

At the corner of 17th St is the imposing **Temple Emanu El Synagogue** (☎ 538-2503), which holds services Sunday to Thursday at 8 am and 5.30 pm, Friday at 8 am and 6 pm, and Saturday at 9 am and 6 pm. North of 17th St on the west side of Washington Ave is the **Miami Beach Convention Center**, home to huge auto and boat shows (see the Special Events section in the Facts for the Visitor chapter) and the Jackie Gleason Theater (see the Entertainment chapter).

Ocean Drive

A walk along Ocean Drive from north to south is a safari through the trendy. To your left is the kind of beach where low-flying planes trail advertisements for nightclubs, restaurants, performances and, in one instance, an enormous full-color poster of Marky Mark in his underwear. To the right are the hotels and sidewalk cafés that seem to want to spill into the street itself. And vehicular traffic would appear to be limited to vintage roadsters, '63 Mustangs and grandiose Harley Davidsons.

Fashion plates will want to head immediately for the residence of Gianni Versace, **Casa Casaurina** (1930), at No 1114, which was for a good while called the Amsterdam Palace. It's a pretty flashy place: a three-story Spanish Mediterranean palace with a small observatory at the top. But unless you're far more influential then we are, you'll just be able to look at the façade wistfully.

But the fashionably impaired needn't worry; despite the Drive's undeniable chic, it's definitely a come-as-you-are affair: the minimum requirement is a pair of cut-off blue jeans, a T-shirt and an optional pair of in-line skates.

The first thing to do, then, is get a drink. As the masses strut, sashay, blade and groove their way past your sidewalk table, order a café con leche, keep an eye peeled for famous models and try to look pretentious and self-congratulatory to fit in. It's great fun.

Get your bearings while checking out the interior of one of the Beach's finest Deco treasures by heading to the roof of the **Park Central Hotel**, No 640. The seven-story beachfront property has a sundeck, and no one seems to mind that visitors just walk past reception, take the elevator to the top floor and gaze out over the city. When you exit the elevator, turn right; just outside the door to the roof on the right is a steep staircase leading to a higher roof overlooking Ocean Drive.

A good time to visit the roof is around 4 pm, when the huge luxury cruise ships chug through Government Cut channel on their way to the Caribbean; the roof offers a stunning view of the ships against the Miami skyline and the beach.

Another attraction of sorts is the hotel's Vampire LeStat room; a room described in Anne Rice's *Tale of the Body Thief* as one that the vampire stayed in. If you ask nicely at the front desk, and they're not busy and the room's vacant (unlikely in high season) they'll take you up and show it to you. You can stay in the room; see the Places to Stay chapter.

Cruising the Drive, a former SoBe tradition where people would drive the length of the Drive in search of a good time, is now illegal.

Lincoln Road Mall

Ocean Drive may have a firm choke-hold on Things Fabulous, but most of the real South Beach begins at the Lincoln Road Mall. Renovated by the city in 1960 and just emerging from a $16.2 million facelift, 'the Road', a wide, pedestrian-only stretch of sidewalk, is the Beach's cultural epicenter, with galleries every hundred feet or so, and sidewalk cafés filled with off-duty models trying to relax.

Other highlights include the **Miami City Ballet** (where you can watch rehearsals through the picture window fronting the Road), the **Colony Theatre** and the **Lincoln Theatre** – a Deco delight that is home to the New World Symphony. See the Entertainment chapter for information on all those venues.

Monthly **Gallery Walks** take place on alternating Saturday nights. These are very popular with locals and visitors alike. Most of the Road's galleries hold openings, and many give away wine and snacks and you can spend several hours popping into them before heading out for a late-night snack or a club. See the Entertainment chapter for more information.

Every Sunday from November to March there's a **Farmers' Market** on the Road between Euclid and Meridian Aves. If you've got kids, note that the Lincoln Road Partnership has arranged kids' activities during the Farmer's Market: meet at the fountain in front of World Resources Café (☎ 534-9095), 719 Lincoln Road.

On varying Sundays throughout the year there is also an **Antiques & Collectibles Market**. Stop in at the Lincoln Road Partnership's offices at 924 Lincoln Road and pick up a free copy of their newsletter, which has monthly schedules.

Even during the week, the Road is abuzz with gallery- and restaurant-goers, as well as the ubiquitous in-line skaters. Running the length of the mall is a center divider of concrete planters filled with lush greenery and awkwardly shaped palms that make a picnic-style late-afternoon snack almost irresistible.

Also, stop in at **Books & Books**, 933 Lincoln Road, the Beach's premiere bookshop (see the Shopping chapter), which frequently hosts visiting authors and has a nice café, a great travel section and an excellent section on Miami-based and -themed fiction, and, nearby, stop into **Flowers & Flowers**, 925 Lincoln Road, to look at their spectacular, and spectacularly expensive, floral arrangements.

Free golf-cart-drawn trams shuttle up and down the Road between Washington Ave and Alton Rd.

Española Way

Designed as a Spanish-style village in the early 1920s, Española (pronounced ess-pahn-YO-la) Way's most prominent feature holds a special place in our hearts: the Clay Hotel & International Hostel, formerly the home of none other than Desi Arnaz, who also had a club here. There's even more irony in the fact that it's now a hostel: the building, which flanks the corner of Washington Ave and stretches halfway down the block on Española, was a totally ritzy place in its heyday. So ritzy, in fact, that Al Capone's S&H Gambling Syndicate took over the middle wing (now rooms 128 to 138) for a gambling casino!

The most striking section is the short block between Washington and Drexel Aves, which is lined with – well, there's no other word but adorable – Spanish-style buildings. It was on this street that Desi himself started the rhumba phenomenon. Nothing like the rhumba . . . .

But the original intent of the development, by NBT Roney, based on designs from several architects, was to be an artists' colony. It was one, on and off, and currently is something of one again. Little galleries and an art center can be found here today. Our favorites are **Studio Russo** (☎ 534-3711) at No 417, where Michael Russo's very odd and wonderful works from . . . well, junk, can be found; and be sure and hit **Ba-BaLú!** (☎ 538-0679) at No 432, which has a very eclectic collection of Cuban mementos, mainly from the Cuban heyday (read: pre-Castro period).

NICK SELBY

KENNETH DREYFUSS

KENNETH DREYFUSS

Beaches

For a city beach, especially an American one, Miami Beach is one of the best around. The water is relatively clear, and relatively warm, the sand relatively white and best of all, it's wide and certainly long enough to accommodate the throngs. The throngs, by the way, are generally rather considerate in that there's usually not lots of litter or broken glass in the sand, but do use caution when walking barefoot.

Note the mega-funky, Ken Scharf-designed lifeguard tower at 10th St. Other non-Scharf (but good local artist-designed) lifeguard towers run from 5th St to 14th St. One drawback is that the ocean here is very calm: there's not much surfing to be done, though you can boogie-board somewhat.

And another shocker for an American beach: topless bathing is permitted in most places, a happy result of the popularity of the place to Europeans and South Americans. Actually, skimpy seems to be the order of the day, and you'll see plenty of thongs and other minuscule coverings around. There *is* a nude beach (see below) but generally speaking on Miami Beach you have to wear . . . something. And you won't feel out of place in a traditional bathing suit, either.

Like a large, accommodating restaurant, the beach has been cunningly and wordlessly zoned to provide everyone with what they want without offending anyone else. So if you find yourself in a place on the sand where the people around you make you uncomfortable, just move a little and you'll be fine.

The most crowded sections of the beach are, of course, in South Beach – from about 5th St to 21st St. Weekends

The Uses of Wires
The wire you will notice if you look up in places near the Promenade is called an ***Erev*** (AY-ruv), and it's there to accommodate highly observant Jews who need to leave their homes for various reasons during the Sabbath (which begins Friday evenings at sunset). Jewish law forbids manual labor of most sorts during the Sabbath. *Very* simply put, the *Erev* acts as something of a connection between the roof of the synagogue and the home, so that when walking within its boundaries, one is allowed a degree of physical labor – such as pushing a baby in a carriage or carrying a *talis*, prayer shawl – on the Sabbath. And it's always a rather interesting sight to see Orthodox Jews trying to avoid the phalanx of joggers and skaters on the Promenade.

Another interesting thing you'll notice if you look up around town is pairs of **sneakers** hanging from phone and power cables. This is said to be evidence of teenage fornication: certain young men tie their sneakers together and toss them over a wire on the occasion of the loss of their virginity. It's rather disturbing just how small some of those sneakers are . . . . ■

are more crowded than weekdays, but except during special events it's usually not too difficult to find a quiet spot. The beaches north of 21st St – especially the one at 53rd St, which has a playground and public toilets – are more family-oriented.

Latin Families For some reason, Latin American families – predominantly Cuban – tend to congregate between 5th St and South Pointe. In this area topless bathing is unwise and can be considered offensive.

Gay The gay beach centers around 12th St, across from the Palace Bar & Grill. It's not like there's sex going on (there isn't); it's just a spot where gay men happen to congregate. There's Fabulous volleyball Sunday afternoons at 4 pm, packed with fun and fun-loving locals.

Nude Nude bathing is legal at Haulover Beach, north of Miami Beach. The area you're looking for is at the northern end of the park between the two northernmost parking lots. The area north of the lifeguard tower is predominantly gay; south of it is straight. There's no sex allowed on any of these beaches and you will get arrested if you're seen trying to get to the bushes.

The Boardwalk There's a boardwalk running from 21st St all the way north to 46th St, and another running for several blocks from South Pointe Park to the north.

The Promenade The Promenade is a Deco-ish, wavy ribbon of concrete at the Beach's westernmost edge (just east of Ocean Drive) that runs from 5th St to almost 16th St. If you've ever looked at a fashion magazine, you've seen it: it's *the* photo shoot site, and if you show up here early in the morning – before 9 am – you'll no doubt see some shoots in progress. All through the day and late into the night, this is where in-line skaters, bicyclists, roller skaters, skateboarders and motorized skateboarders, dog walkers, yahoos, locals and tourists mill about and occasionally bump into each other.

Bass Museum

The Bass Museum (☎ 673-7530) is a wonderful surprise at 2121 Park Ave, directly behind the Miami Beach Public Library, west of City Park. Selections from its permanent collection rotate through the galleries on the ground floor, while a widely varying array of visiting exhibitions rotate through other halls on the ground and 2nd floors. If you go through thoroughly, you can spend two to three hours here. The star of the show here is the tapestry collection, to which the paintings play a definite second fiddle.

Note that the museum is planning an $8 million renovation in the near future, with plans drawn up by none other than Arata Isozaki (who designed LA's Museum of Contemporary Art and renovated the Brooklyn Museum). The museum will try to stay open during the renovation, but whether they will be able to remains to be seen.

The permanent collection in the Main Hall includes Northern European and Renaissance paintings, and an Old Master collection, including works by Peter Paul Rubens & Studio, and two newly restored works: John Hoppner's *Jane, Countess of Oxford with her Daughter* and Gerard Seghers' *Christ & the Penitents*.

Highlights include Rubens' *The Holy Family with St Anne* and *The Flight of Lot*; and Louis-Marie Baader's cotton warp and wool and silk weft *The Return from the Hunt*.

The South Gallery (to the left from the main entrance) contains 16th-century European religious works including Cornelius Cornelisz Van Haarlem's *The Crucifixion Triptych, Four Wings of a Passion Altar* and the enormous *The Tournament* – said to be one of the finest examples of tapestry in an American museum.

The interesting and varied visiting exhibitions seen in the rest of the museum have included, in the past, Passionate Views of the American South: Self Taught Artists from 1940 to the Present, which featured works by Howard Finster, Herbert Singleton and JP Scott; Fellini: Costumes and Fashions; Monumental Propaganda, which focused on salvaging Russia's 'monuments to totalitarianism' from destruction; Through A Glass Darkly: New Works by Judith Schaechter, an artist who works with stained glass in techniques perfected during the Middle Ages; and Louis Slobodken: Mid-Century American Sculptor.

The museum is open Tuesday to Saturday 10 am to 5 pm, Sunday 1 to 5 pm, closed Monday. On the second and fourth Wednesday of the month the museum is open from 1 to 9 pm. Admission is $5 for adults, $3 for senior citizens and students. For special exhibitions admission is $7/5. On the second and fourth Wednesday of the month, from 5 to 9 pm, admission is by donation only (which can be nothing, if you like). You must check all bags and cameras – photography is prohibited without advance arrangement from the curatorial department.

Wolfsonian Foundation

In a foreboding Mediterranean-style building at 1001 Washington Ave on the northeast corner of 10th St, the Wolfsonian Foundation (☎ 531-1001) has a fascinating collection of American and European art, but works from this pool are meted out in trickles in the form of rotating exhibitions that are held on the museum's 5th floor. As we went to press the museum was finishing up its well-received exhibition The Art of Reform & Persuasion 1885-1945, which featured a fascinating look at the strategies of political persuasion in Nazi Germany, New Deal America and Soviet Russia including painting, sculptures, furniture, ceramics and even board games.

The Wolfsonian offers in its ground floor auditorium an ongoing free lecture series, usually running in conjunction with exhibitions; contact the museum for more information. They also run exhibit-related films in the auditorium; tickets are $6, $5 for students and seniors and $4 for Wolfsonian and Miami Beach Film Society (see the Entertainment chapter) members. Call ☎ 531-6287 for ticket and schedule information.

Admission to exhibitions at the Wolfsonian is $7 for adults, $5 for seniors, students and youth aged six to 18, under six admitted free. It's generally open Tuesday to Thursday and Saturday from 10 am to 6 pm, Friday from 10 am to 9 pm, Sunday noon to 5 pm, closed Monday.

Holocaust Memorial

It is difficult to overstate the impact of Miami Beach's Holocaust Memorial. Created through the efforts of Miami Beach Holocaust survivors and beautifully realized by sculptor Kenneth Treister, this is one of the most elaborate, exquisitely detailed and moving memorials we've ever seen. It's something all visitors to Miami Beach should visit, and admission is free.

Like the *Kaddish*, the Jewish prayer for the dead that does not once mention death but rather speaks only of life, the Memorial is a testament to humankind's perseverance and the hope for a better world.

There are five main areas, some of which contain more than one exhibit. Your first glimpse at the memorial, which is at corner of Meridian Ave and Dade Blvd,

NICK SELBY

NICK SELBY

NICK SELBY

Views of *The Sculpture of Love & Anguish*

opposite the Miami Beach Chamber of Commerce, is *The Sculpture of Love & Anguish*: an enormous arm cast in oxidized bronze bearing an Auschwitz tattooed number (the number is intentionally one that was never issued at the camp) rising from the depths – the last reach of a dying person. Climbing the arm is a terrifying series of bronze sculptures of concentration camp victims attempting to climb out of their hell. The detail is nothing short of spectacular, and the sculptures are moving on many levels.

The lily pond in front and surrounding the sculpture is **A Garden of Meditation**, designed to pay tribute to European culture and the lives of the victims.

If you follow the path around the lily pond clockwise you'll reach the **Memorial Wall**, inscribed with the names of Holocaust victims submitted to the project. Continue to the **Dome of Contemplation**, where there is an eternal flame. Note the Star of David, emblazoned with the word 'Jude', which is carved into the wall and allows a star-shaped shaft of light to project inside the dome. The position of the star's projection changes with the position of the sun.

The **Lonely Hall**, inscribed with the names of the major concentration camps, leads from the dome to the main plaza of *The Sculpture of Love & Anguish*, and only now does its force hit the visitor full on. While the figures climbing the arm are visible from over the wall, there's no indication of the level of detail on each character's face until you're inside.

Surrounding the arm is a terrifying gathering of statues from *The Beginning* to *The Final Sculpture*. Words can barely describe the power these sculptures possess. The first sculpture you'll come to after you've passed down the path is one of a crying little girl. When we visited we watched as a man with his five-year-old daughter laid eyes on this statue. The child ran to the statue, held its hand and tearfully looked at her father for an explanation.

As you exit, through the dome again, turn right and walk past **The Arbor of History**, a colonnade of Jerusalem stone topped by vines, and on the wall is a series of photographs etched in black granite. Beneath the photographs are captions, by Professor Helen Fagin, the Memorial's historian, along with a summarized history of the Holocaust.

After the photographs is the main information booth, the Memorial's only weak spot. You can get pamphlets and other literature, including a history of the Holocaust, though they are frugal with supplies. A donation helps. Another problem is getting information from the

Memorial Committee (☎ 538-1663). They're pretty vague on the phone. A better bet is to visit their website (see the Online Services appendix).

The memorial is open from 9 am to 9 pm daily.

Sanford L Ziff Jewish Museum

Jews have been officially 'allowed' to live in Florida since 1763, but evidence suggests that Jews who had converted to Christianity in order to escape persecution and death were here as early as the 1500s. The Sanford L Ziff Jewish Museum of Florida (☎ 672-5044), at 301 Washington Ave in the building that housed Congregation Beth Jacob, Miami Beach's first Jewish congregation, is dedicated to exhibits of the history of Jews in Florida. Their mainstay is *MOSAIC: Jewish Life in Florida*, which features thousands of fascinating items from Russian *samovar* kettles to photographs, business cards, documents and other products of Jewish-owned or -run companies.

The museum is open Tuesday to Thursday and Saturday and Sunday from 10 am to 5 pm, Friday 10 am to 3 pm, closed Monday. Admission is free on Saturday, on other days it's $4 for adults, $3 for senior citizens and students, or a flat fee of $9 per family.

Mid & Northern Miami Beach

Once you pass 21st St on Collins Ave heading north, you're entering the world of 1950s and '60s Miami Beach – the kind of place where people would tell you that they 'Love you, kid . . . and I mean that.' What all the schmoozers and stars and tourists were heading to was a series of monstrous high-rise hotels that line Collins Ave north of the 20s. So with a few notable exceptions – like the lovingly restored **Indian Creek Hotel** at 2727 Indian Creek Drive (see the Places to Stay chapter) – from there up to the city limits is a never-ending string of high-rise condominiums, hotels and apartment buildings.

The other outstanding exception is the **Fontainebleau Hilton Resort & Towers** (see the Places to Stay chapter). As you approach the resort, just before Collins Ave makes its little jog to the left, you see in front of you what appears to be two magnificent pillars, through which the Fontainebleau pool is visible. As you get closer, you'll realize that it's a spectacular *tromp l'oeil* **mural**. The mural, designed by Richard Hass and painted over an eight-week period by Edwin Abreu, covers 13,016 sq feet of what was before 1986 a big blank wall.

The **Eden Roc Hotel & Resort** is, like Fontainebleau,

another notable '50s era resort. And if their pool isn't as spectacular, their health club (see Activities at the end of this chapter) is quickly gaining in popularity.

41st St, also called Arthur Godfrey Rd, lined with kosher shops, delicatessens and even a kosher pizzeria (Shimmies, closed when we went to press but reopening) is the 5th Ave of the Orthodox Jewish South.

North Bay Rd, on the bay side from the 40s to the 60s, is lined with incredible mansions, naturally with private docks, pools and tennis courts. Notable residents are Robin and Barry Gibb of the Bee Gees, and that's an interesting thing about Miami – you can tell a lot about a community by its street names, and here we have places like Andy Gibb Drive, Ronald Reagan Ave, and Arthur Godfrey Rd.

IN BISCAYNE BAY

Between Miami and Miami Beach are about a dozen islands, some more exclusive than others but all visible from the MacArthur and Julia Tuttle Causeways. Most are accessible by bridges.

Port of Miami

Miami is the cruise capital of the world, and when the monstrous liners are docked at the Port of Miami waiting to fill up with people, it's a pretty amazing sight to see. You can't help but notice the ships as you look south from the MacArthur Causeway. On one ship we were flabbergasted when told that the bar we were heading to was on the 14th floor – they're that big.

KENNETH DREYFUSS

It's hit and miss, but the ships are usually in port before the weekend loading up with weekend cruisers. Also, look for another trademark Port of Miami vessel which is in port quite often: the *Chiquita Banana* boat.

Coast Guard Station

If you've seen news images of Coast Guard cutters arriving to the rescue of Cuban rafters or the dismay of drug smugglers, they probably came from this base, from where the term 'heave to and prepare to be boarded' would seem to have been perfected. Tours are not generally permitted, though you can sometimes make out seized drug boats moored at the pier (hint: drug boats are *not* the ones that say US Coast Guard on them) as you pass the base, to the south of the last bridge before you hit Miami Beach traveling east.

Flagler Memorial Monument

On a little island off the west coast of Miami Beach is a monument to Henry Flagler, one of Florida's leading pioneers. It may be argued that Flagler was more responsible for the development of South Florida than any other single person. The monument is accessible only by private boat. If you've got one of those, there are mooring posts available around the island. The water is very shallow, more so at low tide, so be very careful not to beach yourself!

Fisher Island

Carl Fisher, one of the Beach's pioneering developers, bought up this glorious little island, planning to die here – he even built a mausoleum. But after a while he got bored with it, and when William K Vanderbilt II fell in love with the place, Fisher traded the island for Vanderbilt's 250-foot yacht *and* its crew. Things were like that in those days.

Vanderbilt built up a splenderific Spanish-Mediterranean mansion with guest houses, studios, tennis courts and a golf course.

Today, the island is a totally exclusive resort, accessible only by air and private ferry, and the condominiums that line the mile-long private beach range from $600,000 hovels to over $6 million for the awesome pad US President Clinton used when he stopped by. But to understand the opulence one really needs to consider that all the sand on that beach has been imported from the Bahamas. That's right, they brought over boatloads of sugary white sand. Maybe that's why the sun still shines over the island when it's raining in Miami Beach.

You can stay here, at the Inn at the Fisher Island Club (☎ 535-6097); see the Places to Stay chapter.

The island is usually open only to paying guests and residents, but you can arrange a tour if you're especially persistent. The *Eagle, Flamingo* and *Pelican* ferries leave from the Fisher Island Ferry Terminal off the MacArthur Causeway just west of the Coast Guard Station every 15 minutes around the clock. The trip, in air-conditioned comfort of course, takes 10 minutes. If you're driving, they'll even hose off your car at the end of the journey to ensure that any brine that may have collected on your paint job during the voyage is duly washed away! Golly.

Hibiscus, Palm & Star Islands

Hibiscus, Palm and Star Islands are three little bastions of wealth – though far less exclusive than Fisher Island – just west of Miami Beach. There aren't too many very famous people living there now – just very rich ones – though Star Island boasts Miami's favorite star, Gloria Estefan, whose estate is at the eastern end. Developer Thomas Kramer is building a residence here, and he just sold a plot of land for a reported $13 million to everyone's favorite hôtelier, Leona Helmsley. Palm Island was for a short time infamous for its local resident Al Capone.

Star Island is the farthest east, accessed by the little bridge almost opposite the Fisher Island Ferry Terminal. Hibiscus and Palm Islands share a bridge – it's the next one after Star Island's as you head west on the MacArthur Causeway. Generally it's hard to get on to the island's circular drives (you need to get past a security guard) but the islands' drives are public, and if you insist and don't look like a hoodlum you should be able to get in – it's a nice place to pedal through with your mouth hanging agape.

Watson Island

The island nearest to downtown Miami, just east of the mainland, is the grungiest of the lot. Watson Island is home to Chalk's International Airlines (☎ 371-8628/9), which claims to be the oldest-running international airline (the claim has been recently disputed). The airline operates between Watson Island and Fort Lauderdale, Bimini and Paradise Island. But in 1998, the expected relocation of Parrot Jungle to the island will change things considerably. Stay tuned.

Pelican Island

On weekends you can take a free ferry from the causeway west of North Bay Village, about two miles west of 71st St in Miami Beach, to little Pelican Island. It's just a pleasant little place to have a picnic and look at the dozens of pelicans that congregate on and around the island.

DOWNTOWN MIAMI

Miami's downtown skyline is considered one of the nation's most beautiful, or at least most colorful. At night, the towering skyscrapers are lit in neon, and the most unmistakable symbol of downtown is the IM Pei-designed **NationsBank Tower** (1987) at 100 SE 2nd St. The building is illuminated every night, and on special events, the lighting – on seven visible faces of the building – can be custom lit with a combination of seven colors per face. There's no observation deck, but the Sky Lobby on the 11th floor, and the Sky Terrace's Pi's Place Restaurant (☎ 539-7097) – a great deal on food in downtown Miami – are open to the public.

Other funky neon lighting comes courtesy of the Metromover's rainbow-illuminated track, which makes a circuit of downtown. Parking can be a nightmare, but public transport is good, so it may pay to leave the car out of the area; see the Getting Around chapter for more information.

For a downtown, Miami is not exactly the most exciting you'll encounter. Most of the streets are lined with shops selling electronics, luggage and clothing to Latin American visitors, and the place dies very quickly after 5 pm, when the office towers disgorge their yuppies.

Metro-Dade Cultural Center

The Mediterranean-style Cultural Center, with its elevated plaza that is host to occasional outdoor concerts and events, is sort of a one-stop shopping center for culture. The 3.3-acre complex holds two museums and the city's excellent public library. The complex is at 101 W Flagler St (Metromover stop: Government Center). A combination ticket for both the Historical Museum and Center for Fine Arts is $6 for adults, $3.50 for children.

Historical Museum of Southern Florida This is one of our favorite museums, and it's excellent for kids. The Historical Museum (☎ 375-1492, see the Online Services appendix) has displays covering 10,000 years of Florida history. All the exhibits have excellent explanatory materials, all in English and Spanish. Count on spending about an hour to 1½ hours here.

Begin upstairs (starting from the left) with natural habitats, wetlands, coast and ridges; move on through exhibits of prehistoric Florida, Spanish invaders, a Spanish galleon and, our favorite, *L' Orateur*, the most aptly named cannon in history. Continue on to exhibits on the Wreckers, the cigar industry, Indian tribes and the

Boom – including a beautifully restored Miami trolley circa 1920. Exhibits continue through the Depression, tourism in the 1930s, WWII and up to present day. It's not huge, but it's very informative.

Downstairs is a temporary exhibition hall, La Plaza Theater, which has new exhibitions every three to four months.

The museum also runs an admirable program of special events every year with field trips, river cruises and walking tours; some are free and some have fees; contact the museum for their Calendar of Events & Programs (free).

Admission is $4 for adults, $2 for children aged six to 12. On Monday the admission is waived – they still suggest the $4 donation, but you can give what you want (even if what you want is a dime, but please, don't be *that* cheap). It's open Monday to Wednesday and Saturday 10 am to 5 pm, Thursday 10 am to 9 pm, Sunday noon to 5 pm.

Center for the Fine Arts This museum (☎ 375-3000) does rotating exhibitions of fine arts. When we visited they were finishing up Caribbean Visions: Contemporary Painting & Sculpture by French, Dutch and Spanish-speaking Caribbean artists. Contact the museum for a schedule of what's on when you visit.

Admission is $5 for adults, $2.50 for students and seniors, children under 12 free. It's open Tuesday, Wednesday and Friday 10 am to 5 pm, Thursday 10 am to 9 pm (free admission 5 to 9 pm), Saturday and Sunday noon to 5 pm, closed Monday.

Miami Public Library The Miami Public Library is an excellent resource for locals and visitors alike. See the Library section in the Facts for the Visitor chapter for more information.

Wolfson Campus

The Wolfson Campus of the Miami-Dade Community College (☎ 237-3000) at 300 NE 2nd Ave has two art galleries of rotating exhibitions, the Centre Gallery and the Frances Wolfson Gallery. Both are open Monday to Friday 10 am to 6 pm, admission is free.

Bayfront Park

Bayfront Park (☎ 358-7550), a freight port during the first Miami Boom in the 1920s, is today a calm bit of green downtown, essentially between the Hotel Inter-Continental and Bayside Marketplace. There are two

KENNETH DREYFUSS
Downtown Miami skyline

performance venues here: the AT&T Amphitheater (home to Fourth of July and New Year's Eve festivities) and the smaller, 200-seat South End Amphitheater (the site of Bayfront Park After Dark, a free entertainment series). See the Entertainment chapter for more information on all those. The park also houses the JFK Torch of Friendship, and a monument to the astronauts killed in the 1986 explosion of the space shuttle *Challenger*. The area in front of the memorial was renamed Centennial Plaza in 1996, the year of Miami's centennial celebration.

Bayside Marketplace

This is one of those listings we sort of have to put in because everyone else does. Bayside Marketplace (☎ 577-3344) at 401 Biscayne Blvd (it actually runs from NE 4th to NE 9th Sts) is a shopping mall that hordes of tourists just adore, with a bunch of little tourist shops, some restaurants – including a Hard Rock Café, see the Places to Eat chapter – and a *Miami Queen* paddlewheel cruise (☎ 445-7821) around Biscayne Bay Friday to Sunday at 2, 4 and 6 pm. Whee.

Bayside is also home to free concerts every day of the year; see the Free (or Cheap) & Outdoors section in the Entertainment chapter for more information.

This is also the main stop for the Water Taxi, which runs shuttle service to many downtown hotels as well as to Miami Beach (see the Getting Around chapter).

Bicentennial Park

Bicentennial Park, also on Biscayne Blvd but north of the Port of Miami, is similar to Bayfront Park and also has an amphitheater.

Miami Herald Building

The enormous headquarters of the *Miami Herald* and *el Nuevo Herald* (☎ 350-2111), Miami's paper of record (and only major daily) can be toured by advance arrangement, but when we visited, regular free tours had been temporarily discontinued. Call to see if they're running during your visit. If they are, you'll see the Newsroom, the 'Morgue' – library – and production rooms like Paste-up, and the Press Room. The headquarters is right on Biscayne Bay, just east of the main downtown bus transfer center in from of the Omni Mall. The address is 1 Herald Plaza; it's just across the street from the Omni International Mall transit center beneath the Metromover terminal.

Freedom Tower

Freedom Tower (1925) at 600 Biscayne Blvd is the area's other surviving tower modeled after (but not a replica of) the Giralda bell tower at the Cathedral of Seville in Spain. The second is at the Biltmore Hotel, see the Coral Gables section below. The third was the Roney Plaza Hotel, which was later razed to make way for apartment buildings. All three were designed by Shultz & Weaver, a New York architectural firm.

But its fame comes from the fact that it was the 'Ellis Island of the South': the immigration processing center for almost half a million Cuban refugees in the 1960s. The building was for 32 years the home of the *Miami Daily News*. It was placed on the National Register of Historic Places in 1979. Today, despite renovation, it is abandoned, and looms over Biscayne Bay near the entrances to the Port of Miami and Bayside Marketplace.

US Courthouse

Miami's first major post office (1931) later became the Miami Courthouse, because it was, in a kinder, gentler time, large enough to accommodate the needs of the US Government prosecutors. As crime increased, the Feds outgrew the building and now occupy the nearby Federal Building. Today it's open to visitors at 300 NE 1st Ave (☎ 536-4131). The reason to stop here – other than the fact that it's a lovely building that looks as if it belongs more in the Caribbean than in downtown Miami – is to get a look at Denman Fink's *Law Guides Florida Progress*, a mural depicting Florida in the 1930s, including a Cuba-bound PanAm Clipper. The building is open from Monday to Friday 9 am to 5 pm; the mural is in the main courtroom (2nd floor) that also boasts hardwood furnishings like hewn-wood benches, and beautiful arched windows.

Miami Arena

This is the home of Miami Heat and Florida Panthers, Miami's NBA basketball and NHL hockey teams, University of Miami Hurricanes basketball, and host to other events like the Ringling Brothers Circus when it's in town. The Arena (☎ 530-4444) is located west of N Miami Ave at NE 7th St; technically the address is 701 Arena Blvd. See the Entertainment chapter for more information.

Brickell Ave Bridge

The Brickell Avenue Bridge, which crosses the Miami River south of downtown, reopened after a $21 million renovation that took several years (parts for the raising mechanism had to be manufactured), and is more beautiful than ever. It's also wider, and higher, which should speed both cars and boats (it certainly seemed to facilitate the speedboat-borne drug runners who were being chased by DEA agents on the day of the bridge's grand re-opening!). But its claim to fame now is the 17-foot bronze statue by Cuban-born sculptor Manuel Carbonell of a Tequesta warrior and his family atop the towering *Pillar of History* column at the center of the east side of the bridge.

Brickell Ave continues south from downtown across this bridge, where it becomes lined with office towers and some hotels. There's nothing really to see on the south side of the river in this area, with the possible exception of Tobacco Road.

Tobacco Road

Just south of the Miami River Bridge, a small collection of bars line S Miami Ave, including *Tobacco Road Liquor Bar* (☎ 374-1198) at No 626, open 11.30 to 5 am every day. It's something of a Miami tradition; it has Miami's first liquor license, has been here for over 80 years and was a speakeasy during Prohibition. Stop in for a drink while you're here; there are some other little places nearby for snacks as well.

Miami City Cemetery

The original cemetery of the City of Miami was established in July 1897, and you can still visit if that's the sort of thing you like to do. The 9000-plus-grave cemetery has separate white, black and Jewish sections; Julia Tuttle was the 13th burial and she's got a front and center gravesite. Luminaries include many mayors and politicians, about 90 Confederate dead as well as veterans from all wars in the 20th century.

It still sees about 12 to 20 burials a year, though space in the 10½-acre site is dwindling.

The cemetery is at 1800 NE 2nd Ave, not the friendliest part of town. The cemetery manager, Clyde Cates, suggests that if you want to visit you call him a day in advance and leave a message on his answering machine at ☎ 579-6938. Clyde will give visitors an informal tour.

The cemetery's highlight is the grave of Mrs Carrie Miller, who died in 1926. Her husband, William, wrapped her body in a sheet and encased it in a concrete block six feet high: After the body has gone to dust, her sleeping form will remain, reads the epitaph. William had apparently wanted to join his wife in there eventually, but when he finally died he had lost all his money during the Depression. He is buried in an unmarked plot nearby.

In 1996, a murder victim was found in the cemetery, behind the ornate Burdines mausoleum, so Cates recommends only visiting during the day: take Biscayne Blvd to NE 18th St and turn west to the cemetery, to avoid getting lost in the back streets. It's open Monday to Friday 7.30 am to 4 pm, and admission is free.

LITTLE HAVANA

After the Mariel Boatlift (see the History section in the Facts about Miami chapter), the section of town to which Cuban exiles had been gravitating for years exploded into a distinctly Cuban neighborhood, now known as Little Havana. The borders of Little Havana are arguable, but for the purposes of this book, we're saying that they're *really roughly* SW 13th St at the south, SW 3rd St at the north, SW 3rd Ave at the east and SW 37th Ave at the west. Note that while the Cuban influence is strongest in the southwest quadrant of the city, it's pervasive throughout Miami.

Spanish is the predominant language here, of course, and you will absolutely run into people who speak no English; see the Language section in the Facts about Miami chapter for some key phrases, or pick up Lonely Planet's *Latin American Spanish Phrasebook*.

The heart of Little Havana is Calle Ocho (KAH-yeh AW-cho), Spanish for SW 8th St (actually it's Spanish just for 8th St, but what the hell). The entire length of

Calle Ocho is lined with Cuban shops, cafés, record stores, pharmacies, clothing (and, most amusing, bridal) shops, teeming with action. Calle Ocho runs one-way from west to east for most of the length of Little Havana.

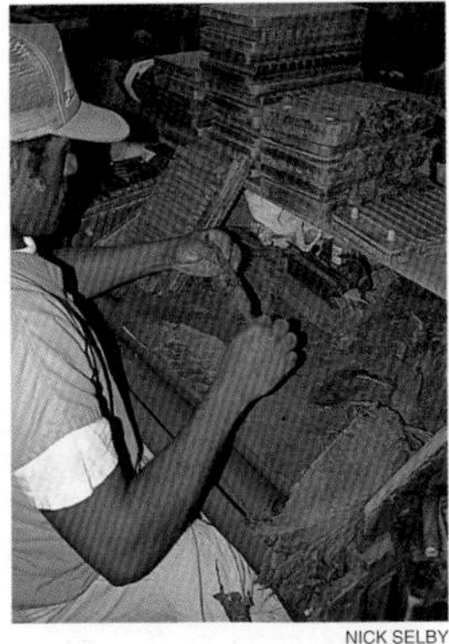

NICK SELBY

Tabaqueros at work at El Crédito Cigars

But while the wall-of-sound-style speakers set up outside places such as Power Records are blasting salsa and other Latin music into the street, Little Havana as a tourist attraction is an elusive bugger. It's not concentrated like a Chinatown; it's actually not really a tourist attraction at all. It's just a Cuban neighborhood, so except for during the occasional street fair or celebration (see Special Events in Facts for the Visitor), you shouldn't expect, like, Tito Puente and Celia Cruz leading a parade of colorfully attired, tight-trousered men and slinky, scantily-clad women in a Carnival or anything like that. More likely you'll see old men playing dominoes.

Which is exactly the attraction the area holds: it's real, it's not putting on airs for anyone, and it could not care less whether you see it or not. So you should definitely go.

The famous green sign reading *Republic Bank Welcomes You to Little Havana* is on Calle Ocho just east of where SW 22nd Ave shoots off to the northeast.

Máximo Gómez Park

The scores of elderly Cuban men playing dominoes here is an example of good government at work: this is a program for senior citizens run under the auspices of the Little Havana Development Authority. The park – named for Máximo Gómez y Baez, the Dominican-born Chief of the Cuban Liberating Army, is open every day from 9 am to 6 pm. This is a fascinating place to sit for a few minutes and watch the action, or join in yourself. The park is at the corner of SW 15th Ave.

A couple of doors (east) down Calle Ocho is the **Little Havana Chess Club** (☎ 643-3622), where somewhat younger men sit indoors playing either chess or

Calle Ocho
As we said, it's just a lot of shops, but some of our favorites are:

- Cervantes Book Store – Mainly Spanish-language books here at No 1898
- España – Religious figures, flamenco dolls and how much more cheesy and kitschy can we get than here at No 1615?
- Power Records – Follow your ears to No 1419 for a huge selection of English and Spanish-language CDs, merengue, jazz Latino, tropical and salsa
- Farmacia Habana – Cuban-style service, American-stocked pharmacy at No 1356
- La Casa de los Trucos – The House of Tricks (No 1343), with costumes, fake blood, trick gum, sex toys and unrippable toilet paper

Of course, there are other sights, see below. Cuban botanicas can be found along Calle Ocho selling Santeria-related items such as perfumed waters named for properties you may desire, like 'Money' or 'Love Me', or the more esoteric 'Keep Dead Resting'.

And you'll want to stop for a guarapo (sugar-cane juice), a café con leche or a thimbleful of zoom juice (espresso) and maybe a little pastry or something. See the Places to Eat section for proper restaurant listings, including the famous Versailles restaurant and an excellent Vietnamese (?!) offering. But for a quick something, try the Calle Ocho Market at No 1390, Karla Bakery at No 1842 (great-smelling and -tasting pastries that always make a line form) or El Rey de las Fritas at No 1177. ■

dominos and smoking a whole lot of cigars. Between the park and the chess club is a little Cuban Chinese restaurant with poor food but perfectly decent espresso (40¢) and café con leche (70¢) to bring out to the park.

El Crédito Cigars

Cigar smoking has really taken the USA by storm once again. Ernesto Curillo, the present owner of this very successful cigar factory is, according to an article in *Cigar Aficionado*, one of the leaders of the American cigar Renaissance. They have several lines, but the hottest

José Martí

José Martí (1853-1895) was born in Havana, and was exiled in 1870 to Spain for 'opposition to Colonial rule'. Eventually Martí would travel and write extensively in North and South America. His anti-racist writings were vast, and he relentlessly pursued his vision of a free Cuba, stirring up anti-Spanish sentiment wherever he could.

Martí traveled throughout Florida, and while he was allowed to return in 1878 to Cuba, he was quickly booted out again by angry Spanish authorities. In 1895, Martí returned to Cuba to take part in the war for Cuban independence, and was one of the first to die in the conflict.

Martí is considered to be one of Cuba's leading writers and a hero of its independence. José Martí Park, between the Miami River and Little Havana at 351 SW 4th St, was dedicated in 1950. ■

product of the moment is their *La Gloria Cubana*, which ranges in price from $44 for a bundle of 25 (six-inch, 32 ring size) to the rare torpedoes, which are $125 a bundle when they're in stock, which isn't often.

You can just stand in front of their picture window looking in at the dozen or so Cuban *tabaqueros* who are hand-rolling cigars, or go in to smell (it's pretty ... shall we say, aromatic) and buy. They're really nice about letting people take photos, so ask if you want one. They're at 1106 Calle Ocho (☎ 858-4162), and are open Monday to Saturday 7.30 am to 6 pm, closed Sunday.

Cuban Memorial Blvd

For two blocks along SW 13th Ave south of Calle Ocho are a series of monuments to Cuban patriots and freedom fighters (read: Anti-Castro Cubans). The eternal flame at the corner of Calle Ocho is the **Eternal Torch in Honor of the 2506th Brigade** dedicated to the counter-revolutionaries who died during the botched Bay of Pigs invasion (see the History section in the Facts about

Miami chapter). Other monuments include the huge brass map of Cuba, 'Dedicated to the ideals of people who will never forget the pledge of making their Fatherland free', and a bust of José Martí.

Cuban Museum of Arts & Culture

The Cuban Museum (☎ 858-8006) at 1300 SW 12th Ave has a small permanent collection and is host to traveling exhibitions of Cuban art. Those exhibitions are probably why the place was closed when we visited: local Cuban exiles have in the past taken offense at the choice of exhibitions. They expressed their displeasure, for example, at the selection of pro-Castro artists' work by bombing the museum. But the museum is still open – by appointment only.

CORAL GABLES

Coral Gables is a lovely, if pricey, city that exudes opulence and comfort. A gaggle of architects and planners under the direction of George Merrick designed the city to be a 'model suburb', with a decidedly Mediterranean theme, huge gateways, and wide, tree-lined streets.

Today Coral Gables, while exciting to multinational corporations and the diplomatic crowds that make their homes here, is a quiet place with a fledgling arts and culture scene.

Lowe Art Museum

One of the most crushing blows to our research schedule was that the Lowe (☎ 284-3535) was closed for renovation. The Lowe has one of the largest permanent collections of art in Dade County – with over 8000 pieces including antiquities, Renaissance and Baroque art; 18th- through 20th-century European and American sculpture and Asian, African, Pre-Columbian and Native American entries as well.

The renovation is adding 13,000 sq feet of exhibition space, and it was scheduled to reopen gradually, culminating in a grand reopening in November 1996.

The museum's open Tuesday, Wednesday, Friday and Saturday 10 am to 5 pm, Thursday noon to 7 pm, Sunday noon to 5 pm, closed Monday. Admission is $5 for adults, $3 for seniors and students. It's at 1301 Stanford Drive, two blocks north of the University Metrorail Station on the Coral Gables campus of the University of Miami.

Architectural Disneyland
George Merrick envisioned what would be called today an 'Architectural Disneyland' filled with theme areas; the idea was to bring people into a place that felt 'old'. He created a **Dutch South African Village** (6612, 6700, 6704 and 6710 SW 42nd Ave and 6705 San Vicente St) modeled after 17th-century Dutch colonists' farmhouses; a tiny **Chinese Village**, one block between Sansovino Ave, Castania Ave, Maggiore St and Riviera Drive; a **Florida Pioneer Village** (4320, 4409, 4515, 1520 and 4620 Santa Maria St), which looks a lot more like New Hampshire than Miami; and the absolutely stunning **French Normandy Village**, on the block between SW 42nd Ave, Viscaya Court, Viscaya Ave and Alesio Ave.

Merrick lost the family fortune after the Depression, and the City of Coral Gables, which had been incorporated in 1925, went bankrupt. Eventually the city's finances were sorted, and Coral Gables grew with Miami but always seemed to attract more money and less attention.

In fact, Coral Gables is one of the few places in metropolitan Miami that's lovely to walk in: the banyan trees that shelter the winding streets actually provide good relief from the sun, and it's relatively safe. ■

Biltmore Hotel

From practically anywhere in Coral Gables you can see the 315-foot-high tower of the Biltmore Hotel (☎ 445-1926), the city's crown jewel, at 1200 Anastasia Ave. The historic landmark hotel, which opened in 1926, has a history that reads like an Agatha Christie novel on speed – a story of murder, intrigue, famous gangsters and detectives set against an Old World European-style backdrop.

Al Capone had a speakeasy here, in what's officially called the Everglades Suite but what everyone – even the hotel management privately – calls the Capone Suite. It was in that room that the owner of just one of the spirits said to haunt the hotel, Fats Walsh, was murdered.

More recently, the hotel was selected as the site of many meetings of 1994's Summit of the Americas, during which Bill Clinton hosted 34 leaders of Latin American countries in the largest summit meeting ever held in the Western Hemisphere.

The hotel's architecture is referred to as Mediterranean-revivalist; the tower is modeled after (but not an exact replica of) the Giralda bell tower at the Cathedral of Seville in Spain.

Enter the upper lobby, look up and drop your jaw in amazement at the detail of the ceiling painting (it *is* a painting) 45 feet above you. Everywhere in the hotel the sense of enormity is apparent: from the pool – the largest hotel pool in the continental USA – to the 18-hole Donald Ross golf course (which actually pre-dates the hotel) to the magnificent conference and dining rooms and suites, everything is built on a superhuman scale.

That pool deserves special mention. It's difficult to describe the impact it has – it may not have as stunning a setting as the Venetian Pool (see below), but it is one of the most beautiful in the world. There's a café out there, and you can sit poolside with an espresso.

You can take free guided tours (run by the Dade Heritage Trust) of the hotel and grounds – you'll get to see the Capone and almost-as-luxurious-but-still-enough-to-drool-over Merrick Suites if they're unoccupied – on Sunday afternoons at 1.30, 2.30 and 3.30 pm; tours leave from the concierge desk in the upper lobby.

And don't miss Storytelling at the Biltmore every Thursday at 7.30 pm in front of the fireplace in the upper lobby. It's free, and you'll hear stories of ghosts, celebs who've stayed here, the construction of the hotel and lots more.

There is, of course, a lot more information about the place – not least of which is the mainstage productions of the Florida Shakespeare Theatre (see the Theater section in the Entertainment chapter) – its health clubs, 10 tennis courts, Sunday brunches, Cigars under the Stars, etc etc, so contact the hotel when you're in town.

Venetian Pool

What with all that building around here, a large quarry was formed. Somebody came up with the absolutely brilliant idea of making the world's ugliest hole in the ground the world's most beautiful swimming pool, which the Venetian Pool (☎ 460-5356) definitely is. It's listed on the National Register of Historic Places, and on our personal list of favorite places in Miami.

It's a spring-fed pool with caves, waterfalls and Venetian-style moorings that's just absolutely fantastic. It's large enough to have a kiddie area, space for laps and room under the big waterfall to just romp around. Different sources come up with different figures, but we're settling on this: the pool holds 820,000 gallons of water. During the winter, the pool's drained and refilled every other night, in summer every night. The water's recycled through a natural filtration process.

And now that a new management has taken over the

dining room, the no-outside-food policy is less painful: they offer things like pasta salads and veggie lasagna ($5.50), chicken stir fry ($6) in addition to the standard hot dogs ($1.75 to 2.75) and hamburgers ($3 to 3.50).

The pool is at 2701 DeSoto Blvd just next to the **DeSoto Fountain**, about two blocks south of Coral Way. Free parking is available. Admission is $4 for adults, $3.50 for teens aged 13 to 17, kids $1.60; Coral Gables residents (with ID) pay $3/2/1.60. Token-driven lockers are available for $1.50. There are no refunds due to weather.

The pool is open (pay attention, this gets tricky): from mid-June to mid-August Monday to Friday from 11 am to 7.30 pm; September and October and April and May Tuesday to Friday 11 am to 5.30 pm; November to March Tuesday to Friday 10 am to 4.30 pm; open year round Saturday and Sunday 10 am to 4.30 pm.

City Hall

Coral Gables City Hall, at the intersection of Biltmore and Coral Ways, is just a neat 1920s building. It has housed meetings of the City Commission since February 29, 1928 – the first commission was made up of Merrick, ET Purcell, Don Peabody, the city's first mayor EE Dammers and the interestingly named Wingfield Webster. Upstairs there's a tiny display of Coral Gables Public Transport from the mid-20th century, and rotating photograph and art exhibits, and oh, yes, look up at Denman Fink's *Four Seasons* ceiling painting in the tower, as well as his framed untitled painting of the underwater world (the historic preservation specialists in the building call it the 'marine' painting) on the 2nd floor landing. It's at 405 Biltmore Way.

Merrick House

There's not much to see here at the residence of the Mericks in Coral Gables (1899); in fact the place is mostly used for meetings and receptions by local clubs. But it's a lovely house (☎ 460-5361) and if the burly and friendly caretaker's around he'll let you wander through for $2 for adults, 50¢ for kids Sunday and Wednesday from 1 to 4 pm. The big draw is the well-maintained organic garden, which has some of the original fruit trees planted at the turn of the century like king oranges, copperleaf and bamboo. It's at 907 Coral Way, and there are good signs pointing the way.

Coral Gables Congregational Church

This lovely church (☎ 448-7421) was Coral Gables'

first (1924); it's directly across the street from the Biltmore Hotel. There are services at 8.30 am in the chapel and 10.30 am in the sanctuary; call and ask if there are any music performances during your stay. It's at 3010 DeSoto Blvd.

Watertower & Entrances

Still in restoration, the Alhambra Watertower (1931) where Greenway Court and Ferdinand St meet Alhambra Circle, looks for all the world like a lighthouse.

Merrick had planned a series of elaborate entry gates to the city, but the bust dried up most of the planning. Of the ones around, worth noting are: Country Club Prado (1927, at Calle Ocho and the Prado Country Club); the Douglas Entrance, *La Puerto del Sol* (1927; at Calle Ocho and Douglas Rd); and the Granada Entrance (Calle Ocho at Granada Blvd).

Colonnade Building

Built in 1925, the former headquarters of Merrick's Coral Gables Corporation is a gorgeous creation, with a central rotunda, arcades and a lavishly ornamental front entrance. It was also once the home of Colonnade Pictures, but the building was combined in 1988 with a new tower directly behind it. Today it's home to the Omni-Colonnade Hotel (☎ 441-2600), as well as shops and boutiques. The building's at 169 Miracle Mile, the hotel address is 180 Aragon Ave, at the corner of Ponce de León Blvd and Miracle Mile.

COCONUT GROVE

Site of the first major settlement in the Miami area, Coconut Grove was, for a time in the 1960s and '70s, a big-time bohemian hangout, but it's evolved – if that's the word – into a highly commercialized area whose main attraction (other than the excellent Coconut Grove Playhouse, see the Entertainment chapter) is now the CocoWalk shopping center, a stylized shopping mall with some restaurants, shops and a cinema. There are a couple of attractions worth the trip.

Barnacle State Historic Site

Opposite the Playhouse, this pioneer residence (1891) (☎ 448-9445) owned by Ralph Monroe is open to the public on weekends. Admission is $1 for everyone. It's at 3485 Main Hwy, open Friday to Sunday (except

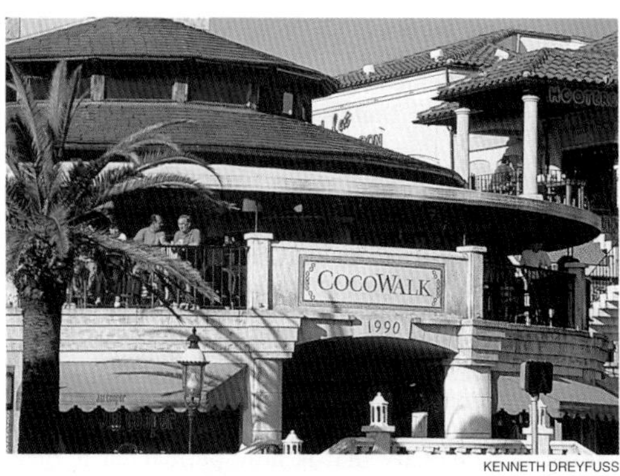

KENNETH DREYFUSS

CocoWalk shopping center

Christmas) with guided tours at 10 and 11.30 am and 1 and 2.30 pm. During the week it's for groups only.

Coconut Grove Exhibition Center

This is the sight of conventions and special events, like the monthly Coconut Grove Cares (☎ 444-8454) antique and jewelry show (see the Shopping chapter for more information).

SOUTHEAST MIAMI

Miami Museum of Science & Space Transit Planetarium

What a total treat for kids – and we were pretty enthralled, ourselves! The Miami Museum of Science (☎ 854-4247) & Space Transit Planetarium (☎ 854-2222) share a building very close to the grounds of the Vizcaya Museum & Gardens (see below), just at Miami's southern city limit. As you enter, the planetarium is to the left, the museum to the right. Before you go inside, take a look at the ceiling painting outside the main doors.

Both the museum and the planetarium are open daily 10 am to 6 pm (ticket sales end at 5 pm), closed Christmas and Thanksgiving. There are separate cash booths for each. Admission for the Museum of Science is $6/4 for adults/senior citizens and children aged three to 12.

The complex is at 3280 S Miami Ave. The planetarium costs $5/2.50 or $6/3 for laser shows. On Friday and Saturday nights from 8.15 to 10 pm there is access to the planetarium's telescopes for $1 (for free Saturday night stargazing, see the Southern Cross Astronomical Society listing, below). Spanish speakers can use audiophones for simultaneous Spanish-language broadcast of planetarium shows, but there's a $20 deposit required for the gear.

A combination ticket for both attractions is $9/5.50.

Museum of Science This is one of the finest science museums in Florida – and Florida has some good ones – for hands on and just plain creatively fun exhibits. The main focus when we went was CyberCity, and many of its exhibits remained after the show closed. Among the draws: about 20 totally tweaked-out Macs and PCs with a T-1 connection to the internet. If you've never checked out the World Wide Web, this was the place to do it. One exhibit of CyberCity that is now permanent is their virtual-reality basketball game, in which you compete with very tall and very talented cyber-players.

But it's much more than geek-stuff: there are excellent exhibitions on creepy crawlers – insects as well as frogs and butterflies; The Body in Action; Everglades and coral reef exhibits in huge showcases with excellent written and audio descriptions (push the button for the audio); and The Slanted Room, which we'll leave to your imagination.

Outside is the Wildlife Center, open during good weather, where you can touch a tortoise, and see exotic birds – if you get there soon enough you may be able to get a look at their rehabilitated Bald Eagle, before they return it to the wild. There are frequent dinosaur exhibits as well. And don't miss their exhibition of Dangerous Animals of South Florida.

Even the museum store is entertaining and prices are pretty reasonable.

Space Transit Planetarium There are no major surprises here, though the free Friday and Saturday space lectures and $1 telescope-viewing sessions hold a special place in the budget traveler's heart. The planetarium does movies, star shows and laser shows, including a daily 40-minute *Best of Pink Floyd* show at 2 pm, and the 44-minute *The Planets*, showing continuously from 2 pm to close. When we visited, they were running a Space Art exhibit in the Planetarium gallery, *Visions of the Universe* by Joe Tucciarone.

Southern Cross Astronomical Society

Every Saturday night, weather permitting, members of the Southern Cross Astronomical Society (☎ 661-1375) set up telescopes for their Friendly Saturday Night at Metro-Dade-run Bill Sadowski Park (☎ 255-4767), SW 176th St and SW 79th Ave. There are free astronomy lessons and just plain star gazing between 8 and 10 pm. They also hold special events throughout the year; call for more information. As we went to press, they were getting ready for their 'Search for Extra Terrestrials at FIU' event. They also run the occasional Explore the Heavens Public Star Party at Crandon Park on Key Biscayne, opposite the tennis center, with slide shows and historical tours. Parking is $2 per car.

Rickenbacker Causeway & Key Biscayne

The Rickenbacker Causeway ($1 toll) links the mainland with Key Biscayne via Virginia Key. The main attraction of Key Biscayne – unless you're a humiliated ex-president (the late, disgraced US President Richard M 'Expletive Deleted' Nixon had a house here) or a multi-squidgillionaire and can afford a condo – is the **Bill Baggs Cape Florida State Recreation Area** (☎ 361-5811). All of the 494-acre park's exotic plants – including about half a million Australian pines – were destroyed during Hurricane Andrew, and the park is in the process of replanting with natives. But all walkways and boardwalks have been replaced, and there are nature trails and bike paths.

The 1845 **Cape Florida Lighthouse** (☎ 361-8779) at the park's southern end has a 1st-order lens (the scale of lighthouse lenses, since you asked, was developed by French physicist Augustin Jean Fresnel (1788-1827), who devised a beehive-like reflecting lens sized from 1st through 6th orders. 1st, the largest, is used at seacoasts, while 6th is used in harbors)

The official address is 1200 S Crandon Blvd; take the causeway to the very end and follow the signs. Admission is $3.25 per carload up to eight people; pedestrians and cyclists $1 per person. The park's open daily from 8 am to sundown.

Crandon Park & Hobie Beaches, public beaches on a five-mile stretch of white sand, are out here as well.

Miami Seaquarium While the advertised star of the show at this excellent 37-acre aquarium (☎ 361-5705) is Lolita, the killer whale, we were far more impressed with what a genuine effort these great folks are making to preserve, protect and explain aquatic life. Case in point, their **Manatee Presentation & Exhibit**, where

Marine Mammal Rescue Team
Seaquarium's manatee exhibit is made possible by Seaquarium's excellent Marine Mammal Rescue Team, whose divers, animal experts and veterinarians patrol the waters of South Florida and respond to reports of stranded manatees, dolphins and whales in the wild.

Team members were overjoyed on June 29, 1992, when the offspring of their male manatee Romeo (he's been here since 1957) and female Acacia (rescued by the team in 1990) was born. Little Indi weighed in at 75 pounds.

Indi became the first captive-bred manatee to become eligible for a release program. After a month in a 'soft-release' program – a secured natural habitat with minimum human contact to teach the manatee to learn to feed on sea grass – Little Indi was released into the wild.

There are only about 1800 of the endangered West Indian manatees left in the world, and the program is dedicated to preventing their extinction. While the program has been very successful, mankind – especially pleasure boaters – continues to threaten the species' existence.

As if to highlight the inhumane practices in designated manatee zones, a hit-and-run boater killed Little Indi near the Julia Tuttle Causeway. His body was found on November 18, 1995 with propeller gashes from head to tail. ■

West Indian manatees are brought after being injured by boat propellers. The manatees are nursed back to health and some are released. There are usually between five and eight manatees here: Juliet has been here since the late 1960s.

In **Red, Whale & Blue**, Lolita the 7000-pound killer whale bounces and splashes (stay about six rows back if you don't want to get wet), and there are Pacific white-sided dolphins as well.

The **Flipper Dolphin Show** in Flipper Lagoon stars a dolphin who sure looks like the one on the TV show (they say it's him) and several Atlantic bottle-nosed dolphins. This lagoon was the set for the original 1960s TV series and the movie.

The presentations at **Shark Channel** are great for little kids if the sharks are hungry. Other shows include **Splash of the Islands** with Atlantic bottle-nosed dolphins, and **Salty's Sea Scoundrels** with Salty the Sea Lion.

Seaquarium's at 4400 Rickenbacker Causeway. The park is open daily from 9.30 am to 6 pm, tickets have to be bought before 4.30 pm though, $18.95 for adults, $13.95 for children (aged three to nine), $16.95 for seniors. There's a AAA discount of 15%, and ISIC holders get $3 off.

Parking is $2. Wheelchairs and strollers can be rented for $4 (no deposit) and a kennel is available at no cost.

Virginia Key Beach This is a lovely city park with picnic tables, barbecue grills and relative peace and quiet. Parking is $2.

Vizcaya Museum & Gardens

While today we recognize ostentation to be a sign of sexual dysfunction, there was a time in Florida history when rich men were rich men, full speed ahead, damn the torpedoes. Such a man was James Deering, who built this opulent palace in 1916. It's a Fabulously splendiferous Italian Renaissance-style villa (it was used as the setting for the splendid dinner party in *Ace Ventura: Pet Detective*) and filled with 15th- to

KENNETH DREYFUSS

NICK SELBY

The height of opulence: Vizcaya mansion

19th-century furniture and decorative arts, but unless you're a real early 20th-century Miami-Faux Venetian architecture or furniture buff, we can't for the life of us justify the admission prices of $10 for adults, $5 for children aged six to 12 ($1 AAA discount).

Okay, okay . . . there *are* undeniably stunning gardens, complete with beautiful fountains. Out back, a stone gondola in the center of the docking area acts as a breakwater, and there's a charming gazebo. The pool is to die for, and there are canals running everywhere. There are narrow trails through the grounds as well.

Tours of the 1st floor, which are included in the price, are available from 10 am to 2 pm; they start every 15 to 20 minutes. All the rooms are roped off, though you can peek in.

The museum (☎ 250-9133) is at 3251 S Miami Ave; tickets can be bought daily from 9.30 am to 4.30 pm, once inside you can stay in the house until 5 pm, the gardens until 5.30 pm. Neither video nor photos are allowed (but we took lots of pictures and no one bothered us).

SOUTHWEST MIAMI

Black Heritage Museum

The Black Heritage Museum (☎ 252-3535, see the Online Services appendix) is a museum in search of a home. It has existed since 1987, when three teachers, Priscilla S Kruize, Dr Paul Cadby and Dr Earl Wells, set out to establish a museum to celebrate the cultures of African Americans, Bahamians, Haitians and other blacks in Dade County.

Since then, they have established three small permanent exhibitions in different locations, and are trying to raise $200,000 to buy a permanent site for the museum. As we went to press, it did not seem likely that they would raise the money by the end of 1996.

The smallest of their exhibitions is the only one really within the Miami city limits. It was opened in 1996 in the entrance to Deering Hospital (☎ 251-2500) at 9333 SW 152nd St.

The two main exhibitions are both outside Miami: the Ghana exhibit is on display at Chapman Elementary School (☎ 245-1055), 27190 SW 140th Ave in the town of Naranja, open Monday to Friday 9 am to 2 pm; and Florida Civil Rights Sit-Ins is at the Mizell Library (☎ 765-4269), Sistrunk Blvd in Fort Lauderdale. Call for hours. Admission to all the exhibitions is free.

National Hurricane Center

If you want to learn a whole bunch about hurricanes,

storms, weather and storm tracking, you can schedule a free tour with the National Hurricane Center (☎ 229-4470) on certain days during the hurricane off-season (December to May). The half-hour tours are normally conducted on Tuesday and Thursday between 11 am and 1 pm. According to the center, tours are not recommended for children younger than 10 years old. And remember that even in the off-season, there are certain periods when the building is blocked out for things like training, scientific conferences, etc, so you should call at least a week beforehand. No groups larger than 20 or 25 people are permitted; a family group of even two is okay – you'll be combined with a larger group for your tour.

The center's on the southwest side of the Florida International University campus; the street address is 11691 SW 17th St at the corner of 117th Ave and 17th St: take Florida's Turnpike to the 8th St exit.

Equestrian Center

Kids go crazy over this center (☎ 226-7886) at Tropical Park (Bird Rd at the Palmetto Expressway) where each weekend purebred horses perform free. You'll see show, quarter and rodeo horses. It's on the grounds of the Metro-Dade Police Stables. The park is usually open from 8 am to sunset, weather dependent.

Metrozoo

While it took a decisive hit from Hurricane Andrew, Miami's Metrozoo (☎ 251-0403, TDD 857-6680, sign language interpreters (five days in advance) 670-9099) is open and operating. Before Andrew this enormous sprawling natural habitat zoo (300 developed acres out of 754 total) was one of the top 10 in the USA, and they're looking to reclaim the title. They'll probably succeed: they have 900 animals from over 260 species, including recent acquisitions of a koala and a pair of Komodo dragons! There are nice waterfalls right outside the entrance and, once inside, the picnic area is to your left.

The landscaping is lovely; animals have plenty of space to move around and there are no bars: cleverly designed moats separate you from them. The buildings themselves are also wonderful: we loved the temple behind the white Bengal tigers. Signage is absolutely excellent.

For a great orientation tour, get on the Zoofari Monorail for one complete circuit (don't let the pre-recorded safety announcements drive you insane).

The monorail's four stops are (1) in front of the amphitheater, (2) the Asian elephant, Wings of Asia and PAWS (the children's zoo, petting area, shows and rides section), (3) in front of the pygmy hippo, Egyptian geese and Arabian oryx, and finally (4) at the northernmost area of the zoo, home to colobus monkeys, black rhinoceros and African elephants.

KENNETH DREYFUSS

PAWS is amazing: in the petting area, kids can play with pot-bellied pigs, Eld's deer (it looks like a white tail), sheep, a ferret, snakes (which are brought out by staff for the kids to touch), a monitor lizard and more. Elephant rides run throughout the day, and the Ecology Theater does shows at 11 am and 1 and 3 pm.

Don't miss the constantly changing wildlife shows in the Amphitheater daily at noon, 2 and 4.30 pm.

Another wonderful feature of the place is the Behind the Scenes Tram Tour, which is a 45-minute ride around the public areas of the zoo and then to other areas, like the veterinary hospital, brooder and hatchery building and quarantine pens. The tours cost $2; check with the admission booth for hours during your visit, and to buy tickets.

Remember where you parked! Metrozoo's enormous parking lot is as confusing as those at major theme parks, so keep track of your car.

The zoo is at 12400 SW 152nd St; take Florida's Turnpike Extension to the Metrozoo exit at SW 152nd St. The zoo's open daily 9.30 am to 5.30 pm (tickets must be bought before 4 pm), ticket prices including tax are $8 for adults, $4 for children aged three to 12; wheelchair rentals are $6 ($10 deposit), single/double strollers $4/7 ($10 deposit); video cameras can be rented for $6 an hour (two-hour minimum, $20 deposit and a drivers license or passport required), video tapes are $4.

Gold Coast Railroad Museum

Just near the entrance to Metrozoo is the Gold Coast Railroad Museum (☎ 253-0063), and if you're at all interested in trains it's worth checking out. Though also damaged badly by Andrew, the museum has been here since the 1950s, when it was set up by the Miami

Railroad Historical Society. They've got over 30 antique railway cars, including the *Ferdinand Magellan* Presidential car, used by US Presidents Roosevelt, Eisenhower, Truman and even Ronald Reagan (for whom the thing was outfitted with three-inch-thick glass windows and armor plating). You have probably seen this train: it's the one in the photograph of newly elected president Harry Truman, which shows him standing at the rear holding a newspaper bearing the famous erroneous headline: 'Dewey Defeats Truman'.

The museum's at 12450 SW 152nd St, open Friday to Sunday 11 am to 4 pm. Admission is $4 for adults, $1 for children under 10 (kids under three are free). Admission includes a train ride, which lasts about 20 to 25 minutes (two miles). Trains leave every hour on the hour between noon and 4 pm.

Weeks Air Museum

Air and history buffs will be delighted with this museum – despite the damage it received from Hurricane Andrew, it's definitely open for business, and has been for a long time. What's nice about this, as compared to other air museums, is that it's truly a history of aviation, not just military aviation, as is often the case. The staff is knowledgeable and dedicated – there's always someone out on the floor to answer questions.

Andrew absolutely flattened the hangar and, with it, many of the museum's priceless aircraft, but a completely dedicated staff has made certain that the museum will rise Phoenix-like from the ashes.

The first area you'll enter will be Hurricane Alley, with exhibits of the planes that were destroyed in the

NICK SELBY

Pitts Special at the Weeks Air Museum

hurricane. Most impressive is the Curtiss JN-4D Jenny with a broken back – you can still see the hand-made brass fittings.

Highlights of the museum include:

- Propeller collection
- J47 jet engine
- Pitts Special 'Little Stinker' (it was 'a pleasure to fly but a stinker to land') aerobatic plane
- YaK trainer, a Soviet bomber from Smolensk
- Beach 17 Staggerwing
- Nose section of 'Fertile Myrtle', the B-29 Superfortress
- Messerschmidt ME-108, the direct predecessor to the 109, the famous fighter plane. Ask about how restrictions on German powered aircraft lead to their engineers' ground-up approach to redesign and reconsideration of aerodynamics.

Also impressive are the museum's exhibits on the Tuskeegee airmen, with videos featuring the black pilots telling their stories in their own words; and their Learn How to Fly a Plane exhibit, in which you attempt to stabilize a miniature plane in a wind tunnel – it takes a cunning hand to work it!

The museum(☎ 233-5197) is in the Tamiami Airport, 14710 SW 128th St. It's open daily from 10 am to 5 pm. The cost is $6.95 for adults, $5.95 for seniors, $4.95 for children 12 and under.

From Miami, take Hwy 836 west to Florida's Turnpike, go south to exit 19 (120th St), then west on 120th St for about two miles to 137th Ave (Tamiami Airport). Turn left (south) and enter the airport, then follow signs.

Fairchild Tropical Gardens

The USA's largest tropical botanical garden, the Fairchild (☎ 667-1651) is 83 acres of lush greenery with lakes, streams, grottos and waterfalls. To call it a tourist attraction detracts from its purpose, which is the serious study of tropical flora by the garden's more than 6000 members.

It was, of course, devastated by Andrew, and their new Windows on the Tropics exhibit at the Fairchild Conservatory was slated to be the completion of the final phase of restoration. The new conservatory was scheduled to offer six 'windows' focusing on distinct areas of tropical flora collected from equatorial regions including Borneo, Madagascar, Brazil and Mexico.

The garden's absolutely excellent visitor pamphlet sets out three trails, with very good and easy-to-follow self-guided walking tours. Signs inside the gardens are very clear. There's a 40-minute tram orientation tour of the entire park, or you can set out on your own. Plan on spending 30 minutes for the Palmetum Walk; 45 for the Upland Walk, and at least an hour for the Lowland Trail, which goes from the rainforest in the southeast of the park, up around the lakes and ends at Hammock Lake.

The park is at 10901 Old Cutler Rd; take US Hwy 1 south to SW 42nd Ave (Le Jeune Rd) south to Cocoplum Circle, turn south on Old Cutler Rd for two miles. The gardens are open daily from 9.30 am to 4.30 pm, closed Christmas. Admission is $8 for adults, free for members and children under 12.

Parrot Jungle & Gardens

Far southwest of Miami is Parrot Jungle (☎ 666-7834), which is more than a parrot show. The lush gardens, set in a hardwood hammock with over 1200 varieties of exotic and tropical plants like heliconias and bromeliads, are home to alligators and crocodiles, orangutans, chimps, tortoises and the very pink flamingoes from the intro sequence on *Miami Vice*. The parrot show is held five times a day; highlights include trained (as in bicycle riding and roller skating) parrots, macaws and cockatoos.

You can bring a picnic, and there's a small café there. If you come, plan on spending at least three hours.

The park is open every day from 9.30 am to 6 pm, tickets on sale until 5 pm. Admission is $11.95 for adults, $10.95 for seniors over 62, $7.95 for children aged three to 10. It's at 11000 SW 57th Ave; take I-95 south to US Hwy 1, and go five miles south to SW 57th Ave, turn left and go three miles to SW 111th St. Note that in 1998, Parrot Jungle expects to move to Watson Island, which will make it a much more major player in the city's tourism market.

Fruit & Spice Park

The Preston B Bird & Mary Heinlein Fruit & Spice Park (☎ 247-5727) is the only public garden of its kind in the USA. It's a very romantic place to go with a date – a 20-acre public facility that shows over 100 varieties of citrus, 50 of bananas, 40 of grapes and a whole bunch of exotic tropical fruits, plants and spices. There's also a nice poisonous plant area. Best of all, after walking through the paths smelling all that, you can buy exotic offerings at the Redland Gourmet & Fruit Store. We'd advise against the durian (which looks like a jackfruit, tastes like sugary fertilizer and smells like an aged corpse), but you can choose from pomello, rambutan, lychee, breadfruit, tamarind and seeds, spices, jellies and jams.

The park also offers an enormous range of classes and activities, from a Banana Workshop to tours of local commercial farms to Chainsaw Etiquette (we swear!) to Tropical Wine Making (all $10), to a Florida Keys Fruit Safari that visits private gardens in the Florida Keys ($25).

It's at 24801 SW 187th Ave (Redland Rd). The park is open daily from 10 am to 5 pm. Admission to the park is just $1 for adults, 50¢ for kids. Tours of the park are given Saturday and Sunday at 1 and 3 pm; the cost for all tours is $1.50/1.

To get there, take US Hwy 1 to SW 248th St, go west, and turn left on SW 187th Ave, and the park's on the left hand side of the road. Stop for a cinnamon bun at Knaus Berry Farm (see the Places to Eat chapter for more information).

Monkey Jungle

In 1933, an animal behaviorist named Joseph du Mond released six monkeys into the wild, and their descendants – now over 60 of them – are the highlight of Monkey Jungle (☎ 235-1611), which also features orangutans, chimpanzees and King, the lowland gorilla. The big show of the day is during the feedings, when the Java monkeys dive into the pool for fruit and treats.

Monkey Jungle is at 14805 SW 216th St. To get there, take Florida's Turnpike Homestead Extension to exit 11 and head west for five miles. Admission is $10.50 for adults, $9.50 for seniors and active military and $5.35 for children aged four to 12. It's open daily from 9.30 am to 5 pm; the ticket office closes at 4 pm. It's a long way to come, but if you're all the way out here, you really should go just a mile further to Burr's Berry Farm for some of the world's best strawberries (see the Places to Eat chapter for more information).

Federal Detention Center

To the southwest of the city is an enormous Federal Detention Center (☎ 577-0010) that you can really only see from the air (which was how we saw it). It holds a number of local villains, drug smugglers and dealers. And a lasting monument to the presidency of George Herbert Walker 'Read My Lips' Bush: this is also the residence of US-deposed former Panamanian strongman Manuel Noriega.

NORTHEAST MIAMI

With a few notable exceptions, northeast Miami is an absolutely uninteresting industrial section of town, packed with warehouses and dust. It's not a very appealing place to head for, unless you're after some specific sights.

American Police Hall of Fame & Police Museum

A police officer is killed in the US every 57 hours. This museum (☎ 573-0070, see the Online Services appendix) is dedicated to memorializing cops who have died in the line of duty – nearly 6000 as we went to press.

It's located in a boxy building with a highly visible and dramatic eye-catcher: a 1995 Chevy Caprice Classic police car on the side wall fronting Biscayne Blvd. While the museum has some fun collections like the cop car from the movie *Blade Runner*, interesting gangster memorabilia and a huge display of confiscated weapons, restraint devices and other cop stuff, it's mainly a memorial – murdered officers' names, rank, city and state are engraved in the white Italian marble that makes up the main floor, where there's also an interdenominational chapel.

But kids love the gore and the descriptions of the execution devices: have a seat in the gas chamber (where it takes 'up to 11 minutes to die' when the cyanide capsules are dumped into the pan of hydrochloric acid); you can also sit in the electric chair ('A tight mask goes over the face . . . to prevent the eyes from popping out of the head as the current surges through the body.') Alas, you can only stand next to the guillotine ('please do not place your head beneath the blade'). You can work a crime scene as a detective, and there's a holding cell here as well.

Finally, lest you complain about the conditions in US prisons, the museum has what I call their 'Yeah, well at least you're not in . . . ' exhibit of jail conditions in third-world countries.

The museum is at 3801 Biscayne Blvd, open daily 10 am to 5.30 pm. Admission is $6 for adults, $4 for seniors and $3 for students and children.

Bacardi Imports Headquarters

The headquarters for the USA's most popular rum company, Bacardi Imports (☎ 573-8511), is in an intricately decorated building (the poorer cousin of the one in

Havana) at 2100 Biscayne Blvd, that's also home to the small **World of Bacardi Museum**, dedicated to the history of the Bacardi family and the rum company, from 1838 to the present. It's filled with mementos and artifacts as well as artwork, paintings and sculptures by family members. Admission is free; it's open Monday to Friday from 9 am to noon.

Little Haiti

Haitians are the third-largest group of foreign-born residents in Florida after Cubans and (strangely) Canadians, and Little Haiti is the center of Haitian life in Miami. As with Little Havana, Little Haiti has absorbed waves of refugees during times of Haitian political strife.

Little Haiti is a colorful neighborhood that is trying very hard, though with limited success, to make itself a tourist attraction. The **Haitian Refugee Center** (☎ 757-8538) at 119 NE 54th St is a community center dedicated to disseminating information about Haitian life in Haiti and in Miami. They are also a good resource for information about community events. The opening of the **Caribbean Marketplace** (☎ 751-2251), a combination tourist attraction and legitimate flea market at 5925-27 NE 2nd Ave has not taken off as planned, but with the growth of the nearby Miami Design District, the

Haiti's 1991 Coup

In late September 1991 the Haitian military led by Lieutenant General Raoul Cedras overthrew the government of constitutionally elected President Jean Bertrand Aristide. The US response was economic sanctions, to be removed only after the return of Aristide to power.

Under Cedras' leadership, Haitian armed forces, which at that time were given extreme legal and institutional autonomy, were responsible for law enforcement and 'public safety'. As human rights abuses – beatings, torture, executions and 'disappearances' – escalated, refugees began to flee to the relative safety (they thought) of the USA in anything that would float.

For the next three years, media images of Haitians being rounded up by the US Coast Guard permeated local media: in the first seven months of 1992 alone, the UN High Commissioner for Refugees (UNHCR) said that the Coast Guard had intercepted and detained at Guantanamo Bay, Cuba, a total of 38,315 Haitians fleeing their country. But the US wasn't letting many in. In fact, of those 38,315, only 11,617 were given the INS stamp of being 'potentially qualified for political asylum'.

prospects are getting rosier all the time. The market is open Monday to Saturday 10 am to 9 pm, Sunday 10 am to 7 pm.

Haitian **botanicas**, which sell voodoo-related items, are worth visiting for beautiful bottles, beads and sequined banners with voodoo symbolism – while they may seem expensive ($100 to 200), they're far cheaper here than at some art galleries around the USA, where the banners are selling as art.

In 1996, the **Roots & Culture Foundation** was planning the first of what it hopes will be annual Roots & Culture Celebrations, with Haitian music, dance, art and food. A five-block section of N Miami Ave – from 54th St to 59th St – was to be cordoned off for the free festival. It was scheduled for May 21, Haiti's Flag Day, commemorating Haiti's emergence as an independent nation in 1804.

There's a pretty bitchin' live music venue here in *Churchill's* (☎ 757-1807) at 5501 NE 2nd Ave – see the Entertainment chapter for more information.

The **Tap Tap**, basically a colorfully painted group taxi mounted on a pick-up truck (the name is onomatopoeic: think of the sound of a third-world truck engine), is a free shuttle between NE 2nd Ave and 36th St to NE 2nd Ave and 59th St from Friday to Sunday.

As pressure mounted from Haitian groups in Miami, which pointed out the historical carte blanche given any Cuban who manages to wash up on US soil, the US Supreme Court upheld a detestable Bush-administration policy that allows the Coast Guard to return refugees it has intercepted on the high seas directly to their home country without the benefit of an asylum hearing. Which the Coast Guard immediately set to.

Through a series of maneuvers (including, some say, a covert payment of cool $1 million by the USA to Cedras) Aristide was returned to power. Cedras resigned, and was granted political amnesty. For the second time in a century, the US sent troops to Haiti to restore democracy.

Which allowed the Clinton administration to say to the rest of the Haitians who were being held at Guantanamo Bay, in essence, to 'please go home now, you no longer have a claim of asylum as your country is again a model democracy'. As if to accentuate the divergent treatment of Haitians and Cubans, Clinton made that move the day after agreeing to allow some 20,000 Cubans at Guantanamo entry to the USA. ■

Design District

Touted as, or at the very least poised to become, the new South Beach, the Miami Design District (roughly bordered by N Miami Ave at the west, NE 36th St at the south, NE 42nd St at the north and NE 2nd Ave at the east) is a collection of antique, tile and specialty shops, art galleries and studios.

Billed in the 1960s as 'the Square Mile of Style,' the area has been a center to the interior decorator and designer industry for about 30 years – with showrooms like Country Floors, David and Dash, Lord Jay, EG Cody and Concept Casual – and is in a neighborhood called Buena Vista. Since about 1993, the neighborhood has been going through something of a renaissance, as owners have ended their 'trade only' sales policy in favor of one that is 'courtesy to the trade and retail'.

The reason people are pegging it as a new South Beach is that conditions are very similar here to those just before the SoBe Boom: higher rents in more fashionable neighborhoods are forcing creative people to move over here. Already the area is home to artists and their studios and galleries, film companies, photographers and dancers – basically anyone who needs lots of space for not a lot of money.

To see the place in its best light, go over on the second Saturday of the month when all the studios and galleries stay open for sort of a gallery walk. They do proper gallery walks as well, on the second Friday evening of the month.

Stop in at the Picadilly Garden Lounge (☎ 573-8221) at 35 NE 40th St for coffee and light meals in their lush little courtyard.

At the northern end of the Design District, the **Florida Museum of Hispanic & Latin American Art** (☎ 576-5171) is one of the few museums in the country to be dedicated solely to the culture of Hispanics and Latin Americans. They have 11 rotating exhibitions per year (the museum's closed in August). A great time to visit is during one of their free Opening Nights, held the second Friday of the month (the same night as Design District gallery walks), which feature local, national and international artists, and, oh, yes, free cocktails from 6 to 10 pm. After you reread that sentence, we'll continue.

Nice, huh? The museum's at 1 NE 40th St; admission is $2 for adults, $1 for senior citizens over 58, students and children aged six to 12.

Museum of Contemporary Art

The Museum of Contemporary Art (MoCA; ☎ 893-6211, see the Online Services appendix) has moved to a brand new and much larger space in the city of North Miami. The museum, which shows excellent rotating exhibitions of contemporary art by local, national and international artists, is also beginning a new permanent collection featuring the works of artists including Ian Hamilton Finlay, Quisqueya Henriques, Alex Katz, James Rosenquist and others.

Past exhibitions include Defining the Nineties, with new art from three US art centers: New York, Miami and Los Angeles; Pierced Hearts & True Love: A Century of Drawings for Tattoos which considered modern tattooing as an evolving art form; Mexican Modernism from the Jacques & Natasha Gelman Collection, the first US appearance of masterpieces from Mexico's modern artists including Gunther Gerzo, Frida Kahlo, Rufino Tamayo, David Alfar Siqueros and Diego Rivera; Robert Chambers, a Miami-based artist's multi-media installation.

To get to the museum, take I-95 to NE 125th St, and go east for 1½ miles; MoCA's at 770 NE 125th St. From Biscayne Blvd, take 123rd St west for one mile, and it will become 125th St. The museum is open Tuesday to Saturday 10 am to 5 pm, Thursday 10 am to 9 pm, Sunday noon to 5 pm, closed Monday. Admission is $4 for adults, $2 for students and seniors; free for children under 12, city of North Miami residents and MoCA members.

NORTHWEST MIAMI

Liberty City & Overtown

From the birth of Miami, blacks were only permitted to live in the northwest quarter of downtown called Colored Town. Later the name was changed to Overtown – it was 'over the tracks'. Overtown was pretty well decimated by construction of freeways and bypasses. There's a locally famous mural of prominent black Miamians on the side of the **Lyric Theatre** at 819 NW 2nd Ave.

Liberty City, farther north and west, is a misnomer. Made infamous by the Liberty City Riots in 1980 (see the History section in the Facts about Miami chapter), the area is very poor and crime is higher than in other parts of the city. And while plans exist to renovate the area by creating a village of cultural and tourist attractions, the prospects of that happening in the near future looked grim as we went to press.

In 1934, a *Miami Herald* series on Overtown's appalling living conditions lead to what would become the first federal public housing project in the southeastern United States; Overtown's residents were shoved into the projects as whites needed the space. The concrete apartment blocks in Liberty City today were built in the 1950s by white contractors to meet the housing demand of the expanding black community.

Whites, fearing 'black encroachment' on their neighborhoods, actually went so far as to build a *wall* at the then border of Liberty City – NW 12th Ave from NW 62nd to NW 67th Sts – to separate their neighborhoods. Part of the wall still stands, at NW 12th Ave between NW 63rd and 64th Sts.

Surprisingly, there is no permanent museum of black history or culture here, though efforts are being made: see the Southwest section below for information on the Black Heritage Museum. For information on Liberty City, Overtown and other areas significant to black history, contact the exceedingly helpful Black Archives History & Research Center of South Florida (☎ 636-2390) open 9 am to 5 pm Monday to Friday (from 1 to 5 pm for specific research projects) in the Caleb Center at 5400 NW 22nd Ave.

Liberty City has a reputation for being dangerous to white visitors; see the Dangers & Annoyances section of the Facts for the Visitor chapter for more information.

ACTIVITIES

Bicycling

See the Getting Around chapter for information on biking around the city. Bike rental is an excellent – and cheap – way to make your way around the Beach, and several places rent bicycles.

Try Gary's Megacycles (☎ 534-3306) at 1260 Washington Ave, which rents bicycles for $3.50/10/35 an hour/day/week, open Monday to Friday 9.30 am to 7 pm, Saturday 9 am to 6 pm and Sunday 10 am to 4 pm, or Cycles on the Beach (☎ 673-2055) at 1421 Washington Ave, where rentals are $3/15/40 an hour/day/week, open Monday to Saturday 10 am to 9 pm, Sunday 10 am to 7 pm. The Miami Beach Bicycle Center (☎ 674-0150) at 601 5th St does bike rentals for $3/14/50 an hour/day/week. They're open Monday to Saturday 10 am to 7 pm, Sunday 10 am to 5 pm. All of these shops sell bicycles as well.

Skating & Running

In-line skating is one of the most popular forms of transportation here. Everyone seems to have a pair of skates, and the streets are excellent for it. Be careful on Washington Ave and remember that there are very few shops that will allow you in with skates on around here. We usually tuck a pair of thong-type sandals in the back of our jeans to wear when we have to carry our skates.

Skate rental is easy but expensive: Skate 2000 has two locations on the beach: one at 1200 Ocean Drive, suite 102 (☎ 538-8282), entered on 12th St; the other is at 420 Lincoln Road, suite 385 (☎ 538-8244). Rentals are $8 an hour, $24 for 24 hours, including all protective gear. On Sunday from 10 am to noon they give free skating lessons. You'll have to give them a $100 deposit (either cash or credit card).

South Beach Rentals, a booth on the Promenade around 8th St, rents skates for $8.50/24. The most expensive option is Fritz's Skate Shop (☎ 532-0054) at 117 5th St. It's $8 an hour, but the $24 daily does not include a $15 overnight fee; they also have a second location at 726 Lincoln Road (☎ 532-1954).

Running is also very popular, and the beach is a very good one for joggers as it's flat, wide and hard-packed. The Promenade is the stylish place for both, but more serious runners may appreciate the running track at Flamingo Park, just east of Alton Rd between 11th and 12th Sts. The entrance is on the 12th St side, east end of the fence, near the PAL building. If you're a serious runner, contact the Miami Runners Club (☎ 227-1500) for information on races and special events.

Surfing

There's not a whole lot of surfing here, but there's some, and X-Isle Surf Shop (☎ 673-5900) is the only surf shop on the beach, at 437 Washington Ave. They rent boards for $25 a day, weekly rates are negotiable, and used boards sell for about $50 to 250, new ones $350 to 500. They're open Monday to Friday 10 am to 7 pm, Saturday 10 am to 6 pm and Sunday noon to 6 pm.

Kayaking & Canoeing

There is something absolutely magical about kayaking through the mangroves, and places where you can are as close as Haulover Beach or South Miami. And the best thing about it is that you don't need any lessons and you can rent all the equipment you need very easily and

NICK SELBY

NICK SELBY

cheaply. We've used Urban Trails Kayak Co (☎ 947-1302) on the bay side opposite Haulover Beach at 10800 Collins Ave, a very friendly outfit that rents one-person kayaks for $8 an hour or $20 for four hours, two-person kayaks for $15/35, including paddles, lifejacket and instructions. There are 19 islands along the Intracoastal Waterway, many with barbecue facilities, and on some you can camp for nothing (an overnight (24-hour) kayak rental is $25/45 one-person/two-person). They're open every day from 9 am to 5 pm.

Sailboards Miami (☎ 361-7245) rents one-person kayaks for $13 an hour, two-person kayaks for $18 an hour. See the Windsurfing section below for directions and the address.

If you really don't feel confident enough to just jump into a kayak and head out on your own, you can take an instructional tour from Mangrove Coast (☎ 633-3364). For $85 a person (including lunch) you get a four-hour paddle in their sea kayaks with rudders, down to Key Largo. The tour runs mainly through mangrove flats and creeks. Take I-95 south to US Hwy 1, turn right at 70th St (the first light after Red Rd), then take the second right turn onto Commerce Lane. Mangrove Coast is on the right side of the street.

Canoeing around the 10,000 Islands, or on the Wilderness Waterway between Everglades City and Flamingo is one of the most fascinating ways to get away to nature; see the Excursions chapter for complete information.

CORINNA SELBY

Ultralights & Skydiving

Miami is an aviation center, and hundreds of small planes fill the skies each day. Ultralight aircraft, in fact, became so popular down here that Dade County built a field specifically for the tiny planes at Homestead General Aviation Airport (HGAA; ☎ 247-4883). Ultralights are small aircraft that are regulated but require no pilot's license to fly. Lessons cost about $75 an hour, and you'll need 10 to 12 hours of training before you can fly solo – contact the Light Aircraft Flyers Association (☎ 460-3356) for information about lessons, upcoming events, or just show up at the field on the second Saturday of each month for their Fly-In and Social Day at HGAA, where there's barbecue breakfast and lunch, talk of flying and, if the weather's good, flying.

Also at HGAA is Skydive Miami (☎ 245-6160, 759-3483), which will get you trained and pushed out of the plane on your first jump ('the most fun you can have with your clothes on') in one day for $129. If you saw the movie *Drop Zone* with Wesley Snipes, you've seen these folks in action – one of their former employees trained Snipes for the film, and most of the jumps – including the huge one allegedly over Washington, DC – were filmed here. They're open every day all year in daylight hours, call the day before.

Windsurfing

The only place we found to rent sailboards was Sailboards Miami (☎ 361-7245) which does short and long board rentals for $20 an hour, $37 for two hours, and holds two-hour 'guarantee-to-learn' windsurfing lessons for $49 for adults, $59 for kids. Private lessons are $25 an hour. They're in the right place for it: Hobie Island, the first right turn after the tollbooths for the Rickenbacker Causeway to Key Biscayne, where the water is calm. They're open daily from 10 am to 6 pm.

Swimming

The best pool in the area by anyone's standards is the Venetian Pool (see the Coral Gables section, this chapter), but you're here in Miami Beach, aren't you? Sitting poolside with a cool drink in your hand is a noble Miami tradition (maybe because of all the models in their skimpy bathing suits?) that's truly a great way to spend an afternoon – or at least part of one.

The excellent T-shaped Flamingo Park Swimming Pool (☎ 673-7750), has six lanes in their 25-yard lap swimming area and a deep-water area. It's open to the public daily from 8.30 am to 1 pm and 1.30 to 6 pm in winter, and admission is free. In the summer, there's adult lap swim every morning from 8.30 to 9.30 am, and the pool is open Monday to Friday noon to 8 pm, Saturday and Sunday from 8.30 am to 8 pm. Admission in summer (yes, admission in the off-season, not the high season) is $1.25 for adults and 75¢ seniors and children. The pool is between Jefferson and Michigan Aves and 11th and 12th Sts, parking adjacent to the pool.

The rest of the really good pools, unfortunately, are at hotels, and hotel pools are restricted to hotel guests and club members (see Health Clubs: you may be able to use some of these pools with a day or week membership). Now we'd *never* ever suggest breaking the policies of a hotel, so the following is clearly intended only to let you know what you're missing.

We have three favorite pools: the one at the Raleigh Hotel (☎ 534-6300) is a class act all the way. Voted most beautiful pool in Florida by *Life* Magazine in 1945, it's as curvaceous as a 1930s Hollywood vixen. Walk through their very posh lobby and straight out to the back. There's a bar at the far end; it's at 1775 Collins Ave, open 24 hours.

If you've ever seen the movie *Goldfinger*, you've seen the excellent pool at the Fontainebleau Hilton – Bond opens the movie sitting poolside here with a cool drink in his hand and saying 'Now this is the life.' He's right. Waterfalls, islands and exotic beautiful people. Getting to the pool – if you're a hotel guest, of course – is much easier from the beach side than through the lobby, where security guards are everywhere. There's a bar and two snack bars (one is beneath the center of the pool), and they frequently have steel bands playing.

The pool at the fiercely fashionable Delano Hotel (☎ 672-2000) at 1685 Collins Ave is, like the hotel, swank. In fact, it's so swank that there's classical music piped in under the water that you can only hear when you're submerged (!). Walk through the lobby, through the restaurant, past the wooden back porch to the gardens, where bed-like lounge chairs (and an enormous chess set) festoon the lawn. The pool's in the garden, and note that there's a table and two chairs in the shallow area. Frozen drinks are $7.

Jet Skis & Motorboats

Jet skis and motorboats kill manatees and fish, rip sea plants and protected sea grass from the bottom (destroying the manatees' food supply) scare swimmers, annoy locals and result in several deaths a year. The waters of Biscayne Bay and the canals are very shallow and tricky to navigate. Many areas of it are protected Manatee Zones. You can rent these hateful machines in various places around the beach, but we wish you wouldn't.

Health Clubs

In an effort to attract travelers, many area health clubs offer week or even one-day memberships. Perks change, but some allow use of nearby hotel pools. Try Club Body Tech (☎ 674-8222) at 1253 Washington Ave ($13 a day, $49 a week, a book of 12 visits $99); Idol's Gym (☎ 532-0089) at 1000 Lincoln Road ($10 a day, $20 for three days and $30 for a week); or the Gridiron Club (☎ 531-4743) at 1676 Alton Rd (the entrance is through the back alley) with aerobics at $70 for 10 classes, the gym $9 a day, $32 a week.

The Spa at the Fontainebleau Hilton (☎ 538-2000) occasionally runs specials for non-guests on a daily or weekly basis, but they don't really advertise it: you'll have to call them while you're here. The main advantage is the access to the Fontainebleau's pool.

The Eden Roc Health Club (☎ 674-5580) at the Eden Roc Resort (see the Places to Stay chapter) at 4525 Collins Ave is a very slick spa that's open to the public for $75 a week, or, for guests, $10 a day, $50 a week. They have, the impossibly accented person on the phone told us, 'Cybex eekweepmun, thahss ahll VR2'. Whatever.

Of course, truly chic people would head to the David Barton Gym on the lower level of the fiercely fashionable

Delano Hotel, which can be summarized as the night club of health clubs: dim lighting, designer furniture in the workout rooms, loud house music and . . . oh yes, exercise equipment. A one-day pass costs $20 ($15 if you bring your local hotel room key), a five-visit pass is $75 and a 10-visit pass, $125.

For a different type of health club, contact the Ronald W Shane Watersports Center (☎ 864-6365), which does crew rowing and other stuff, mainly geared to young students. They're way north at 6500 Indian Creek Drive.

Places to Stay

MIAMI BEACH

From bottom end to top dollar, the Beach has the greatest variety of places to stay in the area. But the information in this chapter is extremely volatile – perhaps as much as the information in the Entertainment chapter. Prices here fluctuate constantly: from the start of our research for this book to the finish, the nightly prices we quote here rose by an average of $5, so you should absolutely expect these to rise. The only exception has been the youth hostels, whose prices remained stable throughout our research.

Camping

This is really not the place for camping but there are some interesting opportunities around. Urban Trails Kayak Co (☎ 947-1302) opposite Haulover Beach on the

Top 10 Hotels

Our personal favorites were: the Clay Hotel & International Hostel for its location and atmosphere, if not luxury; the Indian Creek Hotel, a real Deco treat with an exquisite restaurant, wonderful staff and serene atmosphere; the Mermaid Guest House for being a calm tropical paradise in the middle of the city; the Leslie and Marlin Hotels for their wonderful Caribbean touches; the Lily Guesthouse, a spotless and comfortable (if yellow) retreat; Brigham Gardens and Villa Paradiso Guesthouses, adjacent to each other on Collins with lush gardens, excellent service and nice rooms; and of course, the renovated *grandes dames* of the Miami Beach hotel scene: the Eden Roc and Fontainebleau Hilton Resorts. ■

NICK SELBY

bay side (see the Activities section in the Things to See & Do chapter), rents kayaks, and you can paddle to one of the 19 nearby islands, on some of which you can camp for nothing.

Kobe Trailer Park (☎ 893-5121) is the closest you'll get to a commercial campsite to Miami Beach; they're at 11900 NE 16th Ave in Miami. Tent sites for two people, one tent, with electric hookup, cost $20 year round. The staff is friendly.

The KOA campsite in North Miami Beach closed recently, leaving *Miami-Homestead-Everglades KOA* (☎ 800-562-7732) as the only KOA campsite in the area (which means they have a pool, game room, shuffleboard, bike rentals, laundry facilities, etc). Tent sites cost $24.95 in high season, 'less' in low season. They're at 20675 SW 162 Ave at 200th St in Homestead.

Hostels

There are currently three hostel-style accommodation options – and one impostor – in town. The impostor, whose poorly hand-painted sign says Hostel@WWW (this is an unintentionally hilarious attempt by the owner to inform the hosteling public that he's knowledgeable about the internet) but is actually called the *Plaza Hostel* (☎ 673-2795), has only one thing going for it: it's the cheapest bed in town at $8, with a refundable $10 key deposit. However, it's not really a hostel, but more of a flop house. Rooms are cramped and crowded, mattresses are old, management is gruff and clientele is made up less of travelers (though we saw one) than of unfortunate locals. We don't recommend it, but it's at 426 Meridian Ave at the corner of 5th St.

Of the true hostels, the *Miami Beach International Travelers Hostel* (☎ 534-0268, fax 534-5862) has just a little less of everything than the competition, but that applies to prices as well – it's the cheapest hostel bed in town with dorm bunks at $12 for HI members, $14 for non-HI members (though they're not an HI member hostel). Rooms are a tad worn, and air conditioning only operates between 9 pm and 9 am unless you pay an additional $4 per room per day. They also have basic private rooms for $34.60 for one or two people (no HI member discount) including tax. The hostel's a block-and-a-half from the beach at 236 9th St, just east of Washington Ave. You'll need to show an out-of-state university ID, HI card, US or foreign passport with a recent entry stamp, or an onward ticket, but these rules are only strictly enforced when the place is very crowded – you will always need ID, though. They accept

Visa and MasterCard for reservations only, payment is in cash or travellers cheques.

Perhaps the most beautiful hostel in the USA, the Beach's most established place is the HI member *Clay Hotel & International Hostel* (☎ 534-2988) at 1438 Washington Ave at the corner of Española Way. Set in a 100-year-old Spanish-style villa (with some neat history: see the Miami Beach section in the Things to See & Do chapter), the Clay has clean and comfortable dorm rooms (four bunk beds) for $13 per night or $78 per week including taxes. They also have decent private rooms for $30 single, $33 double, $39 deluxe, and a $2 extra charge for a private bathroom. Private rooms all increase by $5 in winter. All of the above prices are reduced by $1 for HI and ISIC cardholders, and the seventh night is always free. The hostel has an excellent kitchen, awesome garden, a message board and a small bookshop. It's a definite travelers' hangout and information exchange center. The staff is very friendly, if a little harassed due to sheer volume, and helpful. They accept Visa and MasterCard, but not American Express. There's a great bar downstairs with food and drinks.

The most expensive dorm room is darn worth the extra $1 they charge. Perfectly located one block from the beach at 1550 Collins Ave and sporting an Olympic-sized swimming pool, barbecue area and patio and a full kitchen, the *Tropics Hotel & Hostel* (☎ 531-0361; fax 531-8676) has dorm beds (four to a room) for $14 a night or $84 a week. The dorms are spotless, and have steel beds; attached bathrooms and lockers are available. The Tropic's private rooms ($40 a night or $240 a week) are also quite nice, some with great views of the pool and what's in it at the moment. Air conditioning works until 8 am. They accept MasterCard and Visa, but not American Express.

Hotels, Motels & B&Bs

Bottom End The cheapest room on the beach is located in a hotel in which you get exactly what you pay for. Heroically overnamed, the *Waldorf Hotel* (☎ 538-9158) at 816 Commerce St at the southern end of South Pointe, has seven very *very* small private rooms for $10 per night; other – though not necessarily bigger – rooms go for $17 and $20. None of the rooms have baths, kitchens or air conditioning. Check out is at noon ('if you stay one minute longer you'll pay for another day') warns an enormous sign near the entrance, before also admonishing against guests ($5 extra) and violence ('take it outside'). It's not the cleanest or safest of places, but if you're looking to spend as little as possible, this is the place to be.

Somewhat higher on the accommodation chain, the far nicer *Henry Hotel* (☎ 672-2511) has larger, much more comfortable and cleaner rooms with attached bathrooms, refrigerators, hot plates and ceiling fans for $105 a week. Staff is pleasant, and the rooms are perfectly adequate. They're at 536 Washington Ave, next to the Sports Café (see the Places to Eat chapter).

For about the same price – in fact they have a few cheaper rooms – the family-run *Matanzas Hotel* (☎ 673-9417) is not a bad option. The rooms are similar in style and quality to the Henry, but the location is a bit nicer, on the western end of Española Way at No 506. Rooms, which have fridges, stoves and ceiling fans, are $120 a week with a private bathroom and $100 a week ($14.30 a day) with a bathroom shared between two rooms. Just across the street, the *Sinclair Hotel* at No 507 is said to have similar rooms and prices but was closed when we visited.

Middle There are plenty of places on the beach where you can get away with paying less than $50 a night, even in winter. But there are major differences in quality, and two hotels that cost the same don't necessarily give you the same thing. An excellent mid-range like the cheerful James Hotel costs the same as the aging and fusty Shorecrest. Shop around carefully before committing, and always check the rooms before you sign in. Even at the height of the high season, you've got a choice, and don't let anyone convince you otherwise. Also note that true Deco style is small by modern standards, so the more landmark Deco a hotel is, the smaller its rooms are likely to be.

Way down south, the *Hotel Simone* (☎ 672-0431) at 321 Ocean Drive would be a good deal if management wasn't so pro-permanent resident, anti-transient; during low season their little rooms are $30 double, and in high season, for some reason, the price goes down, but you have to pay by the month – it's $600, or $20 a day. There's a $15 key and $30 phone deposit, and you pay in advance. This is really a residential hotel.

The *Berkeley Shore Hotel* (☎ 531-5731) at 1610 Collins Ave is a lovely Art Deco box with a très swirly façade; staff is pleasant enough, if a bit grumpy at first, and they're in the process of renovating the rooms, which currently are a bit worn but clean and cost $35 a day, $180 a week in summer, $50 in winter. The same management runs the cheerier *James Hotel* (☎ 531-1125) about two blocks away at 1680 James Ave, which has clean and

CORINNA SELBY

NICK SELBY

NICK SELBY

KIM GRANT

Top: The Kenmore Hotel's wavy wall
Middle: The Marlin (left), The Breakwater (right)
Bottom: The Colony

large rooms for the same prices, though a friend of ours who stayed there after we researched said that they didn't change the sheets as often as they could have during his stay. In both these hotels, the rooms have full kitchens, bathrooms, air conditioning, television, telephones and free parking.

The *Parisian/Geneva Hotel* (☎ 538-7464) at 1510 Collins Ave is under new management, and the Spartan look of the place suggests it may not last. Too bad; their perfectly nice but not overly clean rooms are $35 to 45 a night, $150 to 200 a week in summer, and in winter $40 to 55 a night, $200 to 300 a week.

The *San Juan Hotel* (☎ 538-7531, fax 532-5704) at 1680 Collins Ave doesn't look too appealing initially and reception doesn't exactly make up for that with charm, but their rooms are surprisingly clean, they all have little kitchens with microwaves. Rooms are $39 a night, $259 a week in summer, $50 to 60 a night in winter.

You'll appreciate the relative remoteness of the 1930s *Kenmore Hotel* (☎ 674-1930, fax 534-6591) at 1050 Washington (corner of 11th St) which is close enough to the scene and the beach but just across the demarcation point for screaming partiers on the west side of Washington. And, it's across the street from the police station. It's got a very distinctive Deco look, with a wavy concrete wall and figure-8-shaped pool, helpful and efficient staff and well-worn (but in a good way) rooms with heavy wooden furniture and Deco-tiled bathrooms. Funky elevator. What's more, it's pretty cheap: rooms are $39 to 59 in summer, $59 to 79 in winter. They have more expensive deluxe rooms, and weekly rates are available as well.

Family-run *Villa Luisa Hotel* (☎ 672-9078, fax 673-9737) has very clean and cheerful rooms, some with an ocean view (actually a slice of the ocean sandwiched between two buildings). It's geared to students and young long-term residents, with rooms for $40 a night, $200 a week in summer, $80 a night, $300 a week in winter. All the rooms have air conditioning, full kitchens and bathrooms. They're at 125 Ocean Drive.

The lovingly restored *Essex House Hotel* (☎ 534-2700, 800-553-7739, fax 532-3827) at 1001 Collins Ave, with its very cool lobby, is a very friendly place with helpful staff and large rooms. And if you're feeling flabby, you can use the South Beach Gym at 1020 Ocean Drive (in the Clevelander Hotel) where hotel guests get a $7 discount on day passes at $8 a day. Rooms are $75 to 95, suites $125 in summer, and $125 to 145, suites $175, in winter.

We like the *Winterhaven* (☎ 531-5571, 800-395-2322, fax 538-3337). Even though the hallways aren't much to look at, the rooms themselves are very sweet, with mosquito netting, ceiling fans and Mediterranean antique furnishings. Rooms are $45 to 85 in summer, $75 to 115 in winter. The hotel's at 1400 Ocean Drive.

Another good option in this price range is the *Carlton Hotel* (☎ 538-5741, 800-722-7586, fax 534-6855) where you get a clean room (small bathroom) with telephone and a huge fridge for $45/50 a single/double in the summer, $60/70 in winter. Rooms with kitchenettes are about $5 more. Each additional person is $10 a night, but you can get a discount for staying a week or longer. There is a swimming pool, free parking (!), free morning coffee and cake, and their staff is very friendly and helpful. It's located at 1433 Collins Ave.

Two friends from Germany stayed at and enjoyed the *Fairfax Apartment Hotel* (☎ 538-3837), an old and slightly crumbling but clean and perfectly pleasant hotel at 1776 Collins Ave, with rooms from $50 to 75 in winter.

The *Brigham Gardens Guesthouse* (☎ 531-1331, fax 538-9898) at 1411 Collins Ave is a charming guesthouse set in a beautiful lush, green garden populated by tropical birds. The large and airy guestrooms (most with kitchens and bathrooms) have convertible futon sofas, and all the rooms have communicating doors. There's a barbecue area out back. They're $50 to 95 a day, $295 to 575 a week in summer, $75 to 125 a day, $375 to 775 a week in winter. This place is very similar in style and personality to its friendly competitor next door, the *Villa Paradiso Guesthouse* (☎ 532-0616, fax 667-0074) at 1415 Collins Ave which charges about $5 per night more and about the same on weekly rates (they say the rates are negotiable, so speak with management).

The *Edison Hotel* (☎ 531-2744, fax 534-4707) at 960 Ocean Drive (entrance on 10th St) is a perfectly acceptable, but rundown, place with rooms for $50 to 65 on weekdays and $60 to 80 on Friday and Saturday. It's much more reasonable by the week at $250 ($35.75 a night). The 'oceanfront' rooms (the higher priced ones above) don't have good views – they're blocked by the auditorium across the street.

The funky old *Bentley Hotel* (☎ 538-1700, fax 532-4865) at 510 Ocean Drive has functional rooms with decent ocean views in some. Rooms are $50 to 75 a night, $150 to 175 a week in summer, $55 to 95 a night, $190 to 225 a week in winter. There's very limited free parking.

The small *Clifton Hotel* (☎ 538-8691, fax 538-8692) at 1343 Collins Ave has clean rooms but well-worn bathrooms for $60 to 70 a day, $330 to 380 a week in summer, $95 to 120 a day, $550 to 630 a week in winter. Service is friendly, if a bit lethargic, and they do 24-hour room service.

The cute little *Penguin Hotel* (☎ 534-9334, 800-235-3296, fax 672-6240) at 1418 Ocean Drive has pleasant, clean and large-ish rooms (fridges available free on request) and nice enough staff. They have a little café and lounge downstairs. Rooms are $63 to 93 a day, $380 to 450 a week in summer, $93 to 133 a day, $580 to 650 a week in winter, suites are $123 in summer, $173 in winter. All prices include continental breakfast. Just up the road, at 1440 Ocean Drive is the beautifully renovated *Betsy Ross Hotel* (☎ 531-3934, fax 531-5282), with its unique mix of Deco and colonial styles on the beachfront. The location at the end of the beachfront promenade gives it really nice ocean views, and the Italian restaurant downstairs looks more expensive than it is (see Places to Eat, next chapter). Rooms are $86 to 116 in summer, $116 to 161 in winter, suites are $156 in summer and $246 in winter.

Island Outpost, a management company that runs several local hotels, including the Marlin and Casa Grande, runs the *Kent Hotel* (☎ 531-6771, 800-688-7678, fax 531-0720) at 1131 Collins Ave, which has the cheapest prices of the company's properties. But you still get most of the same perks as in the others, though the rooms are somewhat smaller. They're priced from $65 to 95, suites $140 (negotiable) in summer; $95 to 115, suites $160 to 175 in winter. There are hammocks in the garden.

The *Lord Balfour Hotel* (☎ 673-0401, fax 531-9385) at 350 Ocean Drive is a newly renovated and cool place with 66 rooms without kitchens but with very cold air conditioning. They'll provide a fridge in the rooms on request at no extra charge. Rooms are $65 a day, $350 a week in summer, $95 a day, $560 a week in winter.

The Deco classic *Park Central Hotel* (☎/fax 534-7520, 800-727-5236, reservation fax 534-3408) at 640 Ocean Drive is one of the classic SoBe hot spots; its pool is fabulous (if small) and its rooftop deck a must-see even if you're not staying here. Rooms, which are also small, are $65 to 130 a night in summer, $125 to 225 in winter. The Vampire LeStat Room (No 607; see the Things to See & Do chapter), while heavily booked, is no extra charge – it was available for $175 per night when we called in April 1996. To get to the roof, walk in past the reception, take the elevator to the top floor and walk out to the right. Good times to go are at about 4 pm, when cruise ships chug out down Government Cut, or on any Friday or Saturday night for a great view of the Drive's action. There's a nice café downstairs in the lobby.

Two hotels owned and operated by the same management company straddle the corner of Ocean Drive and 7th St. The northernmost one, at 700 Ocean Drive, is the *Avalon Hotel* (☎ 538-0133, 800-933-3306), in a gorgeous

Streamline building (1941), and perhaps known more for its trademark white-and-yellow 1955 Lincoln convertible (it's parked out front) than for its rooms, which are very pleasant and clean. Rates run from $69 to 140 in summer, $95 to 175 in winter including continental breakfast and, they say, no hidden service charges. The *Majestic Hotel*, just south of 7th St at 680 Ocean Drive, is similar in everything – decor, price and service – to the Avalon, but in a toss up, the Avalon would win with slightly better everything.

We spent about a month at the *Mermaid Guest House* (☎ 538-5324), which recently was bought and beautifully renovated by a charming and lovely Uruguayan couple, Anna and Gonzolo. When we were looking for a place we stumbled in here, through the long narrow hallway

CORINNA SELBY

The wonderful Mermaid Guest House

and emerged into an absolutely stunning and lush tropical garden that felt more like Bali than Miami Beach – and that's when we knew we'd stay here. The hosts are wonderful and friendly, rooms are absolutely great – all have four-poster beds with mosquito nets, hugely colorful walls and mermaids everywhere. None of the rooms have TVs (though they do have phones and private baths). Say hi to Molly the cat. We can't recommend this place enough: rooms are $75 to 85 in summer, $95 to 105 in winter. The rooftop apartment is $150. It's at 909 Collins Ave.

The very nice new owners of the *Beach Paradise Hotel* (☎ 531-0021, 800-258-8886, fax 674-0206) deserve a shot at it; the rooms are very clean and nice, looking a lot more like LA than Miami. Prices are $75 to 150 a night in summer, $90 to 175 in winter, weekly rates are negotiable. There's free Showtime on cable, parking available and they have a nice lobby café. They're at 600 Ocean Drive.

The *Century Hotel* (☎ 674-8855) at 140 Ocean Drive has the coolest logo of any hotel on the beach – sort of a lizardy thing – and is a darn nice hotel far south enough to keep things quiet even on weekends. Rooms range from $75 to 175 in summer, $125 to 275 in winter. There's a cool bar downstairs, the Lizard Lounge.

The *Ramada Resort* (☎ 865-8511, 800-272-6232) at 6701 Collins Ave is $79 to 99 in summer and $125 to 155 in winter depending on the view. It may say something that Hostelling International held their convention at this hotel in 1994, but we're not sure what.

Service at the *Cavalier Hotel* (☎ 534-2135) was a turnoff when we visited (which was very surprising as it's run by the normally excellent Island Outpost management company), but the rooms were very nice – as were the prices, considering what you get. It's $95 to 135 for a standard room, $135 to 165 for deluxe and oceanfront suites run from $240 to 350. It's at 1244 Ocean Drive.

The Deco landmark *National Hotel* (☎ 532-2311, 800-327-8370, fax 534-1426) at 1677 Collins Ave is a friendly, but standard, old dame of Miami Beach resort life. Nice location on the beach, Olympic-sized swimming pool and a hokey tiki bar make it worth considering, though their pricing scheme has three (count 'em) seasons! Here we go: $95 to 145 in winter, $75 to 105 in summer and $85 to 135 in autumn.

The *Colony Hotel* (☎ 673-0088, 800-226-5669, fax 532-0762) is another Deco landmark, with friendly staff, interesting rooms with teeny televisions but nice touches like potpourri. Prices are $89 to 200 a night in summer, $119 to 200 in winter, including continental breakfast.

There's free Showtime on cable, parking is $14 a day and Discover cards are not accepted. They're at 736 Ocean Drive.

The *Roney Plaza Apartment Hotel* (☎ 531-8811) at 2301 Collins Ave is a hotel totally made up of efficiency apartments that cost $111 to 122 in low season and $132 to 142 in high season.

Island Outpost runs the *Leslie Hotel* (☎ 534-2135, 800-688-7678, fax 531-5543) at 1244 Ocean Drive, where attentive and helpful staff go the distance – this means that baby-sitting services are available. It has many of the same perks as the Marlin (towels, flowers, TV/VCR, etc), but the Leslie is ever so slightly less luxurious. Spotless as is usual with IO's hotels, the relatively (when compared with the Marlin) simple rooms are $95 to 115, suites from $190 in summer, $135 to 150, suites from $250 in winter. They also operate the Cavalier Hotel.

The *Breakwater Hotel* (☎ 532-1220, 800-454-1220, fax 532-4451, see the Online Services appendix) has our favorite beachfront sign, and the newly renovated rooms here are pretty nice too, ranging from $99 to 169 in summer and $109 to 189 in winter. Their bitchin' penthouse suite is $299/450. Rooms have funky tropical decor, and about half have – get this – remote controlled air conditioner thermostats. The pool-view rooms can get loud at night; it's quietest and cheapest in back. Pay-per-view movies are $6.95. They're at 940 Ocean Drive, and there's a nice Italian restaurant downstairs.

Top End The fabulously renovated *Indian Creek Hotel* (☎ 531-2727, fax 531-5651) is a delightfully serene place with excellent service and very friendly staff. When our family came to visit us in Miami, we put them up here. The spotless rooms have been painstakingly restored to their Deco glory. The hotel, at 2727 Indian Creek Drive, is far enough out of the madness 10 blocks south to be a restful retreat from the Fabulous, but close enough to be just a two-minute drive (or 10-minute walk) from the action. The pool out back is really nice, and the Pan Coast restaurant downstairs is one of our favorites (see the Places to Eat chapter). Singles/doubles/suites are $80/90/150 in summer, $100/110/190 in winter.

The charming *Lily Guesthouse* (☎ 535-9900, fax 535-0077) at 835 Collins Ave is pretty yellow, but the rooms (all of which have kitchens and new bathrooms) are impeccably done, bright and have very nice hardwood floors; summer rates are $100 to 175 a night, $525 to 1000 a week, winter rates are $150 to 275 a night, $800 to 1500 a week. Very friendly service and lots of flowers.

Another lovely Uruguayan couple run the elegant

Hotel Lafayette (☎ 673-2262, fax 534-5399) at 944 Collins Ave – the one with the French advertising kiosk outside on the patio across the street from the Mermaid Guest House. It's a quiet kind of place for quiet kinds of people – classical music, no loud parties and a break from the Fabulous world of SoBe. This is one of the best values in its price range not just for the rooms (which are very beautifully done, have fresh flowers daily and really nice bathrooms) but also for the service. The owners will help you plot excursions, pack you a picnic lunch and help you work out all aspects of daytrips and even onward trips. They'll try to get your hometown newspaper, too. Their doubles are $105 to 125 in summer, $135 to 165 in winter, and suites are available as well.

Singer Gloria Estefan's *Cardozo Hotel* (☎ 535-6500, 800-782-6500) at 1300 Ocean Drive looks a bit more expensive than it is: its large rooms (many with hardwood floors and all with TV/VCR and hand-made furniture) are $110 to 135, suites $195 to 360 in summer; $120 to 145, suites $210 to 385 in winter. Downstairs is the Allioli Restaurant (see the Places to Eat chapter).

The gloriously renovated *Eden Roc Resort* (☎ 531-0000, 800-327-8337, see the Online Services appendix) at 4525 Collins Ave is giving the Fontainebleau Hilton a run for its money. With little extras like an indoor rock climbing complex, an Olympic-sized (if not as cool as the Fontainebleau's) pool, and their newly remodeled spa and health club, it's a great place to get away to. Room rates run from $120 to 225, penthouse $1000 in summer, and $195 to 325, penthouse $1500 in winter.

To enter the hot spot of the second, the *Delano Hotel* (☎ 672-2000, 800-555-5001) at 1685 Collins Ave, you need to walk past two hyper-tanned beefcake doormen in white. Once inside, the self-congratulatory staff will allow you to get one of their slick, sparse and minimally appointed rooms for $130 to 175 a day (note: while the bay is one mile west, they refer to the cheapies as 'bay view') in summer, $175 to 225 in winter; the cuter poolside bungalows are $350/450. This place is in demand (Madonna had a birthday do here and owns a piece of the Blue Door restaurant downstairs), so reserve early.

The *Fontainebleau Hilton Hotel & Resort* (☎ 538-2000, 800-548-8886) is probably the most recognizable landmark on the Beach. It opened in 1954, and was taken over by Hilton in 1978. Now it's got three buildings surrounding their absolutely fantastic swimming pool (see Activities in the Things to See & Do chapter). It's a stylish act all the way, with every conceivable amenity, restaurants, bars, a grand ballroom, beachside cabanas, an activities program for kids, seven tennis courts, business center, marina and a veritable shopping mall within the hotel. Room rates in the summer range from $155 to 260 single and $180 to 285 double. Packages during the winter include their Bounceback, which works out to $139 per night per room including breakfast; one-week packages including breakfast, parking and oooh, a drink, are $1020/1170. The Towers Level, the newest addition to the place with keyed entry, concierge service and a bunch of other extras are $270 to 300 single, $295 to 325 double. The hotel is at 4441 Collins Ave.

Tucked away and accessed through its lush courtyard, the *Hotel Impala* (☎ 673-2021, 800-646-7252, fax 673-5984) at 1228 Collins Ave, is a European-style hotel with rooms that have oversize bathtubs, TV, VCR, stereo with CD player, etc. The place is lovely to look at, and the staff manages to create an atmosphere that's elegant but not arrogant. Room rates include continental breakfast and are $159, suites from $225 to 315 in summer, $189 and $269 to 369 in winter.

And in a recess at 834 Ocean Drive, the *Casa Grande Hotel* (☎ 531-8800, 800-688-7678, fax 531-5543) is a great deal for the admittedly high price; service is exquisite and rooms are beautiful, all with TV, VCR, CD/stereo, full kitchens, and tons of luxurious perks, like turndown service each evening and chocolates or flowers on your pillow. All the furniture's Indonesian, there are laundry and room services, staff is perfect, etc . . . . In summer, per night: studios $150, one bedroom $200, one bedroom with ocean view $225; in winter it's $175/225/250. They also have two- and three-bedroom suites for up to $1000 a night, call for more information. Valet parking is $10.

The elegant, Mediterranean-style *Ocean Front Hotel* (☎ 672-2579, fax 672-7665) is a pleasure to write about. It's chic but not pompous, exclusive but not pretentious, and expensive but not really that expensive when you look at what you get. Twenty-two of their 27 rooms have an ocean view, and if you're really wanting to part with some cash for a treat the penthouse suite is almost sinfully luxurious, complete with rooftop terrace, a Jacuzzi and some beautiful furniture. All the rooms have hair dryers. Their pricing scheme is straight out of Kafka, but the least expensive rooms with ocean views are $150 to 175 (single or double) and without a view is $125 to 155. Other rooms range from $190 to 365, and the penthouse is $385 in summer, $425 in winter – other room rates only change by about $5 or so between summer and winter. It's at 1230-38 Ocean Drive.

For a special occasion, the Caribbean-style rooms at the landmark *Marlin Hotel* (☎ 673-8770, 800-688-7678, fax 673-9609) are well worth the steep price tag of $200 to 325 a night year round (but this is negotiable in summer) including continental breakfast, as the service is superb, the place astonishingly clean, the rooms are all unique, and the location at 1200 Collins Ave is right in the thick of things. All rooms (actually they're suites) have TV, VCR and stereos (with a CD collection), a small book collection, kitchens, bathrobes and beach towels, all-natural soaps and shampoos and evening turndown service. Look for the vintage pink Caddy convertible outside. They have a rooftop patio for parties, but no pool.

La Voile Rouge Beach Club & Hotel (☎ 535-0099, fax 532-4442, 800-528-6453) is about as exclusive as you'd want to get on the beach: the entire place, whose complex sports two swimming pools and a gaggle of burly security men ('you talkin' ta *me*?'), has but eight suites, which range from $300 to 700 in summer, and $450 to 900 in winter. The rooms are simply spectacular, though smaller than you'd hope at $900 a pop, and all are individually styled – Morocco, Art Deco, Santa Fe – you get the idea. Their Raffles-like restaurant does lunches on their lovely terrace, and the whole thing costs a lot but they treat you right. It's definitely the most luxurious and pampered stay on the Beach. It's at 455 Ocean Drive.

You can also stay at the *Inn at the Fisher Island Club* (☎ 535-6097) on exclusive Fisher Island (see the Things to See & Do chapter). Room rates range from $330 to $1295 a night, though they do offer a honeymoon package starting at $940 for three nights, double occupancy.

DOWNTOWN MIAMI

Unless you're here on an expense account or with a rich friend who's paying, the city of Miami isn't really the best place: what are here are mainly the big chains, a couple of notable and relatively cheap hotels, and the rest are flop houses that we don't recommend at all. The chain hotels here – Sheraton, Hyatt, Holiday Inn, Inter-Continental – offer no surprises whatsoever: they all have business centers, concierge service, expensive dry cleaning, restaurants and 'nightclubs' where industrial transmission cog salesmen named Dieter and Hans-Joachim boogie the night away, waving fists with the thumbs-up sign up and down on the dance floor.

For what you get for your dollar, in terms of proximity to the action and just plain neighborhood ambiance you will do far, far better staying on the Beach than in the city, but hey, if you're game, so are we.

Bottom End We really like the *Miami Sun Hotel* (☎ 375-0786, 800-322-0786) at 226 NE 1st Ave, which is surprisingly clean and tidy and perfectly located for a downtown hotel. It's also got friendly service, lots of gleaming white tile in the lobby, and very clean, if small, rooms. There's a café downstairs, but skip their secretarial and photocopying services in favor of nearby Office Depot (see the Shopping chapter). Rooms range from $35 to 55 year round.

Royalton Hotel (☎ 374-7451), 131 SE 1st St, is slightly rundown, but they keep it clean, and we love that old-fashioned elevator. Year round, singles are $42.50, doubles $49.50, triples $58.

The *Leamington Hotel* (☎ 373-7783) at 307 NE 1st St is not a bad option; year-round prices here are $39.40/45/50.65, and they, too, have one of those old-fashioned elevators. It's clean and nice.

Middle The *Miami River Inn* (☎ 325-0045, see the Online Services appendix) is a charming place right on the river at 119 SW South River Drive (between SW 1st and 2nd Sts). If we had to stay downtown and you were paying, this is where we'd do it. They have lovely rooms, six cats and excellent and friendly service. Rooms run from $49 to 89 in summer, $69 to 129 in winter.

Of the big chain hotels, the *Holiday Inn* (☎ 374-3000, 800-465-4329) at 200 SE 2nd Ave is the cheapest option downtown. They have a special summer rate of $59 (standard) and $89 for a 'king-size room' including two breakfasts; rooms normally range from $79 to 149, suites from $150 to 375.

The utterly unexciting *Dupont Plaza Hotel* (☎ 358-2541, 800-432-9076, 800-327-8480), on the site of the ground-breaking of the original city of Miami, is yet another standard business hotel option. A one-bedroom apartment is $95, so why would anyone want standard hotel rooms, which range from $99 to 105 (but ask for the corporate rate of $85)? Prices include two breakfasts; suites are $125 to 450. They're at 800 Biscayne Blvd Way.

Top End Other downtown options include the *Sheraton* (☎ 373-6000, 800-325-3535) at 495 Brickell Ave, which has rooms on their corporate floor from $119 to 144, and, if you're stupid, you can ask for a standard room priced from $144 to 184.

There are two Hyatts (☎ 800-233-1234) in the area: the *Hyatt Regency* (☎ 358-1234), downtown at 400 SE 2nd Ave, and *Hyatt Regency Coral Gables* (see below). Rooms range from $135 to 160.

The *Hotel InterContinental* (☎ 577-1000, 800-327-0200) at 100 Chopin Plaza has standard rooms for $159 to 189 and deluxe or superior rooms are $199 to 289.

CORAL GABLES

The *Hyatt Regency Coral Gables* (☎ 441-1234) at 50 Alhambra Plaza, is pricier than its downtown counterpart at $149 to 217. They are everything you'd expect from a Hyatt: we treated ourselves to a stay here and had a very nice time indeed, thank you very much.

The *Biltmore Hotel* (☎ 445-1926, 800-727-1926, 800-228-3000) (see the Things to See & Do chapter) has rooms from $159 to 199 in low season, $179 to 219 in high season; one-bedroom suites $269 to 299/349, honeymoon and Eisenhower suites $399/449, and the tower suite (the Capone) is always $1800 a night. It's at 1200 Anastasia Ave, Coral Gables.

Places to Eat

MIAMI BEACH

There's a bounty of restaurants on the beach, catering to absolutely every style and budget. You can get by incredibly cheaply if you stick to Cuban and fast food, and you may be in for some new taste treats. Try local favorites like guarapo (sugar cane juice), Cuban coffee (respectfully referred to by SoBe locals as 'zoom juice') and café con leche, but don't expect some kind of chi-chi Seattle stuff: this is an over-sweetened (they put sugar in for you unless you specifically tell them not to) industrial-strength product, and Western palates may find the stuff ghastly. Haitian specialties include pumpkin soup. Whatever you're in the mood for, you'll find it on South Beach. There are a lot of cheap places here, but there are a lot of expensive ones as well, so it's easy to spend more than you want to on food – strategy pays off, and you always pay for convenience.

See the Dangers & Annoyances section in the Facts for the Visitor chapter for a word on the notoriously poor service you can expect. Remember that many places – like the News Cafe and the 11th St Diner – include the tip in the check (in fact, the News Cafe includes a tip on takeout orders as well, whether you like the service or not!) so always look to see if this has been done – don't tip twice!

Because the restaurant scene in Miami Beach is so vast and varied, this section

One artist's interpretation of the effects of zoom juice on the central nervous system.

Top Five Food Values
With a ton of restaurants around, some excellent value can get hidden in all the ink. There's lots of competition, a lot of great value to be had, but here's what we say are the top five values in dining. Note that each of the five locals to whom we showed this list strenuously and loudly objected to a different one of the five – which tells us that it's pretty accurate.

- Large burrito at San Loco (Miami Beach)
- Anything at Exquisito (Little Havana)
- Anything at Sports Café (Miami Beach)
- Thai chicken salad at Granny Feelgood's (Miami Beach and downtown)
- All-you-can-eat sushi lunch for $9.99 at Sho Bu (Coral Gables)

has been organized by price category from Budget (under $7) to Middle ($7 to 15) to Top End ($15 and up), with sub-categories by food style – Mexican, Italian, seafood, etc.

Coffee Bars

This is not Seattle, or even Atlanta, when it comes to the coffeehouse scene, but there are a few alternatives to the reprehensible-to-Seattlites 'zoom juice' served at the Cuban places around town. *Aurora Cafe* (☎ 534-1744) at 1205 17th St has excellent espresso and cappuccino plus exotic coffees from around the world, a very slick yet unpretentious space and a little library packed with lefty publications. They also do some food as well.

Starbar Café (☎ 674-7070), aside from having the best iced coffee and cappuccino on the beach ($1.75 to 3) and a really wonderful, starfishy atmosphere, swell staff and clean toilets, serves up whopping sandwiches (about $5.95), and a huge bowl of miso soup with noodles and wok-fried vegetables for $3.75. They also do decent salads for $5.95. They're at 1360 Collins Ave, open Sunday to Thursday 9 am to midnight, Friday and Saturday 9 to 2 am.

Hollywood Juice & Smoothie (☎ 538-8988) isn't really a coffeehouse (though they do serve cappuccino and espresso), but we think it's a great place, so here it is: great fruit shakes and smoothies for $3.25 to 4.50, wheatgrass juice for $1.75 an ounce, and healthy sandwiches. They're at 704 Lincoln Road.

Java Junkies (☎ 674-7854) at 1446 Washington Ave on the corner of Española Way, does all sorts of coffee miscegenation as well as the usual espresso ($1.50), cappuccino ($2.50), rolls, pastries and buns. It's a pseudo-nouveaux bohemian hangout.

The *8th St Coffee Bar* (☎ 672-7500) at 760 Ocean Drive has been highly recommended.

Budget

American *Hamburg* (☎ 672-5344) at 214 Española Way right next to the Respectable Street Cafe has excellent hamburgers – a quarter-pound beef, turkey or veggie burger is $2.95; half-pound is $3.95; fries are 92¢. They have sandwiches and other entrees as well, like grilled chicken breast for $5.45, but they're most beloved for their burgers and the fact that they're open every day from 11 to 5 am (and they deliver until late) – a good place to head after a concert or a night of clubbing and pubbing.

Great Dane Garden (☎ 535-0120, fax 535-6314) at 1542 Alton Rd, has healthy and delicious sandwiches (no red meat) for $3.25 to 3.75, soups for $2.25 and $2.50 and salads from $3.50 to 6.25. They bake their fabulous breads daily, and they'll deliver within one hour for a $1.25 fee.

The mega-hip sandwich folks at *Tommy to Go* (☎ 674-8755, fax 674-9046), 458 Ocean Drive, serve up healthy huge hero sandwiches, from simple offerings like roast beef and cheese ($4.25) to downright suspicious, like grilled vegetables with chèvre ($5.75). It has fun and friendly staff, takeout and limited daytime delivery only (no eat-in) and is open 7.30 am till 9.30 to 11 pm depending on business and season.

Despite its faux-frog name, baguettes and pretentious translations ('cornichons' = French pickles), *La Sandwicherie* (☎ 532-8934) is as American as a failed S&L. Which means that it has great – and great big – sandwiches; create your own for $4 to 7, salads from $5 to 7. No beer or alcohol but they do have fruit juices and sodas. It's at 229 14th St, in the alley (which does smell a bit ripe now and then). They have about four stools and a small sandwich bar. The place is open from noon to 5 am every day, and they'll deliver between noon and 3 pm.

The *Villa Deli* (☎ 538-4552, fax 673-6404) has been around forever, and it deserves to be: great cheap eats, breakfast (eggs, grits or potatoes, bagel or toast, cream cheese or butter, coffee or tea) for $1.98; after 10 am and on Sundays it's $2.48. Lunch and dinner are similarly cheap, with sandwiches from $4.95 to 7.50, and a dinner combo from 3 to 7 pm for $5.95. They're at 1608 Alton Rd.

Granny Feelgood's (☎ 673-0408) at 647 Lincoln Road serves mainly vegetarian food, and though they do let a little chicken and turkey slip in here and there, you'll *never* see red meat on the menu. Their portions are simply breathtaking, and *two* can fill up on their $6.95 Thai salad, which has loads of veggies and some grilled sliced chicken topped with a peanut sauce. The waiters could technically slap a $1.50 'sharing' charge on you, but they rarely do in practice. They also have great breakfast specials for about $3, and soya pancakes for $2.95. It's a great, friendly place with good service and definitely worth hitting. They also have a juice bar and outdoor café, open Monday to Thursday 9.30 am to 10 pm, Friday and Saturday 9.30 am to 11 pm, Sunday 9.30 am to 9 pm.

The Light (☎ 531-2721) is a wonderful vegan and vegetarian restaurant that opened just before we went to press. They have daily specials but some menu items include sweet & sour vegetables (tempeh, mushroom, celery and broccoli) or potato, soy, carrot, onion, tomato and eggplant stew for $7; vegetable rice for $2.50 and desserts like apple crisp, banana (soy) cream pie and strawberry pie for $2.50. The address is 901 Pennsylvania Ave, but it's at the corner of 9th and Washington, through the municipal parking lot.

The *News Cafe* (☎ 538-6397) at 800 Ocean Drive is an absolute South Beach landmark, though over the years the prices have gone up and the service has gone down. It's trendy enough to be painful, and they're open 24 hours. Their famous dish is the tomato bruschetta ($5.50), perfect with an iced tea for a light snack while watching the skaters wiggle by down Ocean Drive; also try their plain omelet ($5) or pasta dishes from $6.25 to 9.75. They add a 15% tip to all checks.

NICK SELBY

People watching at the trendy News Cafe

Eating Out in Multicultural Miami

Miami's smorgasbord of multicultural cuisine can leave some visitors scratching their heads. Miami food is a mixture of American Southern, Cuban, Spanish, Caribbean, African and European foods. Highlights to look out for are Jamaican jerk dishes, heavily spiced, marinated and grilled dishes usually of chicken but also beef and fish; Creole dishes, usually shrimp but also chicken in a tomato-based sauce with peppers, garlic, onions and celery served on rice – shrimp in a sauce – you'll like it. Jambalaya is a tomatoey rice dish usually featuring ham or sausage, onions, garlic and peppers.

Gumbo is derived from the Bantu word for okra. Its only consistent property is that it's a stewlike substance served over rice. The stew is thickened first with browned flour and then with either okra (a slimy vegetable) or filé powder, made from sassafras leaves. There are lots of variations on gumbo: the most popular is shrimp and crab, but look out for more exotic varieties like squirrel and oyster (!), duck and sausage, or Z'herbes, a vegetarian version.

Note that Haitian and Cuban food sometimes involves goat, which can be stringy. You'll also see dolphin on the menu in many restaurants. This is dolphin fish, and *not* the friendly and protected sea mammal. The other name for dolphin fish is mahi mahi. Alligator tail is served in some restaurants (mainly in boring deep-fried nuggets, which may as well be Chicken McNuggets®, but also served marinated and grilled, which is excellent) and is not from protected gator but from those raised on federally licensed alligator farms. ■

KENNETH DREYFUSS

Exotic offerings at a West Indian market

Cuban *La Cueva del Camaron Restaurant* (☎ 672-7680) at 1120 15th St east of Alton Rd is a family-run restaurant specializing in dad's shrimp Creole ($8.95) but with daily specials of chicken, steak, liver and onions or pig's feet with beans and rice for – hold on to your hat – $1.95. Other main courses are $2 to 6. It's a very nice place, and they have a $1.99 breakfast special that's a great buy, with eggs, bacon or ham, café con leche and Cuban toast. They're open Monday to Friday 7 am to 7 pm, Saturday 7 am to 5 pm, closed Sunday. Just down Alton Rd at No 1439 is the *Chicken Grill* (☎ 672-7717), serving up grilled chickens for $6.99 and a leg/thigh with rice and beans for $3.29. They have a window counter serving zoom juice (30¢) and café con leche ($1). The restaurant's open from 8 am to 11 pm, closed Sunday.

Closer to the center of town at 820 Lincoln Lane North (one block north of Lincoln Road, just west of Meridian Ave) the *Los Hispanos Restaurant* (☎ 531-3786) is a tiny, hidden-away local hole-in-the-wall with dependable specials from $4 to 7, all served with rice, beans and plantains. Baked chicken $3.99, grilled cheese sandwich $1.30 and breakfast specials from $1.25 to 1.99. Smoking section is to the left (ha ha). They're open Monday to Friday 7 am to 6 pm, Saturday 7.30 am to 4 pm, closed Sunday.

Las Americas (☎ 673-0560) at 450 Lincoln Road is an interesting place for a sandwich at night (about $2.95) or breakfast (their special has more than most and costs $2.39); in the evenings there's entertainment in the form of someone plinking on their old piano. They're open daily 8 am to 11 pm or midnight, depending on business.

The 24-hour café con leche market has been cornered by *David's Café* (☎ 534-8736), at 1058 Collins Ave at 11th St. Not-awesome Cuban food in the $3 to 6 range, an OK breakfast for $2, it's really here as an emergency stopgap when you're starving at 3.15 am and don't want pizza (see next page).

Most of the waiters at *Puerto Sagua* (☎ 673-1115) have been there for over 30 years, serving up humongous portions of good Cuban food for reasonable prices (though we heard just as we went to press that they went up substantially – friends tell us to add about $1.50 to each of these prices): soup of the day is $2.95, arroz con pollo is $5.25, ropa vieja (shredded beef) is $6.75 and their specialties like filete de pargo grillet (grilled red snapper) top off the menu at $11.75. Good breakfasts cost $2. They're open 7 to 2 am daily at 700 Collins Ave, and have probably the best Cuban café con leche on the beach, because they give you the elements (espresso and steamed milk) in separate cups and don't pre-add sugar. Breakfasts, though, can be a tad greasy.

At 941 Lincoln Road Mall, near the corner of Michigan Ave and just near Books & Books, the *Lincoln Road Café* (☎ 538-8066) is another long-time Cuban spot famous for its infuriatingly slow service and reliably decent food. They've got sandwiches from $2.75 to 4.75, and very good poultry dishes from $6.95 to 7.95. For dessert, skip the glucose-tolerance-test-sweet tres leches ($2.50) in favor of their arroz con leche (rice pudding) for $2. They're open Monday to Saturday from 8 to 1 am, and Sunday from 10 am to 5 pm; sit outside here during Gallery Walks drinking coffee and save yourself some cash over the trendy nearby competition.

We would be remiss in our duties to omit the SoBe landmark *Mappy Cafeteria* (☎ 532-2064), with its excellent (though slow) service, good food and a killer location right at 1390 Ocean Drive that assures cameo appearances in movies shot in the neighborhood like *Miami Blues* and *The Specialist*. The prices are higher than most other Cuban places, but it's worth a visit: reliably good breakfast specials from $2.75 to 4, decent fish and seafood from $8 to 12, meat and chicken $5 to 8, good Cuban sandwiches $3 to 4.50. They're open daily from 7 am to 11 pm.

David's Café II (☎ 672-8707) at 1654 Meridian Ave is the upscale brother of David's Café on Collins Ave, with shorter hours, higher prices, very cheery staff and better food. Main courses average $7 to 9, a Cuban sandwich is $4.25, and they have a full bar and have we mentioned friendly service? They're open Sunday to Thursday 7 am to 11 pm, Friday and Saturday 7 am to midnight.

Mexican The battle of the burrito has come to South Beach, with two extremely worthy contenders and a couple of wanna-be's (including a Taco Bell at 1665 Washington Ave). After lengthy consideration, we've decided that *San Loco* (☎ 538-3009) at 235 14th St between Washington and Collins Aves has the best burrito in town, hands-down. They serve up terrific and overstuffed burritos ($2.75 to 5.75), enchiladas ($3.50 to 5) and tacos ($1.50 to 4) in the restaurant, where really lovely staff take good care of you. They also don't throw bushels of cilantro at the food. They're open Sunday to Thursday 11 to 5 am, Friday and Saturday 11 to 6 am. Excellent salads are $3.75 to 5.75, and beer and sodas $1 to 2.75. No credit cards are accepted.

The somewhat awkwardly located *Mrs Mendoza's Tacos al Carbon* (☎ 535-0808) at 1040 Alton Rd, serves up even bigger burritos that have less garlic and heaps more cilantro, for $3.99, tacos with chips and salsa for $2.99, guacamole and chips for $3.09 and rice and beans for $1.60. The atmosphere may seem more fast-food than San Loco, but they're not kidding about their salsa – when they say hot, it's head-blowing, ulcer-slammin' hot! They're open Monday to Thursday 11 am to 10 pm, Friday and Saturday 11 am to 11 pm, Sunday noon to 9 pm, there's no smoking in the restaurant and they don't take credit cards.

If you love cilantro, you'll love *El Rancho Grande* (☎ 673-0480), where they put it in absolutely everything they serve. It's a comfortable and cozy sit-down and more formal affair than the other two, but it has great lunch specials with main courses from $3.49 to 6, and fajitas from $7.99 to 9.99. All the food is served in terra cotta dishware, burritos come smothered with two types of melted cheese and sour cream, along with rice and beans and guacamole, but salads are a bit mean-portioned. Prices almost double at dinner time. Margaritas (rocks only, not frozen ones) are $3.50 a glass, $9 a half-pitcher or $17 a pitcher; other Mexican hootch available as well. They're at 1626 Pennsylvania Ave (near Lincoln Road Mall) and are open for lunch Monday to Friday 11.30 am to 3 pm, and dinner Sunday to Thursday 5 to 10 pm, Friday and Saturday 5 to 11 pm. Closed for lunch on Saturday and Sunday.

Titi's Taco's (☎ 672-8484) has been around for quite a while (it's pronounced tee-teez), and for a place with outside tables along Ocean Drive it's okay on the drinks, but we're not so hot on the food. They've got half-decent black bean soup for $2.95, two tacos for $5.95 and appetizers from $3.50 to 8.75. A good-size bean and cheese burrito is $3.95. They're at 900 Ocean Drive, open Sunday to Thursday 10 to 2 am, Friday and Saturday 10 to 4 am.

Pizza Washington Ave is lined with pizzerias selling slices and pies, and pizza can be had all over South Beach. Most places are open way late on weekends. Pizza Hut (☎ 672-1900), Little Caesar's (☎ 531-4494) and Dominos (☎ 531-8211) all deliver, but if you want a pie you should do your best to try some of the beach's excellent homegrown product before resorting to the white-bread chains. For a real Italian-style pizza, head for the Sports Café (see Middle – Italian, below). We think that for delivery pizza, the *Bella Napoli* (☎ 672-1558) restaurant at 1443 Alton Rd is the best on the beach; they sell large (18-inch) pies for $7.50 (!) and a large pie with garlic, mushrooms, peppers and onions is $11.90. There's a $1 delivery charge and a $5 minimum order on deliveries, or you can eat in the restaurant, though it's a bit threadbare. They're open Monday to Friday 11 am to 11 pm, Saturday and Sunday noon to 11 pm.

A worthy runner-up for either takeout or eat-in is *Master's Deli Pizza* (☎ 672-2763/4/5, fax 674-0799) at 1700 Alton Rd, which does real New York-style pizzas; their large pies with two toppings are $9.99. Both of these places have beer and wine, the latter has more indifferent service and sometimes loud video games.

Some of Washington Ave's better slice offerings include: *Ciccio's Pizza* (☎ 534-7155) at No 1405 has a $2.99 special for two slices and a medium soda; $9 large pies, or one large pie with one extra topping and four sodas for $10.50. They're open Sunday to Thursday 10 to 3 am, Friday and Saturday 10 to 6 am. *Pucci's Pizza* (☎ 673-8133) at No 1447 does $2 slices and $11 large (18-inch) pies, open Sunday to Thursday 11.30 to 4.30 am, Friday and Saturday 11.30 to 6 am. *Lincoln NYC Pizza* (☎ 672-2722) at No 1595 has the two-slices-and-a-medium-drink deal for $3.50, plain large pies $10. It's open daily from 10 to 5 am.

Da Leo Pizza Via (☎ 538-0803) was, at press time, slated to open in the former home of Gertrude's, the highly mourned failed coffee shop that was popular despite its reprehensible service. Da Leo, which also runs what's said to be a first-rate Italian restaurant (see Middle, Italian, below), plans to serve traditional Italian-style pizzas priced from $7 to 11. It's at 826 Lincoln Road.

Bagels This is the New York Jewish capital of the Southern USA, and bagels are everywhere. A bagel is a disk-shaped bread product made from heavy dough that has been boiled and then baked. The result is a substantial and chewy roll with a uniquely textured coating – the closest comparison would be a real Bavarian *Brez'n*, but that's not really it. Just eat one. Originally ethnic Jewish, the bagel has insinuated itself into the American menu and can now be bought in most big cities from coast to coast. They are usually offered in plain, sesame, poppy, onion, garlic, combinations of the previous or, more rarely, salt. They're available in any diner and in most restaurants that serve breakfast, but several bagel specialists have opened on the beach and in the state; most open early for breakfast (between 6.30 and 7.30 am), but all have fantastically confusing closing hours on different days. Suffice it to say that they close in the early evening.

Brooklyn Bagels (☎ 534-7373) at 941 Washington Ave, claims that the water for their bagels is imported from

New York City (which has, believe it or not, some of the purest and sweetest water in the USA). Whatever, the bagels are darn good, and they sell for about $1.50 with cream cheese; add a cup of coffee and that's the breakfast special, 7 to 11 am, for $1.99.

The chi-chiest entry is *Offerdahl's Bagel Gourmet* (☎ 534-4003) at 1500 Alton Rd, which has cream cheeses flavored with such exotic ingredients as scallions, sun-dried tomatoes and strawberries and other toppings like honey and whipped peanut butter. Any of the above, and more, on a bagel is $1.90 to 2.70, butter only is 80¢, and a bottomless cup of coffee is $1.10. If you're an idiot, you could pay $1.30 to have a *larger* bottomless cup. They were discussing a name change as we went to press.

The *Bagelry* (☎ 531-9877) at 1223 Lincoln Road is far less pretentious, with 45¢ bagels, 85¢ with butter and $3.70 with tuna salad.

Fast Food There's nothing special about the fast food on the beach, but the *Miami Subs* chain sells slightly up-market sandwiches and salads for less than $5, and extras like beer and cheap champagne. The beach also has a *Koo Koo Roo*, which does healthy, low-fat poultry dishes and veggie sides, and *Pollo Tropical*, doing very inexpensive and delicious grilled chicken. All Pollo Tropicals have playgrounds. Other than that, there are the usual offerings from McDonalds, Burger King, KFC, Taco Bell, Dunkin Donuts, et al.

Middle

American *LuLu's* (☎ 532-6147) is another of our favorites, and we're very thankful that the fire that totaled it in late 1995 wasn't bad enough to keep it from re-opening. It's a kitschy, Wonderbread, Americana, Elvis-and Be-Bop setting where you can get the best dang chicken-fried-steak ($7.95) and blackened chicken ($8.95) south of the South. They do respectable baby-back ribs ($10.95), and really big salads from $4.95 to 7.50. It's a very fun place, sit anywhere, smoke anywhere, have a Blackened Voodoo or Dixie beer and kick back. Their specialty desserts are worth trying as well: like sweet potato/pecan pie ($3.50) or banana chocolate pie ($3). They're at 1053 Washington Ave.

Fifty feet up Washington at No 1065 is the *11th St Diner* (☎ 534-6373), an original Art Deco diner trucked down from Wilkes-Barre, Pennsylvania, renovated and serving really good three-egg omelets ($4.25), sandwiches ($2.50 to 6.25), and American favorites like fried chicken and meat loaf from $7.25 to 14.95. It's open 24 hours, every day. Service is usually pretty slow – it's cheerful enough, though – and don't forget that they include the tip in your check. Excellent mural in the smoking section.

The Strand (☎ 532-2340) is a posh place with many expensive items but there's one key exception when they do special dinners: meatloaf for $6.75. It's not every night, so call first. See the Entertainment chapter's nightlife calendar for information on weekly magic shows with Michael Hayes. They're at 617 Washington Ave.

Jeffrey's (☎ 673-0690) at 1629 Michigan Ave is said to be very good – it certainly looks romantic, with artwork, candles and Tiffany lamps. Appetizers include artichoke and shrimp for $8.50, chicken salad plate for $7.50 and stuffed mushrooms for $4.25; some main courses are the vegetarian plate for $9.95, crab cakes for $13.95 and veal cutlet for $11.95.

Asian *Charlotte's* (☎ 672-8338) at 1403 Washington Ave has very good Chinese food, and it's a fine local hangout. Our favorites are their curry shrimp ($8.95) and Singapore fried noodles ($8.95).

Sushi's a happening thing on South Beach, and our favorite place for it is *Sushi Hana* (☎ 532-1100) at 1131 Washington Ave. The place is cavernous, but there are four traditional *tatami* tables in back, and service is usually very friendly (if rushed). There's free (and great) salad when you sit down. À la carte sushi is 75¢ to $2.50, temaki rolls $3 to 3.50, rolls from $2.75 to 9, and sushi/roll combinations (big enough for two people to share) are $15.50. *Sushi Rock Café* (☎ 532-2133) at 1351 Collins Ave also has excellent sushi and darn good service at slightly higher prices for sushi, slightly lower for combinations and temaki rolls. But the music's awfully loud in the evenings. *Toni's Sushi Bar* (☎ 673-9368) at 1208 Washington Ave is said to be good (and it's certainly crowded); à la carte sushi is $1 to 2.25, sushi entrees run from $12 all the way up to the gigantic sushi-boat at $60. They also do more expensive seafood dishes for $12.95 to 18.95.

World Resources Café (☎ 534-9095) at 719 Lincoln Road does a Thai-based world cuisine menu, with inexpensive appetizers ($3 to 4) and curries ($5 to 6) along with more expensive fare. It's a great place to be on weekends, Gallery Walks and on full moon days for their rotating and eclectic outdoor entertainment schedule. Just next to Sushi Hana at 1137 Washington Ave is the *Thai House* (☎ 531-4841) with veggie dishes from $6.95 to 8.95, Pad

Thai noodles for $7.95, satay chicken $8.95 and higher-priced specialties. *Thai Toni's* (☎ 538-8424) at 890 Washington Ave is renowned for its more expensive specialties, but the service is excellent and the place itself very chic.

Canton Inn (☎ 673-2218) at 843 Lincoln Road is an old-fashioned kind of Chinese restaurant that feels as if you're walking back into the 1950s – especially the prices of the set lunch specials ($3.25 to $5.25) served Tuesday to Sunday 11.30 am to 3 pm. Dinner entrees average $8.

Our friends tell us that *Yeung's Chinese Restaurant* (☎ 672-1144) at 954 41st St delivers for a $1 charge some pretty respectable food – though some dishes, like vegetable dumplings ($4.75) and shredded duck with Chinese veggies and rice noodles ($9.95) are better than others, like crispy chicken ($8.95).

Cuban Gloria Estefan's *Larios on the Beach* (☎ 532-9577) deserves special mention in a category of its own. Fight through the crowds to get at the hostess (they don't pretentiously stand outside flagging people in) and apply for a table (no reservations accepted). The atmosphere is better than the food (which is good but not outstandingly so) and it's definitely worth it once. Try the paella ($38 for two people, takes 45 minutes) or the less expensive fish Creole ($8.25). Otherwise, you can squeak out for under $20 or so for two people by getting three or four appetizers (like the huge Cuban sandwich for $4.35) and one drink each. They're at 820 Ocean Drive.

European The *Dab Haus* (☎ 534-9557) at 825 Alton Rd has excellent German food like bratwurst, currywurst and knoblauchwurst for $5.95; Sauerbraten for $8.95 and pork and chicken schnitzel for $7.95. They also do crèpes – we like the mushrooms, potatoes, red cabbage and cheese for $7.75.

Stephan's Gourmet Market & Café (☎ 674-1760) just south of the Clay Hotel at 1430 Washington Ave is a market bursting with fresh and delicious Italian produce, cheeses, meats and spices, and their kinda sexy dining room has a special that's a very good deal on a date: $21.25 (including tax) for dinner for two with bread, an entree that changes nightly, salad and a bottle of wine. Nice penne with sautéed mushrooms in goat cheese sauce.

Renzi's Café (☎ 531-0480) at 1400 Ocean Drive at the Winterhaven Hotel, does Ocean Drive Italian with funny waiters. It's only moderately priced for lunch but it gets expensive at dinner: pastas at lunch $6.50 to 7.95, at dinner $9.50 to 13.95; main courses run from $9.95 to 12.95 at lunch, $12.95 to 19.95 at dinner.

The *Raleigh Bar & Restaurant* (☎ 534-1775) is a gorgeous place to come before or after trying to gain access to their pool; it's also rather reasonable considering the FQ (Fabulous Quotient) of the place: for lunch main courses like roasted vegetables Provençal are $7.50, tuna burger with ginger soy sauce is $13, but grilled jumbo shrimp gazpacho is $7.50. Sunday Brunch is a chi-chi affair (wild mushroom omelet with fresh herbs and goat cheese at $9.50) and dinner gets very expensive. It's a nice place, though, at 1775 Collins Ave.

Grillfish (☎ 538-9908), across from the Warsaw Ballroom at 1444 Collins Ave, has a wonderful atmosphere – Greek? Mediterranean? 'Gay' said the waiter – it's elegant but tuxedos are forbidden, and the mainly Italian seafood dishes are very good: grilled salmon and rainbow trout are $11.95, but they also do chicken (piccata is $7.95). Appetizers run from mussels at $4 to shrimp scampi at $6.25. The restaurant is open till 'elevenish, one-ish on the weekends'.

The *Booking Table Restaurant* (☎ 672-3476) at 728 Ocean Drive does a filling and terrific surf & turf sampler appetizer ($8.95) that has salmon steak and chicken breast, and rosemary chicken pizzas (they're small and $8.95), but their dinner prices are just a tad high at $12.95 (grouper or dolphin) to $15 (tuna or salmon steak). They include a 15% tip in your check.

Lyon Frères et Compagnie (say that 10 times fast) (☎ 534-0600) is one of the Lincoln Road Mall's main meeting points. They're a combination gourmet market, chi-chi coffee joint, wine bar and French salad bar/café that has seats inside (no smoking) and outside on the sidewalk. Free wine tastings take place most Friday evenings. Salads are sold by the half pound, and are $2.50 to 6 (careful construction is key to escaping cheaply). Their pre-wrapped sandwiches are 'European' (accurate if that means 'small') and cost $3.95. Focaccia is $4.95. Saturday and Sunday brunch is currently a good deal with an omelet for $3, but staff say the price should rise. It's at 600 Lincoln Road.

Café Papillon (☎ 673-1139) at 530 Lincoln Road is a good place to stop for lunch along the Road – soup and half a large sandwich is $5.95, and Italian sandwiches (like tomato, mozzarella, basil and oil and vinegar) are about $5. There are newspapers on sticks, and a casual, if close, atmosphere.

One of the Beach's hottest spots, the *Van Dyke Hotel Restaurant* (☎ 534-3600), at 846 Lincoln Road, serves adequate food in a very chic setting that's usually packed to the rafters and taking over half the sidewalk. Service is very friendly, and even efficient, and if you could just get rid of the models preening, posing and prodding each other it would be a better place to eat the $6 to 9 burgers and chicken burgers, $8.75 open roast beef sandwich, and the house specialty, eggplant parmigiana, for $8.25. There's nightly jazz upstairs. Watch that included tip.

The Paramount (☎ 535-8020) at 1040 Lincoln Road, is a local favorite with imaginative food and reasonable prices. Appetizers are great, like toasted yellow pepper risotto cakes with pesto shrimp ($5.95), main courses like lasagna ($9.95) and grilled tuna with caper lime butter $13.95.

Haitian & Caribbean *Tap Tap* (☎ 672-2898) at 819 5th St is a charming and interesting place that should be seen if you're here. It's a wonderful place to have a drink – try Haitian Barbancourt Rum, available in several grades – and their $4 pumpkin soup is awesome. There's unique Haitian hand-made furniture and murals throughout the restaurant, and live music and other entertainment rotates through often – check the *New Times* or *Wire* for more information. The tiny and tropical *Norma's on the Beach* (☎ 532-2809) at 646 Lincoln Road is only moderate for lunch – dinners become expensive. They do good Jamaican specialties – lots of jerk seasoning – and dishes average $8 for lunch and $18 to 20 at dinner. Grab a cold Red Stripe or Dragon Jamaican beer ($3.50), and be happy, mon.

Mango's Tropical Café (☎ 673-4422) at 900 Ocean Drive next to Titi's Taco's has an incredible Haitian tropical mural that goes all around the room and over the bar. Their specialty is the Caribbean-style jerk chicken wings, an order of 10 is $5, 20 is $10; also try Cassie's chef soup (chicken, shrimp and veggies with noodles) for $6.95.

Italian It's a local's favorite, it's definitely our favorite, and the only reason *Sports Café* (☎ 674-9700) is in the Middle category as opposed to Budget is out of respect. This unpretentious and comfortable café's unfortunate name disguises a family-run place that feels as if you've walked into a Roman café – not a slicked up American version of a Roman café but a real one! When you sit down they give you freshly baked bread with a spiced extra-virgin olive oil dipping plate. The homemade pastas are simply the best we've ever had in the USA and maybe even in Italy (and we like our pasta!); simple pasta dishes like basil-tomato sauce are $6.95, lasagna

$7.25, and daily specials from $7.25 to 8.95 – don't miss their crab ravioli in pink cream sauce topped with freshly ground Romano cheese and black pepper. Their pizza is made Euro style – smaller, thinner crust and a different method of layering the toppings – and it's first rate. Can it get better? Yup. Suave and attentive service, a good and inexpensive wine list and fish and chicken specials as well. They accept Visa, MasterCard, travellers cheques and cash, and they're open from 11 to 1 am daily. They're at 538 Washington Ave.

Another pleasant and inexpensive Italian place is *Café Volare* (☎ 535-0081), at 635 Collins Ave, whose owner gleefully informs us that he never uses canned tomatoes and only uses fresh, homemade bread and pasta. It's certainly inexpensive, but dishes tend to be salty – specify you don't want it salty when you order. Pastas range from $5.95 to 6.95, main courses from $7.95 to 13.95. They serve an excellent arugula salad and interesting *focaccina al rosmarino*. Service is very friendly (men: take a date here and he'll make you look like a regular and valued customer), but there's a tendency to try and upgrade your order through chit chat ('Maybe you wanna nice-a glass of Italian wine widda dat?'). They're open daily noon to midnight.

PaneCaldo Restaurant (☎ 538-1440) at 1440 Ocean Drive (beneath the Betsy Ross Hotel), has authentic Italian food in a sophisticated setting; do try the excellent ravioli d'aragosta allo Zafferano (homemade lobster ravioli in a saffron cream sauce; $10.50), and the very nice tagliatelle integrali vegetariane (whole wheat pasta with a tomato-onion spinach sauce; $8.95). When you sit down they give you a sample of three types of breads with various dipping plates, like crushed olives and chopped tomatoes. Appetizers are $2.75 to 7.50, salads from $3.50 to 6.50.

The Beehive (☎ 538-7484) at 630 Lincoln Road is a quirky place with solid Italian foods either inside or out back in their wonderful Deco courtyard. Pastas for lunch run $4.95 to 10.95, for dinner they're $5.95 to 10.95, and good pizzas from $5.50 to 12.95. Wednesdays are especially fun, as it's Drag Night in the courtyard (from October to May), with all the servers in varyingly outrageous drag – reservations are requested, and there's a two-drink minimum or $5 cover charge.

Da Leo (☎ 674-0350), 819 Lincoln Road, is darn worth trying; tables spill outside in the evenings, and people seem both happy and well fed; generous portions of pastas run $6.95 to 7.95, main courses $9.95 to 15.95. It's open for $7.95 set lunch (make-your-own salad, two pastas and a soup) from November to May, and dinner year round.

Osteria del Teatro (☎ 538 7850) at 1443 Washington Ave has an expensive but very good Italian menu, but if you get there before 7.30 pm there's a fixed price $16 dinner that's worth every penny.

Mexican Everything on the menu at *Tita* (☎ 535-2497) is under $11; we liked the vegetarian burrito ($7.50) and the jalapeño smoked chicken breast with the works (vegetables, rice, beans and guacamole; $8.75). It's a small place (54 seats) with an industrial Mexican, earthy kind of feel to it. They're at 1445 Pennsylvania Ave.

Top End

American *Embers* (☎ 538-0997) at 1661 Meridian Ave is a reincarnation of the Embers from Miami Beach's 1940s heyday, and the atmosphere is very chic. The current owners bought up the recipes from the former ones – like one for the dressing on the famous Embers salad ($5), and the cuisine is sort of New-Age-classic-American with appetizers like crab cakes ($9.95), steamed citrus-scented artichoke ($7.95), and main courses like David's signature bourbon-glazed filet mignon and the four double chops of their rack of lamb, both at $26.95. Pasta is somewhat cheaper, like rigatoni at $14.95. There are specials on Mondays and Wednesdays.

Chinese *Chrysanthemum* (☎ 531-5656) at 1248 Washington Ave is open for dinner only. They serve quite a variety of fish and seafood dishes, like shrimp Imperial (with cashew nuts and bamboo shoots) for $13, crispy fish in lemon sauce for $11.80, but also orange and garlic frog legs for $14.95 and duck for $13.80. On their menu they indicate which meals are low-calorie ones.

The *China Grill* (☎ 534-2211) at 404 Washington Ave may be expensive, but it's the place to bring a date you want to impress: a friend says, 'It will cost a packet, but you will get laid!' Food is served family-style (well, maybe *wealthy* family-style) in large bowls intended to be shared. Menu items include grilled dry-aged Szechwan beef ($26.50 for one person, $46 for two), sizzling whole fish ($22/34), grilled rosemary scallops ($23) and wasabi crusted grouper ($22). It's slightly – oh, slightly – cheaper at lunch time, but it comes highly recommended. For the cheapest and best deal they have, show up between 6 and 7 pm for their pre-event dinner for $24.96 per person including an appetizer and two of five entrees (but not tax or tip).

French *Les Deux Fontaines* (☎ 672-7878) is at the Ocean Front Hotel, 1030-38 Ocean Drive. Open for lighter lunch fare and more substantial dinners, this patio restaurant sits above Ocean Drive – close enough to people-watch but far enough away to keep the riff-raff away from your saumon au papilotte. It is a nice spot to have some paté and bread ($5.35) or escargot ($7.80) and a glass of wine at lunch. At dinner time, prices shoot upwards, though like the hotel in which it's located, it's not as expensive as it looks or feels – main dinner courses average about $15 per person without wine, tax or tip. There's a decent wine list (French and American).

Joe's Stone Crab Restaurant (☎ 673-0365) at 227 Biscayne St is as close as Miami Beach gets to a world famous restaurant. It's been around since 1913, and open only during stone crab season from October 15 to May 15. There's seating politics (the restaurant's maitre d' was described in the 1994 *Zagat Survey* as being 'the wealthiest man in Miami'), but at the end of the day it's just reliably excellent stone crab and seafood dishes. At a price, to be sure: medium stone crab claws (six per order) are $16.95; 'selects' (seven per order) are $21.95, and large (five per order) are $28.95 – and if your appetite is robust, you can easily polish off two orders per person. Other dishes can be cheaper, like broiled swordfish steak ($16.95) or grouper ($13.95). There's also takeout service available, if you don't want to fight the crowds, and if you're feeling decadent in, say, Duluth, you can order an overnight air shipment of Joe's stone crabs to anywhere in the USA by calling them before 2 pm at ☎ 800-780-2722. The cost, including shipping, for one order of selects is $57.95, but two orders is only (relatively) $79.90.

Pan-Asian/Caribbean *Pan Coast Restaurant* (☎ 531-2727) at the wonderful Indian Creek Hotel is one of our absolute favorite places to eat: if you have one splurge in Miami Beach (dinner for two with wine will run about $60), we say do it here. The intimate (there are only about eight tables) restaurant is supervised by chef Mary Rohan, who calmly walks out of the kitchen now and then to bursts of applause from diners. Two things that are always on the menu are the tempura shrimp with mustard-miso sauce ($9) and the mache greens-sautéed wild mushrooms-Roquefort-pine nuts salad with roasted red pepper vinaigrette dressing ($8). For main courses, which change twice a week, there are dishes like oven-roasted five-spice chicken, in mushroom sauce with herb-roasted potatoes and roasted vegetables ($15) or sautéed 'salmon' swordfish with watermelon-papaya-ginger salsa, mango-basil sauce and spicy chips ($18). But Mary's always willing to cater to vegetarians, and as the above dishes indicate, she does it imaginatively. Three thumbs up!

Nemo Restaurant (☎ 532-4550) at 100 Collins Ave has a very interesting Asian menu with oyster-miso soup ($6), wok-charred salmon and sprout salad and, that old Asian stand-by, pan-roasted chicken with mashed potatoes and dried cranberry dressing, both for $16.

Thai *Pacific Time* (☎ 534-5979) at 915 Lincoln Road has excellent Thai and other Pacific Rim food in a very elegant setting. They also do a lot of fundraising and community minded projects, but service can get a tad snooty. Best deal is their prix-fixe dinner for $19.95 per person (between 6 and 7 pm), with scallion pancakes, grilled ginger chicken and Tahitian crème brulée.

Seafood *South Pointe Seafood House & Brewing Company* (☎ 673-1708) at 1 Washington Ave on Government Cut in South Pointe Park, is a very elegant seafood restaurant with attentive service and very good food. Their lunch menu is the same as the dinner menu, but lunch dishes are about $5 cheaper. If your company's paying, try the blackened swordfish with orange sauce and red onion marmalade ($19), or their very good shrimp scampi ($15). Pastas are $13 to 22. Wash this down with some of their excellent beers that are microbrewed on the premises (see the Bars section in the Entertainment chapter for more information).

Kerry Simon, the chef at New York's Plaza Hotel during the reign of Ivana Trump, runs the lovely *Max's South Beach* (☎ 532-0070) at 764 Washington Ave. Even if you're not up for the rather pricey main courses (like the $11 hamburger) or the specialties like salmon tandoori, black beans and Cayenne onion rings ($19.95) it's still a great place to stop in for one of their excellent Black Ties or 007 Martinis ($6.75).

Other *Allioli* (☎ 538-0553) at 1300 Ocean Drive is in the same building as the Cardozo Hotel (see Places to Stay), both also owned by Gloria Estefan. They provide a romantic, elegant and softly lighted atmosphere, while serving Spanish food with Italian/Cuban influence. For lunch roasted chicken with rice and vegetables is $9.50, churrasco $12.90 and their sandwiches $5.25 to 6.95. For dinner you'll have to part with a little more, pastas are $10.50, paellas $14.95 to 18.95 and meat and seafood $14.95 to 22.

Fellini Restaurant (☎ 532-8984) has good Italian food in a very nice atmosphere and prices aren't outrageous either: entrees run from $11.50 (grilled chicken with grilled veggies) to $14 (grilled salmon with veggies) to $19 for medallions of beef with porcini mushrooms and mashed potatoes. They're at 860 Washington Ave.

Casona de Carlitos (☎ 534-7013) at 2232 Collins Ave may not be as good as a restaurant actually *in* Buenos Aires, but for a *parrillada* (Argentinian barbecued side of beef) you could do a whole lot worse then this one at $29.95 for two people. Argentinian food is heavy on the red meat – another favorite is their barbecued filet mignon at $19.95.

The *Leslie Hotel Café* (☎ 538-5386) is good for snacks and sandwiches, even if it is really yellow and the prices are all totally odd. For a decadent splurge, the Skyy Hyy is a neat idea – two shots of Skyy vodka, an ounce of sevruga caviar, with a sashimi tuna-ponzu dipping sauce for $23.69. Sandwiches are a little more reasonable; mojo marinated grilled chicken on Caesar salad is $8.93, and Angus burger with cheddar and fries is $6.78. They're at 1244 Ocean Drive.

MIAMI

Downtown

Most places downtown cater to the 9 to 5-ers, and therefore close early, and most are closed on Sunday.

Foodcourts There are two good foodcourts offering a variety of Chinese, Mexican, Indian, pizza, sandwiches, etc, all for $1 to 6; the better of the two is at 243 E Flagler St, the other at 48 E Flagler St (upstairs), where you'll also find a *Granny Feelgood's* (see the Miami Beach Budget section above).

Cafés & Restaurants *Pi's Place Restaurant* (☎ 539-7097) at the NationsBank Tower at 100 SE 2nd St is open for snacks and lunch Monday to Friday from 11.30 am to 2.15 pm. You can get a decent lunch for less than $5, and the view of downtown is pretty slick.

Café Nash (☎ 371-8871) at 37 E Flagler St, inside the Seybold Building Arcade is a fairly small place which seems to be quite popular among the business people downtown. They are open for breakfast and lunch only, omelets $3.25 to 4.95, lots of different salads $3.25 to 7.50, sandwiches $2.95 to 6, platters including two side orders $4.50 to 7.50.

The checkered *Downtown Diner* (☎ 375-8077) at 4 SW

1st St smelled darn good when we were there. Continental breakfast is $1.99; two eggs, potatoes, bacon or sausage, toast and coffee is $2.99; sandwiches $4.95 to 6.95 and platters (including two side dishes) are $5.95 to 7.95. They're open Monday to Friday 7 am to 4 pm, Saturday 8 am to 2 pm.

La Cocina de Mama Stella (no ☎) is extremely small: there are maybe five tables outside and the kitchen is more or less outside as well, but the food looks and smells fantastic, though the staff's English is extremely limited. Cuban dishes all cost $4.99. They're next to the Royalton Hotel at 121 SE 1st St.

Panini Coffee Bar (☎ 377-2888) is an indoor/outdoor café, French-ish and trendy by downtown standards. They serve coffees and pastries (60¢ to $2.95), as well as sandwiches on wide French bread ($4.75 to 5.75), salads ($2.50 to 5.95) and soup by the cup/bowl ($1.95/2.95), and are at 16 NE 3rd Ave, open Monday to Saturday 8 am to 6 pm.

We walked by *La Cibeles Café* (☎ 577-3454) at 105 NE 3rd Ave and it looked worth a try; they do Cuban dishes from $4.25 to 6.95. The *San Villa Oriental Restaurant* (☎ 371-9359) at 230 NE 3rd St does Philippine, Chinese, Japanese, Singaporian, Korean, Thai, Malay and Indonesian food cheaply: lunch is $2.50 to 5.95, dinner $5.95 to 8.50 and seafood dishes $10.95. It's open daily 10 am to 10 pm (at least).

Oriental Express (☎ 374-0177) at 59 NE 2nd St has a lunchtime buffet with dishes like veggie chow mein ($3.95), chicken or beef with broccoli ($4.85) and shrimp with tofu ($5.25). Everything comes with soup and rice.

Cacique's Corner (☎ 371-8317) is another Cuban place at 100 W Flagler St near the downtown bus center. Platters (including three side dishes) are $4.50 to 8.95, chicken sandwiches $3.25, Cuban sandwiches $3.50.

The inevitable *Hard Rock Cafe* (☎ 377-3110) at 401 Biscayne Blvd in Bayside Marketplace is perhaps known more for the gigantic rotating electric guitar on its roof than for its food, which is perfectly fine (some is great) and not as expensive as we would have thought: enormous and excellent sandwiches like the VLT (veggie, lettuce and tomato) for $6.99, smoked barbecue beef on a pretzel roll $8.50 and full entrees from $8.99 to 16.99. It's open 11 to 2 am daily. Also in

NICK SELBY

the Bayside Marketplace (actually near the flag entrance to it) is *Las Tapas* (☎ 372-2737), which is said to have excellent little samplers of Latin foods.

Tobacco Road (☎ 374-1198) at 626 S Miami Ave has been around for over 80 years. It's primarily known as a blues spot, but they also do good burgers with a variety of toppings from mundane (cheese) to strange (eggs) for $5 to 8, and they make home-made ice cream. They're open every day from 11.30 to 5 am. Next door is *Tacos by the Road* (☎ 579-0059) at No 638, which does an admirable selection of tacos ($3.21), burritos ($4.59 to 4.99), and nachos with beef ($4.79). And finally, *Fishbone Grille* (☎ 530-1915) at No 650, has fresh fish daily either grilled, blackened, sautéed, baked, Française or Oriental blackened. Prices change according to what's on the chalk board. They have a very decent seafood gumbo ($3.95 to 4.95), and some interesting pizzas from $7.95 to 9.95.

East Coast Fisheries (☎ 373-8493) is Miami's oldest fish restaurant. It's right on the Miami River at 360 W Flagler St, and has been renovated so you can now watch the boats while you eat. Entrees range from $8.50 to 19. It's a very big lunch crowd and popular for dinner.

Joe's Seafood Restaurant (☎ 374-5637), also on the Miami River, has a deck where you can sit outside. It's at 200 NW North River Drive.

Little Havana

Las Palmas (☎ 854-9549) at 1128 Calle Ocho gets top billing for price and the fact that they're open 24 hours. Carne con papa is $1.99, Cuban sandwiches are $2.50. *El Pescador* (☎ 649-8222) at 1543 Calle Ocho has very friendly service and excellent Cuban dishes for about $2.50 including rice, potatoes and bread. We liked the *Calle Ocho Marketplace* (☎ 858-1828), a combination lunch-counter (pan con bistec/Cubano/media noche sandwiches are $2.50/2.50/1.75); coffee stand (guarapo $1.75, zoom juice 30¢, café con leche 60¢) coin laundry and food market at 1390 Calle Ocho.

El Rey de las Fritas (☎ 858-4223) at 1177 Calle Ocho has grumpier service but decent food; fritas with cheese for $2, Cuban fries for $1.75 and a steak sandwich for $3.25.

We really like the *Exquisito Restaurant* (☎ 643-0227) at 1510 Calle Ocho, for cheap coffee, great atmosphere and excellent food; most dishes are less than $5.

El Palacio Luna (☎ 285-9088) is a neat Cuban-Chinese place with chow mein for $4.50, curry chicken at $5.95 and honey garlic chicken at $6. They're at 1444 Calle Ocho.

We've heard great things from everyone about *Hy Vong Vietnamese Restaurant* (☎ 446-3674) at 3458 Calle Ocho, but somehow never got the chance to go in: One Lonely Planet staffer reports: 'It's just the best Vietnamese food I've ever had, and I love Vietnamese food: the best is their *bun* – thin sliced meat with vermicelli; and their squid salad marinated in lime juice and onions – get there early: it looks like a dive but the food is cheap and great, so it fills up fast.'

Don't expect the food at the very famous *Versailles* (☎ 444-0240, 445-7614) to match the gaudiness of the decor: that decor and the atmosphere are why you're here. The cavernous and unbelievably glitzy (in a 1980s Scarface-Miami Vice kind of way) restaurant is a Little Havana Cuban landmark, and you really should go out

Cuban Cuisine
The most common Cuban foods are pork, beef, rice, beans, eggs, tomatoes and lettuce, and rice, lemon and orange. *Yuca* (manioc or casava) is a starchy root vegetable that can be boiled or baked. Garlic and onion, rather than spices and chile peppers are used for seasoning. Another common seasoning in Floridian Cuban food is *mojo*, a garlic citrus sauce. Common accompaniments are rice *(arroz)*, black or red beans *(frijoles negro o rojo)*, yuca and especially, *plantains* – a larger cousin to the banana, served fried. When done right, fried plantains are crispy outside and sweet and starchy inside. The darker the plantain, the sweeter the fruit.

Cuban Specialties The most common dish offered at Cuban restaurants is *carne asada* (roasted meat), usually *puerco asado* (roast pork) or *carne de cerdo* (pork). Other dishes include *bistec* (steak), *arroz con pollo* (chicken and rice); *ropa vieja* (literally 'old clothes' but actually shredded skirt steak stew served with rice and plantains); and *filete de pescado* (fish fillet).

Other types of seafood are: *calamar* (squid); *camarones* (shrimp); *jaiba* (small crab); *langosta* (lobster); *mariscos* (shellfish) and *ostiones* (oysters).

Meat and poultry include *bistec, bistec de res* (beefsteak); *cabra* (goat); *cabrito* (kid (small goat)); *chorizo* (spicy pork sausage); *cordero* (lamb); and *jamón* (ham).

Sandwiches Sandwiches available at *loncherias* (snack bars) are interesting, made by slicing Cuban loaves lengthwise, filling them with ingredients and toasting (and mushing) them in a *plancha* – a heated press. The biggies include: *Cubano* (pork or ham and cheese, of your way to do a meal here during your trip. It can be great fun with a group and a pitcher of (weak) sangria ($9.50). Service is fine but the food pushes hard at the average barrier. Live with it: ropa vieja ($6.85), palomilla (Cuban steak) with fries or plantains ($7.50) or with white rice, black beans and plantains ($8.50); or vaca frita, shredded beef grilled with onions ($7.50). It's open Monday to Thursday 8 to 2 am, Friday 8 to 3.30 am, Saturday 8 to 4.30 am, and Sunday from 9 to 2 am. The restaurant is at 3555 Calle Ocho.

Many Cubans say that the food at *Islas Canarias* (☎ 649-0440) is the best in Miami; at any rate it's about the same price and much better for food than the Versailles. It's at 285 NW 27th Ave. There are several others that have been recommended to us on Calle Ocho: try

sometimes with mustard and pickles, depending on how much you look like a *gringo)*; *pan con lechón* (extra crispity-crunchity pork, and *mojo)*; *palomilla* (steak sandwich with fried onions), and *media noche* or *midnight* (ham, cheese and roast pork on a roll).

Desserts Most desserts *(postres)* are small afterthoughts to a meal. They include *arroz con leche* (rice pudding); *crepa* (crepe, thin pancake); *flan* (custard; crème caramel); *galletas* (cookies/biscuits); *gelatina* (jello); *helado* (ice cream); *pastel* (pastry or cake) and watch out for that *tres leches* (literally 'three-milk' cake, actually a glucose-tolerance-test disguised as a pudding).

Tea & Coffee The big players are *café con leche* (coffee with hot steamed milk, half and half); *café con crema* (coffee with cream, served separately); espresso served in thimble-size shots, also called 'zoom juice'); *té de manzanilla* (camomile tea); and *té negro* (black tea).

Fruit & Vegetable Drinks Pure fresh juices *(jugos)* are popular all over Miami, and readily available: the fruit is normally squeezed before your eyes. Every fruit and a few of the squeezable vegetables are used – ever tried pure beetroot juice?

Licuados are blends of fruit or juice with water and sugar. *Licuados con leche* use milk instead of water. Possible additions include raw egg, ice, and flavorings such as vanilla or nutmeg.

Aguas frescas or *aguas de fruta* are made by mixing fruit juice or a syrup made from mashed grains or seeds with sugar and water. ■

La Carreta (☎ 444-7501) at No 3632, a lot like the Versailles but a little less glaring and in your face. *Guayacan* (☎ 649-2015) at No 1933 is about the same price as all the others, and a Nicaraguan version of the Versailles: lots of glitz and flash.

Coral Gables

Numero Uno on our list of places to eat in Coral Gables is *Daily Bread* (☎ 856-0363), which does superb falafel and gyro sandwiches ($3.50) in addition to being a Middle Eastern mini-supermarket that sells baklava, olives, tahini and halvah, along with their own excellent brand of pita bread – $1.10 for a bag of five. They're at 2486 SW 17th Ave (they've got another location at 12131 S Dixie Hwy), open Monday to Saturday 9 am to 7 pm, but no falafel after 6 pm, closed Sunday.

Monte's (☎ 445-0996) at 2330 Salzedo Ave is an interesting place: run by Indians, it specializes in French dishes at dinner time, but very few Indian ones. No matter; it's a great place for lunch. Try the breaded steak ($5.25), lasagna ($4.35) or beer batter fish ($5.75), or sandwiches from $1.70 to 5. At dinner the prices go up: appetizers run from $2 to 4, main courses from $7 to 11.50 and it's BYO alcohol if you'll be wanting any.

Sho Bu (☎ 441-1217) is worth it if you're a) a sushi fanatic and b) able to eat *a lot* of sushi: this place offers all-you-can-eat sushi for $9.99 at lunch, $11.99 at dinner. The stuff is small but good. There are several caveats: 15-piece limit on eel, 20 on shrimp tempura, there's a 90-minute maximum sitting time on Friday and Saturday, and you always have to pay for each uneaten piece, especially uneaten rice – and you can't take it out in a doggy bag. Still up for it? It's at 265 Aragon Ave. No smoking during dinner Friday to Sunday.

Everyone tells us that *Tropical Chinese Restaurant* (☎ 262-7576) at 7991 SW 57th Ave is *the* best place in Miami for dim sum: the *New Times* gives it a Very Good, and we have four people who called us to recommend it during our research.

Restaurant St Michel (☎ 446-6572) is one the most romantic (and expensive) restaurants in Miami. It's a four-star place on the ground floor of the Hotel St Michel, at 162 Alcazar Ave. Reviews are decidedly mixed on food (entrees range from $15 to 25) with dishes like sautéed Florida Keys yellowtail, Citrus beurre blanc and filet mignon with cabernet sauce and caramelized red onion marmalade with chipolte mashed potatoes (whew). Most people agree that the desserts are excellent and everyone agrees that the place is absolutely charming, so maybe stop in for some coffee and a nice piece of cake.

There's a newly established and moderately priced 'restaurant row' on Giralda Ave between Ponce de Leon Blvd and Miller Ave with about a dozen places serving all kinds of food from Italian to French bistro. *Las Puertas* (☎ 442-0708) at 148 Giralda Ave is said to be a fine gourmet Mexican. A real treat for those looking for fresh seafood, inventive presentation and just good salsa.

Coconut Grove

There are a couple of little places in CocoWalk shopping center; we like *The Cheesecake Factory* (☎ 447-9898) which does about 25 kinds of cheesecake from $4.75 to 5.30 a slice. They also have burgers from $6.95 to 7.50; pizza, like roasted pepper, ricotta and sun-dried tomato for $8.50, and Thai Chicken pizza for $8.95; and a mean Sunday brunch including eggs Benedict and spicy Cajun Benedict ($8.50), and Mike's Breakfast Pasta (spaghetti, scrambled eggs, bacon, garlic and onions) for $9.50.

Johnny Rockets (☎ 444-1000) at 3036 Grand Ave, right across the street from CocoWalk is an excellent 1950s-style hamburger joint – they even use the old-fashioned Coca Cola glasses. Burgers are $3.55, a No 12 cheeseburger (with red sauce, pickles, lettuce and tomato) is $3.80; chicken breast sandwiches are $4.95, and a BLT is $3.95. They're open until 2 am on Friday and Saturday, and deliver in the Grove. They have another branch at the Dadeland Mall (see the Shopping chapter).

Planet Hollywood Miami (☎ 445-7277), owned by a gaggle of action figures like Sylvester Stallone, Arnold Schwarzenegger, Bruce Willis and Demi Moore, spends boatloads of cash on promotions, but we don't take advertising so we're not even going to describe the place. But the food prices are a lot more reasonable than one would think: pastas from penne with fresh broccoli, cauliflower, zucchini, squash and peppers, carrots and onions in a pesto cream sauce at $9.95 to Thai shrimp at $11.95, and generous portions of chicken or beef fajitas for $10.95. They're at 3390 Mary St. Reservations are recommended on weekends.

On the day before we went to press, a friend called in a panic and said we *had* to include *Le Bouchon du Grove* (☎ 448-6060) a bistro that *South Florida Magazine* called as 'French as de Gaulle'. It has very friendly, if heavily accented, staff, in a very relaxed atmosphere, but it's pricey: count on a three-course dinner for two without drinks to run at least $55 to 60. Specials when we called were, appropriately, frog legs with garlic butter, and some sort of 'whaht feesh' wrapped in a cabbage leaf, both at $14.95. Locals go there to hide from the tourist chaos. It's at 3430 Main Hwy.

Southwest

These are *way* west but absolutely worth the trip, especially if you're visiting Monkey Jungle or the Fruit & Spice Park. *Burr's Berry Farm* (☎ 251-0513) has simply the best strawberries in the USA. Not just strawberries, but huge, fist-sized, sumptuously sweet, breathtakingly fresh, unbelievably, nay, *sexually* satisfying strawberries. People come from miles around – a *lot* of miles (there's a private air strip out back for well-known customers who, yes, *fly* there for these berries!) – and stand in the ever-present line to buy quarts ($7) or pints ($3.50). They also make the best strawberry shake we've ever tasted (about $2.50) and sell hot dogs ($1), jam ($4.50) and chili sauce and pickles ($3.75). They're open from Christmas to May only, 9 am to 5.30 pm every day. It's one mile west of US Hwy 1 on Monkey Jungle Rd, at 12741 SW 216th St in Goulds.

Farther out, *Knauss Berry Farm* (☎ 247-0668) at 15980 SW 248th St, a couple of miles west of the Fruit & Spice Park, have similarly heavenly cinnamon rolls that create similarly long stagnant lines on Saturdays as people wait to grab them. They also have the same sort of strawberries, jams and jelly offerings as Burr's but with the addition of bread, cakes and brownies. Cinnamon rolls are 40¢ or $4.25 a dozen.

Northeast

Step back into the past at *S&S Restaurant* (☎ 373-4291), a classic '40s-style diner with downright sassy service ('Keep yer shirt on, hon!'), great food (except for the crab cakes, which were execrable) like humongous burgers ($2.75), baked macaroni & cheese ($4.75) and more adventurous entries like shrimp Creole with two veggies and bread ($5.50). It's a small horseshoe-shaped lunch counter that's always very crowded and there's usually a wait of a few minutes for a seat. Lots of cops. It's at 1757 NE 2nd Ave.

Another Miami tradition is the *Rascal House* (☎ 947-4581). While service here is just as snappy, and the atmosphere equally diner-ish (though this place is much, much bigger than S&S), the Jewish food is uniformly great. Our favorite is the Lake Erie whitefish salad ($11.30), but just get anything: we've been here several times and never had a bad or even a not great meal. Expect to wait in line when you come; the line for the counter is usually shorter than that for proper tables. Sandwiches, like corned beef, tongue (yech!) or roast beef are $5.95, but some, like liverwurst or salami are $4.65. Don't miss the grilled salmon for $12.75. The restaurant is at 17190 Collins Ave (at 172nd St) in North Miami Beach.

Aventura There's nothing much of note in Aventura except a shopping mall, an unreliable storage facility and three excellent places to eat, should you happen to be in the neighborhood. *JD's Pizza & Subs* (☎ 652-4455, 652-3387) at 1620 NE 205 Terrace (just beneath the west side of the overpass of the Ives Dairy Rd entrance to I-95) doesn't look like much, but their pizza is absolutely divine – we stop here just for a slice ($1.60) whenever we can. They sell small/medium/large pizza pies for $10.60/12.30/16.95, lasagna for $5.90. There's no toilet, and service is from gruff, large Italian men. Video-game tables. These guys have two other locations, both in the middle of nowhere: Miami Lakes off Palmetto at 6828 NW 169th St, and Miami Springs at 5683 NW 36th St.

In the Promenade Shops Mall at 20475 Biscayne Blvd sits one of the best diners anywhere, *Turn Bagel* (☎ 933-3354) a family-run place with uncommonly and frighteningly friendly service from the kind of uniformed waitresses that call people 'hon', 'sweetie' and 'sugar'. Breakfast is the best time to come (they throw some free mini-Danish pastries on the table when you arrive) with eggs, potatoes and a bagel for $2.49, but they also do lunch specials from 11.30 am to 3 pm like a quarter-chicken with French fries for $4.99. Bagels to go are 40¢ or $4.20 for a dozen.

The *Unicorn Village Market Waterfront Restaurant* (☎ 933-8829, 933-1543) in the waterways development northeast of the Aventura Mall, is a market and restaurant. The restaurant serves healthy and delicious food, but it's not strictly vegetarian, so everyone can eat. At lunch, sandwiches run from $5.95 to 6.95, salads $4.75 to 7.95, and specials like Chinese chicken stir fry or steamed veggie platter are $6.95. At dinner, veggie entrees include spinach lasagna and angel hair pasta in tomato sauce for $11.95, other dishes like grilled honey-mustard chicken $13.95. The supermarket is a Babylon of fresh and organically grown vegetables, fruits, meats, cheeses, wines, natural products like vitamins and skin care creams – everything is good, prices aren't bad and service is excellent. The fruits and vegetables may be the best in Florida – absolutely hands down the best in Miami. It's at 3565 NE 207th St.

Northwest

Design District *Piccadilly Garden Lounge* (☎ 573-8221) at 35 NE 40th St for coffee and light meals in their lush little courtyard. They do a very nice Caesar salad (for two) for $7, and beef dishes from $13.95 to $26.

We've had a couple of recommendations for the *Charcuterie Restaurant* (☎ 576-7877) as a lunch spot. It's at 3612 NE 2nd Ave, open Monday to Friday from 11.30 am to 3 pm.

Entertainment

To call Miami Beach a trendy nightspot would be a little like calling New York a fairly large city: this is one of the most totally fashionable places in the country right now for clubs and nightspots. But nightlife around here is far more than clubs: the New World Symphony is an unexpected treat, and legitimate theater is very active in the area. There's an art scene here that's evolved from a couple of grungy studio-galleries into a driving force in the American art world. And sports fans can go nuts in a city that has professional football, baseball, basketball and hockey franchises, jai alai, NASCAR racing, horse racing and respectable college teams.

NICK SELBY

Ocean Drive on a Sunday

BARS

There are perhaps more bars than street corners in Miami Beach, so we're listing ones that we or our friends recommend. Remember to bring photo identification like a driver's license, passport or national identity card because if you look under 30 you will be asked for ID. The strictly enforced drinking age in Florida is 21.

Note that all the restaurants along Ocean Drive have outdoor seating, and unless it's very crowded – like on a weekend or holiday – you can usually sit in one of those places with a drink or two without having to order food. A few of our favorite places to sit on the Drive are the *Clevelander's* oddly shaped bar in front of their pool at No 1020; the *Booking Table* at No 728 for their cheap appetizers and relatively friendly service; and the Speakeasy Bar & Lounge, a '20s-theme lounge at the *Ocean Front Hotel* at No 1230.

Watering Holes

Mac's Club Deuce Bar (☎ 673-9537) at 222 14th St is the oldest bar in Miami Beach, established in 1926. It's definitely a prime local hangout, and it's easy to see why: there's no trendiness here, just a dark but friendly and welcoming room with a pool table and juke box, and no-nonsense service. They're open daily from 8 am to 5 am, bottled beers are $2.25 to 3.25, well drinks are $2.50 – what more could you want?

Over on Alton Rd, the comfy *Irish House Bar & Grill* (☎ 534-5667) at No 1430 is another local spot with a happy hour of varying specials Monday to Friday from 5 to 6.30 pm, two pool tables, some video games and a jukebox. Pitchers (depending on the brew) are $8 to 12.

Ted's Hideaway (☎ 532-9869) at 124 2nd St is a pretty classic hole-in-the-wall open 24 hours. They have, surprisingly, a pretty good beer selection with things like Weissbier for $3.25, Red Stripe, Corona, Fosters and Caribe for $3, and a two-for-one happy hour from 4 to 6 pm and 2 to 4 am. They also have three pool tables.

Nearby, *Rolo's Bar* (☎ 532-2662) at 38 Ocean Drive looks like a café (the food is expensive and the service unbelievably slow) but we're listing it for it's selection of beers, by far the best on the beach. They have a couple hundred types of beer from Louisiana Abita Turbo Dog ($2.95) to Aussie Razor Edge ($3.50) to Polish Zywiec ($3.50) to orgasmic Belgian beers ($6.95).

The *Palace Bar* (☎ 531-9077) is *the* gay bar and restaurant; very popular on weekends and before the beach and Tea Dances. It's at 1200 Ocean Drive.

Brandt & Break (☎ 672-9958) is politely described by a friend as a 'redneck pool hall that's a great place to hang out' at 653 Washington Ave.

West End (☎ 538-9378) at 942 Lincoln Road is a primarily gay but all-welcome place that has a great happy hour from 8 am to 3 pm daily, and on Thursday and Sunday from 8 to 5 am, it's *three*-for-one drinks (!). They have three pool tables and are open daily 8 am to 5 am – check in *Wire* for their semi-regular drag shows with singers, drag magicians and dancers.

821 (☎ 534-0887) at 821 Lincoln Road is a great local hangout; there's live music on many nights and lesbian night on Thursdays (See Cabaret and Gay & Lesbian sections below).

Jam's Taverna & Grill (☎ 532-6700), 1331 Washington Ave, is open Monday to Friday 11.30 to 5 am, Saturday and Sunday noon to 5 am, with happy hour from 5 to 8 pm (two for one). They have three pool tables, large-screen TVs where they show sporting events, the music is usually fairly loud and they serve bar food like burgers and sandwiches for $2 to 8.

If you *really* like pool, there's always *Sterling Club Billiards* (☎ 531-2114), a pool hall/bar with 12 pool tables and loud rock music at 1242 Washington Ave.

The *South Beach Pub* (☎ 532-7821) is a friendly local

hangout, with open-mic nights Sundays. They're at 717 Washington Ave.

The *Cosmic Cafe* (☎ 532-6680) adjacent to the Clay Hotel & International Hostel, 410 Española Way, was undergoing a change of management when we visited, but it's a very nice setting – low lighting, a nice curved bar and decent drinks. It was open 9 to 2 am daily under the old management and did drinks and bar food.

Theme Bars

At *Virtua Cafe* (☎ 532-0234, see the Online Services appendix) virtual-reality games (which change daily) are $5 for five minutes, but if you like to watch there are monitors that allow you to see the game from the point of view of the person playing. They also have two flight simulators, and for $1 you can sit at the bar and join in on a nationwide interactive computer trivia game for the whole night. They've also got a pool table and some dancing. Bar food (pizza, burgers or sandwiches) is $3 to 7. It's worth checking out; Fridays there's unlimited virtual reality for $10. They're at 1309 Washington Ave.

Tap Tap (☎ 672-2898) at 819 5th St is a Haitian restaurant and bar (see the Places to Eat chapter) that also does art shows, is home to community meetings and is generally a cool and colorful place to hang out drinking Haitian Babencourt rum ($4.60) or African Ngoma beer ($4). It's open Sunday to Thursday 11.30 am to 11 pm, Friday and Saturday from 11.30 am to midnight.

If you've been to Berlin and liked it, you'll probably like *The Berlin Bar* (☎ 674-9300) at 661 Washington Ave: People in Black, slick atmosphere, you get the idea. They do some live music and entertainment from 5 pm to 2 am daily.

Chili Pepper (☎ 531-9661) at 621 Washington Ave is a bar and concert space with live music on Sundays. There's never a cover charge and they've got specials throughout the week. Tuesday is Brit Night with $7 pitchers and $1 drafts of English beer; Mondays from 8 to 10 pm there's free pool (other times the pool tables cost $10.50 to 12.50 an hour with a one-hour minimum). They're open Sunday to Thursday 9 pm to 3 am, Friday and Saturday from 9 pm to 5 am.

Dab Haus (☎ 534-9557) at 832 Alton Rd has the best selection of German beers, wines and schnapps in the area; they have Dortmunder pils and Alt Tucher hefe weizen, dark hefe weizen and Kristall weizen, Königs pils and Hacker-Pschorr all from $2.50 to 4, and wines by the glass from $3 to 4. They're also a darn serviceable German restaurant – see the Places to Eat chapter.

Bar None (☎ 672-9252) at 411 Washington Ave has a permanent exhibition of the paintings of Mr Sylvester 'Stop or My Mom Will Shoot' Stallone. And if that's not enough, it's a big Eurotrash hangout – good place to go wanna-be-star-spotting. It's open Tuesday to Sunday from 10 pm to 5 am.

Penrod's Beach Club (☎ 538-1111) at 1 Ocean Drive is kind of a beach blanket bimbo-theme place, with a pool, a semi-private stretch of beach with volleyball, dancing, and nightly drink specials like Wednesday margarita night when 32-ounce drinks are $2. Penrod's has another stand at 14th St at Ocean Drive.

If you're looking to see a place that's packed on weekends with Causeway Crawlers, like secretaries from Kendall, who usually get drunk enough to start dancing topless on the tabletops, *Mezza Notte* (☎ 673-4343) is the place for you. The bar and restaurant is at 1200 Washington Ave; show up early on weekends.

Microbreweries

South Pointe Seafood House & Brewing Company (☎ 673-1708) at 1 Washington Ave on Government Cut in South Pointe Park is a really fun place to sit and drink some excellent microbrewed beer – for $2 you can get a sampler with a small cup of each of their beers, and regular servings range from $4 to 4.50. We liked Government Cut light (the light's the color, not the calories) and Jeff's Pacific Ale. Alas, their Oatmeal Stout . . . well, let's just say Guinness has nothing to worry about. They do a happy hour Monday to Friday 4 to 7 pm with free appetizers and $1 off drinks.

Abbey Brewery (☎ 538-8110) opened just as we went to press, so dammit we didn't get to taste any of their offerings, which are the Abbey Brown, Oatmeal Stout, Porter Christmas and Indian Pale Ale ($3.75 a pint). They also have about 13 other beers on tap from $3 to 4.25. Happy hour is Monday to Friday from 4 to 7 pm, $1 off all drafts. They have a small range of appetizers and bar food, and they're open every day from 1 pm to 5 am, 1115 16th St at Alton Rd.

Live Music

The best jazz club in the area is the *MoJazz Bar & Lazy Lizard Grill* (☎ 865-2636) at 928 71st St. They're closed Monday, and have live jazz Sunday and Tuesday to Thursday from 8.30 pm to 12.30 am, Friday and Saturday from 9.30 pm to 2.30 am. There are no age restrictions and cover prices range from nothing to $10

What's Happening & Where to Get Tickets

The best places to check for what's on during your stay is in the papers: the best of those are *Wire*, the Friday Weekend section of the *Miami Herald*, or the *New Times*.

On the internet, a very useful source is the Single Source (see the Online Services appendix) which gives a daily listing of special events around the area.

Tickets to specific events can always be bought at the venues themselves, and usually through Ticketmaster of Florida (☎ 358-5885), an omnipotent force in the ticketing world which can give you concert and event information and sell you tickets over the phone when you give them your credit card number.

There are also several telephone numbers you can call in Miami for pre-recorded information on upcoming events:

Cosmic (and Comet) Hotline from Miami Planetarium	☎ 854-2222
Jazz Hotline	☎ 382-3938
Moviephone	☎ 888-3456
WLVE Entertainment Line	☎ 800-237-0939
WLYF Information Line	☎ 651-5050, option 2
ZETA link	☎ 800-749-9490

depending on who's playing and where you're sitting. There's half-price cover on weekends before 8 pm or after midnight. Acts are varied – from the University of Miami jazz band to the 'Jumpin' Jewish Sounds' of Klesmer meets Jazz to the MoJazz Band on Friday and Saturday.

Rose's Bar (☎ 532-0228) is one of the only places around where you can hear live local bands like Manchild, The Goods, Day by the River and Darwin's Waiting Room. They're at 754 Washington Ave. The *Lizard Lounge* (☎ 674-8855) in the Century Hotel at 140 Ocean Drive is a quiet, often deserted place to have a coupla beers, with a very nice outside garden. They do an excellent Sunday brunch for about $20 outside in their front courtyard.

Respectable Street Cafe (☎ 672-1707) at 218 Española Way is a nightclub that has a couple of live bands a week; other standard nightclub specials include Tuesday G Spot ladies night (no cover for ladies). Call for show dates, which vary.

The *Cameo Theater* (☎ 673-9787, 531-4993) at 1445 Washington Ave also has live bands occasionally; see the Nightclubs section.

In Little Haiti, *Churchill's* (☎ 757-1807) has been around for 50 years. It's an English pub with satellite TV broadcasts of English football and rugby, eight draft beers, about 50 bottled beers and live rock music on most nights. They're at 5501 NE 2nd Ave, open Monday to Saturday 11 to 3 am, Sunday noon to 3 am.

Little Havana Nightlife

One of the best spots in Little Havana is *Cafe Nostalgia* (☎ 541-2631), with real Cuban music in a totally great atmosphere of Cuban memorabilia and a small dance floor. It's open Thursday to Sunday 9 pm to 3 am. The house band is complimented with musicians who stop in to jam, like those in androgynous singer Albita's band across the street at *Centro Vasco* (☎ 643-9606), where she's been performing forever. The club, at 2235 Calle Ocho is a frequent haunt of Emilio and Gloria Estefan.

STRIP JOINTS

Sex is a large part of Miami's allure: the city is packed with young, beautiful and half-naked people, partying and posing through the sultry nights. Spoken or unspoken, Miami promises sex with a fine degree of sleaze as much as it promises beaches. Whether you're straight, gay or bi, there's a pervasive atmosphere of dangerous sensuality and untold passion. Most of this is interaction in clubs, bars and on the beach, but there are a couple of venues where sex is the featured attraction.

Neither offer sex acts but both of which have nude dancing and table dancing. *Club Madonna* (☎ 534-2000), 1527 Washington Ave (the one the pop star Madonna sued, not the one she goes to), is open nightly 6 pm to 6 am; there's a $10 entry charge. On Monday and Tuesday they hold striptease contests.

De JaVu Showgirls (☎ 538-0355) at 2004 Collins Ave is a classic beach strip joint, with great '60s vintage posters.

NIGHTCLUBS

Miami Beach nightclubs come in and out of vogue at a rate that can only be compared to that of pre-Beatles rock bands – it's like on *The Jetsons* when the daughter tells her father 'No, Daddy, that band was groovy *last* week!' Indeed, in the course of just three months, four very popular and very fashionable nightspots here went bust and disappeared. Celebrities move in and out of the scene – like the guy who changed his name to an unpronounceable symbol before rocketing to failure,

Boom Boom Boom . . . Busted!

Early in the winter 1995-96 season, Miami Beach police carried out raids on several popular nightclubs. They came looking for illegal drugs, under-aged partiers and, if they could find it, some illicit sex would look good on the report as well. The clubs hit were Glam Slam, Paragon, Twist and Groovejet and the next day the media had a field day showing photos of half-naked tourists being hauled off by cops.

As a result of the raids, several clubs closed, and were closed at the time of writing, though they all are expected to reopen at some point. Club owners and city officials continue to meet to discuss the problems of illegal activity in nightclubs, and police send undercover agents around the clubs periodically.

The moral of the story is that taking, buying or selling illegal drugs in Miami Beach nightclubs is probably a really bad idea. ■

Madonna, Madonna's brother, Madonna's hair stylists, Madonna's . . . well *you* know. Hell, even Mickey Rourke had a club that he ran when he wasn't outside punching people. Clubs here rise meteorically and fall like the 1987 stock market: the information in this section is the most volatile in the book.

Nightclubs on South Beach are generally a healthy mix of gay, lesbian and straight, though several are more exclusively gay. In this chapter we've listed the ones that are mixed with the ones that are straight, as the lines are very blurry. If a place is predominantly gay, they'll probably put up a polite sign: 'Welcome to the Warsaw Ballroom. This is a gay nightclub.'

There are theme nights at many local clubs; for an idea of what's available, see the Nightclub Calendar section below.

Straight & Mixed

Amnesia (☎ 531-8858) is the home of South Beach's most famous Sunday Tea Dance (post-beach, pre-club), but Amnesia's not exclusively gay: many nights are mixed. There's also a dance floor out in the courtyard – dance under the stars – at 136 Collins Ave.

Bash (☎ 538-2274) at 655 Washington Ave is pretty much the hottest predominantly straight nightclub on the beach, owned by Sean Penn and Mick Hucknel. It has a cool, good dance floor inside and another one in the courtyard outside.

Don't you *know* who I am?!?

For reasons best left to psychology, the more offensively, awfully, breathtakingly rude a doorman and the more ruthlessly exclusive a club, the larger the clamoring hordes of short-skirted women and big-tipping men trying to gain entry.

'If you're not dressed to the nines and walking with an attitude that says you totally fuckin' belong here, forget it, baby,' counsels Melanie Morningstar, who writes the Nights Out with Morningstar column at *Wire*. Morningstar helpfully added that she's seen people successfully get in by offering bribes of up to $100 and even sexual favors to doormen at nightclubs.

Why anyone would pay $100 (the average nightclub cover charge on the Beach is about $10) or risk death by anonymous sex to some lanky little thug to get into a place where drinks cost $8 a pop is beyond us, but there it is. But clearly, to get into some of the more popular clubs, all you can do is try one or more of the following strategies:

- **You're Polite** Don't be meek, but don't act as if you're Sean Penn (unless you happen to be Mr Penn, in which case . . . Hey look! A photographer!).
- **You've Got Attitude** You're a lean, mean, partying machine, and don't let no one mess with you. Oh yeah, you're gorgeous, too.
- **You're Cool** When the competition is as fierce as it is here (it's about equivalent to the atmosphere in a department store three days before Christmas), a second's hesitation is enough to keep you milling about on a crowded sidewalk filled with wanna-be's.

Cameo Theatre (☎ 673-9787, 531-4993) is a predominantly straight dance club in a renovated theater at 1445 Washington Ave, which sometimes has really good cutting edge music acts, like Cafe Tacuba from Mexico and reggae from Burning Spear Reggae – check in *Wire* for what's up.

Club Cabana (☎ 534-1665) in the Club Cabana Hotel, 161 Ocean Drive opposite the Lizard Lounge has a gorgeous backyard on the beach where you can dance under the stars.

Glam Slam (☎ 672-4858) was closed when we went to press, but was one of the most popular clubs on the beach for years, and it is expected to reopen. It's at 1235 Washington Ave.

Groovejet (☎ 532-2002) is *the* after-hours spot in town

- **You're Dressed Properly** Standard nightclub garb here is as it is in New York, Paris or anywhere else: look expensive. Or at least interesting – drag queens, Star Trek characters and other Fabulously, outlandishly or outrageously dressed people get in as well.
- **You Know Someone** and/or
- **You Are Famous**

on Thursday, Friday and Saturday. Do not annoy Gilbert, the 'celebrity doorman' from New York, and don't even think of showing up until at least 2 am. It's at 323 23rd St.

Les Bains (☎ 532-8768) at 753 Washington Ave, the sister club to one in Paris, has a surplus of modeling types and big-haired, yellow-suited men with lots of gold chains.

Liquid (☎ 532-9154) is an impossibly exclusive place that people are clamoring to get into – and unless you're dressed pretty Fabulously, forget it (though they do a come-as-you-are night, see Calendar below). It's run by a gaggle of people including Ingrid Casaras and Michael 'the brother' Ciccone. It's at 1439 Washington Ave.

Twist (☎ 538-9478) at 1057 Washington Ave is a darkish (a few small lamps spread a dim light) place with music videos and a very nice wooden bar. Bartender and their press say it's for everyone ('never a cover, always a groove') but it's a predominantly gay crowd.

For a glimpse at the Causeway Crawler crowd, hit *Temptations* at 1532 Washington Ave.

Dig the floating toys in the bar-moat at *Swirl* (☎ 534-2060); in the back garden the tables have sandboxes and toys – more funky than South Beach slick – they do Afro tea parties where guests are given Afro wigs. There are couches in the outdoor patio. They have nightly specials – it's a Fabulous spot, with lots of cheery locals. It's at 1409 Washington Ave.

Gay & Lesbian

The gay night scene at South Beach, according to a famous local quip, can be summed up as men that 'look like Tarzan, walk like Jane and talk like Cheetah'.

Hombre (☎ 538-7883) at 925 Washington Ave is totally gay, somewhat sleazy but fun all the same; they've got an outdoor bar as well that is said to be very cruisy and touchy.

Mary D's Ladies Night at *821* (☎ 534-0887) is the best known and most crowded lesbian night on the beach, with the Cabaret for Women every Thursday. Performances start at 9.30 pm, two-for-one drinks from 6 to 9 pm. 821 is at 821 Lincoln Road.

The Kremlin (☎ 673-3150) is a pretty exclusively gay disco (but on Fridays it's very welcoming to all) that does salsa and hot Latin nights during the week, and lesbian nights on Saturday. Check in *Wire* for theme nights, which change all the time. They're at 727 Lincoln Road.

Warsaw Ballroom (☎ 531-4499) is the longest lasting (it's been around for at least five years) and hottest gay nightclub on the beach; it's one floor plus a balcony. They have always been innovative with foam parties and dick dancers. Downstairs is the new *Warsaw Bar*, an amazing carved wooden bar. There are amateur strip nights on Wednesdays and After Tea on Sunday. It's at 1450 Collins Ave.

Loading Zone (☎ 531-5623) may be the answer to trendy South Beach-brand gay bars (where leather more often tends to mean shoes), with dark corners and less attitude – trendy attitude that is. It's in the alley between West Ave and Alton Rd at 14th St.

Paragon (☎ 534-1235) is an enormous gay nightspot at 245 22nd Street that closed just before New Years Eve 1996; it's said to be reopening but stay tuned.

Nightclub Calendar

There's something happening every night at South Beach nightclubs, bars and lounges, and while the players and the highlights change all the time, here's an idea of the kind of things the local clubs were up to on weekends at the time of writing. Remember, some of this will be different when you visit, so check the *Wire* Calendar section, the *New Times* or just ask around for current information.

Thursday *Groovejet* does Groove Girl Thursday, two-for-one drinks for women all night; *Liquid* does a 'come-as-you-are' local's night ('oh, gracious Trend Gods, we thank thee for thy generosity'); it's Ulypian Thursday at the *Marlin*: bring a board game; *Kremlin* becomes packed with Superhunks; and *Twist* does a two-for-one happy hour from 1 pm to 3 am (!); it's Teen Night at *West End*, 18- to 21-year-olds admitted free to see dancing go-go boys.

Friday *Liquid* does their 'dress to kill' Unadulterated weekends on Friday and Saturday night: Main Room dance, Situation Room hip hop, acid jazz, funk and alternative; it's open-mic No Shame Theater at the *Area Stage* (see Theater, below); *Kremlin* has Hot Tropical Salsa night; and *Amnesia* does Coliseum, the 'extra large' gay night.

Saturday Grand Central night at *Amnesia* with dancing out under the stars; *Kremlin* does Saturday Nights for Women; the *Speakeasy Bar & Lounge* has Prohibition nights; *Liquid* continues Unadulterated weekends; House, tribal music at *Swirl*; let's get really queasy and drink $1 Jaegermeister shots all night at the *Tudor Hotel Lounge*; *West End* does Old Time Drag Shows with Bridgett Buttercup and Taffy Lynn at 11 pm and 1 am.

Sunday The famous Sunday Tea Dance at *Amnesia*; and After Tea at the *Warsaw Ballroom*; Open-mic night at the *South Beach Pub* and The Cigar Social Club at *The Space*; *Liquid* does X-TRA LARGE – make it a Manwich night gay Sundays; it's Retro Night at *Bash* with disco, swing, funk and soul.

Monday Drag Nite With Kitty Meow & the South Beach Divas at *Caffe Torino* at 11.30 pm, for the next few minutes the best drag show on the beach; the Teeny Weeny Martini Party at the *Leslie Café & Martini Bar*.

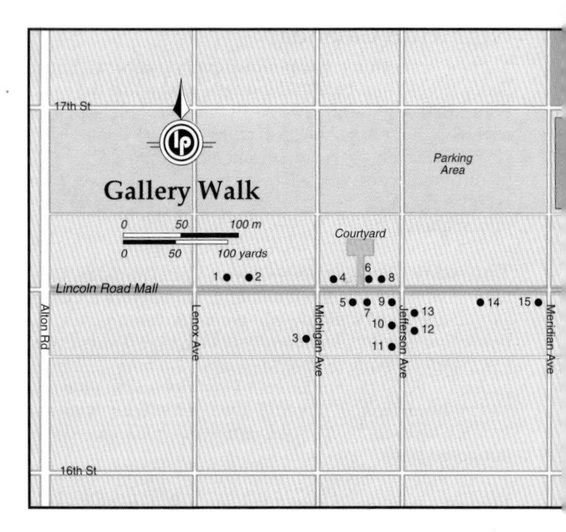

Tuesday Playing with Marvella at *Swirl* with games like Bingo for shots and strip Twister.

Wednesday *Warsaw Ballroom*'s famous $1000 amateur strip contest; the Dating Game at *Caffe Torino* starts at 10 pm – reserve; there's also magic at *The Strand*.

GALLERY WALKS

There are Gallery Walks on the second Saturday of the month (except in August) along Lincoln Road Mall. These have evolved into more than just popping into the galleries, which hold openings during the Walks, and now most locals who attend make an entire evening of it, with dinner before and some clubbing afterwards. There's no set way to go about it, you just show up and pop in to what's open.

Some galleries, from west to east along the Road and around that participate (if no street is indicated it's on the Road):

- ClaySpace
  No 1037, ☎ 534-3339 – ceramics
- Ground Level
  No 1035, ☎ 534-3339 – varying exhibitions
- Galleria Del Sol
  1628 Michigan Ave, ☎ 674-7076 – Latin American and local art

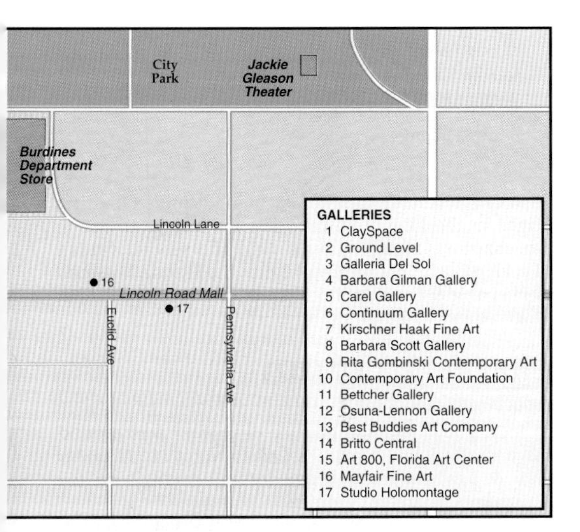

- Barbara Gillman Gallery
  No 939, ☎ 534-7872 – contemporary Latin American and American art
- Carel Gallery
  No 928, ☎ 534-4384 – 19th- and 20th-century oil painting
- Continuum Gallery
  No 927, No 120, ☎ 538-3455 – nonprofit visual arts center
- Kirschner-Haack Fine Art
  No 922, ☎ 531-7730 – contemporary American, European and Latin American art
- Barbara Scott Gallery
  No 919, ☎ 531-9171 – American contemporary painting, sculpture, jewelry
- Rita Gombinski Contemporary Art
  No 900, ☎ 532-4141 – Israeli and original Gombinski painting, sculpture
- Contemporary Art Foundation
  1630 Jefferson Ave, ☎ 674-9541 – Latin and Ibero-American art, new concept stuff
- Bettcher Gallery
  1628 Jefferson Ave, ☎ 534-8533 – classically influenced abstract painting
- Osuna-Lennon Gallery
  1635 Jefferson Ave, ☎ 673-3324 – 17th- and 18th-century paintings and sculpture, antique furniture, early-20th-century painting
- Best Buddies Art Company
  1637 Jefferson Ave, ☎ 534-8779 – art, T-shirts and sculpture
- Britto Central
  No 818, ☎ 531-8821 – expensive vodka bottles and other pop art

- Art 800
  No 800, ☎ 672-6003 – contemporary art at the Florida Art Center
- Mayfair Fine Art
  No 701a, ☎ 534-1004 – Russian art
- Studio Holomontage
  No 630e, ☎ 532-8880 – holographic art in many forms

Also of interest, though not such an event, is **Opening Night** in the Design District (see the Things to See & Do chapter), a gallery walk held the second Friday of each month. On Opening Nights, the Florida Museum of Hispanic & Latin America Art (☎ 576-5171), 1 NE 40th St, gives away free cocktails from 6 to 10 pm.

CABERET & COMEDY

People in South Beach aren't here to laugh, they're here to look good, and the paucity of cabaret acts around town shows it; see Mary D's Ladies Night at *821* under Gay & Lesbian clubs above for information on the Thursday Cabaret for Women.

The *Comedy Zone* (☎ 672-4788) at 1121 Washington Ave spotlights national comedy headliners (which basically means that they've appeared on Comedy Central, VH1 or MTV, or Leno or Letterman) Thursday to Sunday. Tickets cost $10 on Thursday and Sunday and $12.50 on Friday and Saturday. The rest of the week admission varies. There's gay comedy Tuesday and amateur night on Wednesday with free admission.

CINEMA

There's a standard, googleplex-type cinema at every major shopping mall. The Omni 10 AMC Theater – with the most annoying recorded information telephone line on earth at ☎ 358-2304 – at the Omni International Mall does cheap shows of first-run films every day: before 4 pm, matinees cost $3.50. 'Private shows', between 4 and 6 pm, are just $2.75. After 6 pm, the cost is $4.75 for adults, $3.50 for students with an ISIC, seniors and kids under 13.

Miami Beach Film Society The film series at the Wolfsonian Foundation (see the Things to See & Do chapter) is often co-sponsored by the Miami Beach Film Society (MBFS; ☎ 673-4567), a fascinating organization that also runs series independent of the Wolfsonian. The idea is to use Miami Beach's venues to make viewing a film more fun, so events run the gamut from Inflatable Rubber Raft Drive-In at the Raleigh Pool for a screening of *Skirts Ahoy* to the annual *Food in Film: Movies to Dine for* series, which began in early 1996. That festival was shown at a number of Miami Beach restaurants and co-sponsored by *Gourmet* magazine – which was so excited about the success of the series that it announced that it would expand the idea to run nationally. Tickets in 1996 were $45 per person including dinner and cocktail hour, though that's expected to rise – a lot.

Contact the MBFS for information on what's on during your visit.

Alliance Cinema This little cinema (☎ 531-8504, 534-7171), tucked into the recess just east of Books & Books at 927 Lincoln Road, does independent films by lower-budget filmmakers that ordinarily wouldn't make it to Miami. It began as a projection screen in the window of Books & Books and finally has grown into its own permanent space here. Movies change generally on Fridays, except when a title has been held over due to popular demand. Every six months or so, they hold an 'Anti-Film Festival' featuring films (about half of them locally made) with a 'quirky, edgy' bent. The Alliance also shows films on Sundays at Bar-Cinema Vortex at 1663 Lenox Ave, in the tiny doorway opposite the SunBank ATM, and next to Common Space Exhibition, a small art gallery.

Colony Theatre The Road's second Deco theater (after the Lincoln Theatre, see Classical Music, below), the 1934 Colony (☎ 674-1026) is a 465-seat venue with great acoustics, which hosts some concerts (Melba Moore was here when we visited) and theater, and also shows independent and gay- and lesbian-oriented films. They're at 1040 Lincoln Road.

PERFORMING ARTS

Theater

Area Stage *Area Stage* (☎ 673-8002), 645 Lincoln Road, presents cutting-edge original works with a strong emphasis on local talent. Ticket prices are $17 for adults, $8 for students under 25 with ISIC, based on availability.

Edge Theater The *Edge Theater* (☎ 531-6083) is another cutting-edge house at 405 Española Way on the 2nd floor above Java Junkies.

Florida Shakespeare Theatre *Florida Shakespeare Theatre* (☎ 446-1116, see the Online Services appendix) performs at their new mainstage at the Biltmore Hotel, 1200 Anastasia Ave in Coral Gables (see the Things to See & Do and Places to Stay chapters). The new theater was built after Hurricane Andrew destroyed the company's former home at the Minorca Playhouse. The name is misleading: the company, which performs year round on mainstage and on tour, handles Shakespearean works as well as classic and contemporary works. One former season, for example, included *Hamlet*, Eugene O'Neill's *Desire Under the Elms*, *Top Girls* by Caryl Churchill and *Cobb* by Lee Blessing. Tickets to the performances cost $25 for adults, $15 for seniors, children and students; opening nights costs $30/20.

Jerry Herman Ring Theatre The *Jerry Herman Ring Theatre* (☎ 284-3355, see the Online Services appendix) is at the University of Miami's Coral Gables campus. Actors including Sylvester Stallone, Steven Bauer, Saundra Santiago and Ray Liotta are alumni. They have planned a number of experimental and studio productions as well; details will be announced.

Jackie Gleason Theater for the Performing Arts The *Jackie Gleason Theater* (☎ 673-7300) at 1700 Washington Ave is the Beach's premiere showcase for Broadway shows, the Florida Philharmonic, the Miami City Ballet, the Concert Association of Florida and other big productions. Originally built in 1951, the place was actually the home of the Jackie Gleason television show.

The Miami Broadway Series runs the gamut from David 'Presto – CUT!' Copperfield to The Who's *Tommy*; there's a children's Story Theater series with productions of kids' favorites; and there are musical concerts by the likes of Liza, Donna and Ray Coniff. Ticket prices change by performance, but hover in the $30 to $50 range for Broadway shows and concerts.

Gusman Center for the Performing Arts This venue (☎ 374-2444) at 174 E Flagler St is a renovated 1920s movie palace now home to a huge variety of performing arts – including the New World Symphony and the Florida Philharmonic – and the annual Miami Film Festival. They hold traveling shows, so it's not easy to nail them down, but as we went to press the offerings on tap were Broadway show revivals, a local theatrical and performance group, concerts (including the heartfelt crooning of Mr Mel Torme), variety shows and the annual Miami Film Festival, an international festival held in February. Ticket prices change for each performance.

NICK SELBY

Miami Beach's theatrical jewel

Coconut Grove Playhouse This lovely theater (☎ 442-4000) celebrated its 40th anniversary in 1996, but the facility has been here for 70 years. The Playhouse gained fame and attention when José Ferrer was appointed artistic director in 1982, and constantly swaps shows with Broadway in New York – it sends some, and some of the more popular Broadway road shows stop here. There are two stages, the main Playhouse stage and the smaller Encore Room.

Tickets to the Playhouse cost $30 from Sunday to Thursday, $35 on Friday and Saturday, some student discounts apply. In the Encore Room, tickets are $22 Sunday to Thursday and $27 on Friday and Saturday. The facility is at 3500 Main Hwy, at the corner of Charles Ave, two blocks south of the CocoWalk shopping center.

Spanish-Language Theater For Spanish language theater, check in the Spanish press, or contact *Teatro Las Mascaras* (☎ 642-0358), *Teatro de Bellas Artes* (☎ 325-0515), *Teatro Martí* (☎ 545-7866) or the *Manuel Artime Performing Arts Center* (☎ 525-5057). The *African-Caribbean-American Performing Artists* (☎ 758-3534) stage performances at various venues around the city.

Classical Music

There are classical concerts by the Florida Philharmonic and visiting orchestras throughout the year at venues like the Jackie Gleason Theater for the Performing Arts, the Gusman Center for the Performing Arts, and Dade County Auditorium. For information about concerts throughout the city and state, contact the excellent Florida Concert Association (☎ 532-3491), at 555 17th St.

New World Symphony See the Music & Theater section in the Facts about Miami chapter for background on this wonderful orchestra. The *New World Symphony* (NWS; ☎ 673-3331) performs from late October to late April in both the Lincoln Theatre in Miami Beach or the Gusman Center for the Performing Arts downtown. And while their concerts are going on, the Symphony also does a traveling series to South America, Israel, Monte Carlo and Japan.

Michael Tilson Thomas, the NWS's artistic director, conducts a healthy majority of the performances himself, though a host of guest conductors – and artists – also appear. Among past offerings are the Opening Nights Series, featuring music from Brahms, Copland and Shostakovich; a Gourmet Series highlighting Rachmaninoff, Rimsky-Korsakov, Mozart, Strauss and Wagner; a Twilight Chamber Series; and a Baroque Festival.

About 30% of the performances are free, and in September there are a host of pre-season free concerts as well. The NWS has recently received grant money to allow their musicians to hold a series of free concerts featuring music of their choice.

Ticket prices for the remainder of the concerts cost from $18 to 43, depending on performance and seating. Tickets can be bought from the box office at the Lincoln Theatre, or through Ticketmaster offices.

Lincoln Theatre The Beach's theatrical jewel, the beautiful *Lincoln Theatre*, 555 Lincoln Road, is more than just host to the New World Symphony: they hold a wide variety of performances here including South Beat Concerts, 'An Evening with Four Poets Laureate', free Musicians' Forum concerts and performances by visiting artists. Stop in when you're here or call the Lincoln Road Partnership at ☎ 531-3442 for specifics.

Dade County Auditorium Besides being home to the Florida Grand Opera, the auditorium (☎ 547-5414), 2901 W Flagler St, also sees classical music concerts held by the Concert Association of Florida, the Miami Symphony Orchestra and the San Francisco Symphony. To get to the auditorium, go west on Hwy 836 to the 27th Ave exit, south on 27th Ave to Flagler St (the third light), turn right and the auditorium is on the right.

Opera

The Florida Grand Opera and the Greater Miami Opera Association (☎ 854-1643), which runs a program of visiting artists, perform at the Dade County Auditorium in Miami (see above).

Dance

There are performances by dozens of nonprofit dance organizations all over the area and the state of Florida; the best resource for information on what's happening when you're in town is the Florida Dance Association (☎ 237-3413) at the Miami-Dade Community College Wolfson Campus, 300 NE 2nd Ave, Miami, FL 33132. If you call or write them and let them know where you'll be and when you'll be there they'll send off a schedule of performances and events.

Miami City Ballet The *Miami City Ballet* (☎ 532-7713) at 905 Lincoln Road regularly performs at the Jackie Gleason Theater, the Bailey Concert Hall in Davie, the Broward Center for the Performing Arts in Fort Lauderdale and the Raymond Kravis Center for the Performing Arts in West Palm Beach. They also give holiday performances of *The Nutcracker* at several venues. Finally, the company goes on the road around the US and internationally.

They also run Family Day at the Ballet, an introduction to the ballet for children by the company's dancers and Artistic Director Edward Villella, in which performances are preceded by a talk by the director and the opportunity for children to meet ballerinas. Tickets for kids are $6 to 16. They also run DanceTalks, a series of talks hosted by Villella before each new repertory program, which touch on 20th-century dance and choreography.

Ballet Flamenco La Rosa Part of the Performing Arts Network (PAN), the *Ballet Flamenco La Rosa* (☎ 672-0552) is a professional flamenco dance company that performs flamenco with live music. They run on a very loose schedule, so call for individual performance dates and prices, but as an idea, when they perform at the Colony Theatre, about three times a year, tickets are $20 for adults at the door, $18 in advance and $15 for students and seniors. They also perform at local festivals and special events. They hold classes every day for children and adults ($10) in all forms of dance, including jazz, modern, creative movement, flamenco, ballet, Latin dancing and yoga.

PAN provides rehearsal space as well as holding performance series, lectures, demonstrations and workshops. They're all in the purple and yellow building at 555 17th St just behind the Jackie Gleason Theater.

Free (or Cheap) & Outdoors

Bayfront Park After Dark (☎ 358-7550) is a series of free concerts at Bayfront Park's South End Amphitheatre from February to May on Thursday nights at 6.30 pm. Past series included Abeng Frummers & Dancers, Celtic music and Irish dancing, New World School of the Arts Dance Troupe and FIU dance troupe, and the New World School of the Arts jazz band.

But Bayfront Park's most famous for its *American Birthday Bash* Fourth of July celebrations at both the South End and the much larger AT&T Amphitheatres: this is South Florida's largest Fourth of July event. The event features music, kids' rides, watermelon-eating contests and a fireworks celebration.

There are frequent free concerts on Lincoln Road. There's free jazz every night in the 2nd-floor lounge at the *Van Dyke Hotel* (☎ 534-3600) at 846 Lincoln Road. On Friday and Saturday, Toni Bishop and her band play from 10 pm to 2 am, and Sunday to Thursday there are trios playing from 8 pm to midnight.

From May to December *SunTrust Twilight Music Series* on the third Saturday of each month features jazz-oriented (but not exclusive) concerts, from February to April the Lively Lunchtime concert series is held every Thursday from noon to 2 pm. We particularly like the *Full Moon Concerts* outside World Resources Café (☎ 534-9095) at 719 Lincoln Road, where everyone gathers on the night of a full moon to hear live music ranging from African drumming to jazz to folk to dijeridu concertos. They also do regular World Beat performances on Friday nights from 8 to 10 pm.

There are about a dozen concerts a year at *South Pointe Park*, though they're not scheduled and are usually associated with special events; check in *Wire* or the *Herald* during your stay. The *New World Symphony* holds outdoor concerts as well, and on the Fourth of July does a performance at North Beach Open Space Park, on the beach between 72nd and 82nd Sts.

Shopping complexes in the area are also a good bet for free concerts: there are free concerts every day of the year at the *Marina Stage*, an amphitheater facing the bay at Bayside Marketplace (☎ 274-7982). The concerts are widely varied and run the gamut from oldies, top 40 and rock & roll to Caribbean and reggae to jazz and calypso. Daytime concerts are held Wednesday through Sunday from 1.30 to 5.30 pm; evening concerts are held Sunday to Thursday 7 to 11 pm, Friday and Saturday 8.30 pm to 12.30 am.

CocoWalk Mall (☎ 444-0777) in Coconut Grove, holds free concerts in March and April only; there's less variety than at Bayside.

GAMBLING

The casino initiative which would have undoubtedly turned South Beach into a nightmare failed, so until the developers and high-rollers can figure out a way to bribe officials or dupe the public (and they probably will manage both at some point), gamblers are rather limited in their choices. You need to be over 21 to bet.

For casino-style action (we're split on this one: Corinna loves it and thinks it's 'fun' while Nick avers that he'd rather sit home and flush dollar bills down the toilet, which would be more fun and perhaps cheaper) *Sea Kruz* (☎ 538-4002, 688-7529) runs lunch and dinner gambling cruises. They go three miles into international

KENNETH DREYFUSS

Calder Race Course

waters, where their full casinos are legal, and then just cruise up and down the coast. It's a buffet-style affair, and while there's live music, the real action is the casino, which has nine blackjack tables, craps, roulette, slot machines and – hey, don't worry if you blow all your cash – they've thoughtfully provide ATMs on board and can also do Visa cash advances.

The cost of the cruises varies, and there are frequent specials, like second person free, etc, but at the time of writing the most you'd ever pay was $37 for lunch all week and dinner Thursday to Sunday, and $45 for dinner on Friday and Saturday. Cruises leave from the 5th St Marina just south of the MacArthur Causeway on the southwest tip of Miami Beach at 12.30 and 7.30 pm Sunday to Thursday, 1.30 and 7.30 pm Friday and Saturday. Lunch cruises last from four to five hours (it's best to leave the nest egg in the RV).

SPECTATOR SPORTS

Pro Sports

Football Attending an American football game may be one of the most intense experiences in spectator sports here, and Miamians get more than a little crazy when it comes to their *Miami Dolphins* (☎ 620-2578), a successful NFL team that was coached for what seems like a thousand years by Don Shula, who retired in 1995. Preseason games begin in August, and during the season (from September to January) there are usually at least two home games a month at Joe Robbie Stadium, a mile south of the Dade-Broward county line at 2269 NW 199th St. On game days there's bus service between downtown Miami and the stadium. If you're a real football nut, you can watch the team practice at their training facility (☎ 452-7000) near Fort Lauderdale. Take I-95 or Florida's Turnpike to I-595 west, to the University Drive exit, turn left, to SW 30th St, make another left and the facility's half a mile down on the right hand side of the road.

Baseball The *Florida Marlins* (☎ 626-7400) are a relatively new National League baseball team that lose quite often over at Joe Robbie Stadium during the season from May to September.

Basketball The *Miami Heat* play National Basketball Association games at the Miami Arena (☎ 530-4444) between November and April. Tickets cost $14, 21 and 28.

Hockey The *Florida Panthers* play National Hockey League games at the Miami Arena (☎ 530-4444). Panther Pack tickets, sold from 10 am on the day of a game (noon on Sunday games) are $9; reserved seats are $20, 24 and 30.

College Sports

The University of Miami dominates college sports in the area, and the *Hurricanes*, or Canes, football team dominates UM sports. You can see the Canes play football at Orange Bowl Stadium. Ticket prices are $16 for general admission, $23 for reserved seats.

The Hurricanes play college baseball at Mark Light Stadium. Tickets cost $5 for adults, $3 for children under 17 and senior citizens; the Florida and Florida State series cost $6/4.

Hurricane basketball is played at the Miami Arena. Tickets cost $13 for sidecourt seats; in the endcourt they're $9 for adults and $2 for children under 17.

Auto Racing

The Metro-Dade Homestead Motorsports Complex (☎ 230-5200) is a brand new $50 million racing center that debuted in November 1995 with two NASCAR races. The *New York Times* quipped that it would have been hard to imagine anyone in Homestead wanting to see something coming at them at 200 mph after Hurricane Andrew, but the complex (run by Miami Motorsports, which ran the Miami Grand Prix – now held here at the complex – through downtown Miami) holds five major race weekends a year, and if Formula One racing comes here as well, there could be many more. The complex is on the east side of the City of Homestead, at 1 Speedway Blvd.

Horse Racing

For horse racing there's *Hialeah Park* (☎ 885-8000) at 2200 E 4th Ave in Hialeah (Metrorail stops right there), with its French-Mediterranean-style clubhouse that was built in 1925. Races are from March to May, though you can always come in to get a look at the park's grounds and flamingoes (they raise them). Admission is $1 to the grandstand and $2 to the clubhouse.

Calder Race Course (☎ 625-1311) is an indoor raceway with horse racing from late May to mid-January, and the Festival of the Sun Tropical Park Derby from November to January. They're way north at 21001 NW 27th Ave.

Tennis

The annual Lipton Championships (☎ 442-3367) are a 10-day tournament played at the Tennis Center at Crandon Park, on Key Biscayne. There are two tennis tournaments associated with the FedEx Orange Bowl Football Classic: the Rolex-Orange Bowl Tennis Tournament and the International Tournament for players under 14.

Jai Alai

Jai alai, a fascinating and dangerous Spanish game in which players hurl a *pelota* – a *very* hard ball – at over 150 mph, can be seen (and bet on) at *Miami Jai Alai* (☎ 633-6400); admission is $1, $2 for reserved seats and $5 for Courtview Club seats. Matinees are on Monday, Friday and Saturday from 1 to 5 pm, evening games from 7 pm to midnight. The arena is at 3500 NW 37th Ave, near MIA; from Omni International Mall take Bus No 36, which stops right in front.

Shopping

WHERE TO SHOP

South Beach

See the What to Buy section below for items that are better to buy in South Beach than anywhere else. Shopping malls now dominate the shopping scene so totally that there's really nothing left of a local shopping scene anywhere in South Beach. While Lincoln Road, Washington Ave and Alton Rd are lined with galleries and little knickknack shops, if you want to buy something big, you're probably going to end up in a mall. It's frustrating, but there it is. One happy exception is the Burdines (☎ 674-6311) at 1675 Meridian Ave. This is a branch of the once-mighty Burdines empire of grand Southern department stores, but even this old dame is showing signs of creakiness, and prices when we've gone in have been higher than in comparable shops in shopping malls.

Downtown Miami

Right in the heart of downtown Miami, especially along Flagler St, is a huge collection of shops and boutiques selling . . . well, selling export-ready electronics mainly to Latin American visitors. There are over 300 shops, and most of them are the sort in which you'll have to bargain your heart out to get a good deal on electronics products

CORINNA SELBY

Tile mosaic – Alton Rd

that you'd probably be far better off buying at Circuit City – which offers a 30-day money-back guarantee, a better selection and fixed prices. But if you're up for a haggle, this is the place to head!

Specialty Chain Stores

There are several large specialty retailers in the area. When we're shopping for something we usually call the big shops first, as their price gives us a good idea for price comparison with other places. Check the ads in the *Miami Herald* for specials and sales. Many of these stores have more than one location, so ask when you call about the one nearest you. The larger clothing stores are below, in Shopping Malls.

Sports Authority (☎ 682-0717) sells sporting goods, golf clubs, bicycles, running, hiking and climbing equipment and a small selection of backpacks.

Circuit City (☎ 933-8616) has several locations around the area selling a decent range of electronics, computers, appliances and other gizmotronics. Incredible Universe (☎ 716-5800) at 7800 NW 29th St has taken the PT Barnum approach to selling electronics – balloons for the kids, big bright colors and a veritable three-ring circus of bleeping things.

The Wal-Marts (☎ 470-4510), K-Marts (☎ 252-3577) and Searses (☎ 937-7500) of the world are there to be one-stop shopping centers for just about anything you could need, from padlocks to plates, diapers to garbage disposals (pronounced dispose-all in the south) and everything in between. If you need something, stop in any of them and they may have one of 'em.

Eckerd (☎ 538-1571) is a chain of pharmacies around the state, some open 24 hours. Walgreens (☎ 261-2213) is a chain of (get this:) combination pharmacy/liquor stores throughout the area, so if you should ever need a shot of whiskey and a bandage . . . .

Shopping Malls

Massive shopping malls have so saturated the shopping scene here that it's difficult to find many items without entering one. And the insidious nature of the malls and the huge shops is that lower wages lead to higher employee turnover. In Sports Authority, a major sporting goods chain, we complained to a manager that we couldn't find one person who could tell us whether they had tents with no-see-um netting. 'Well,' he told us, 'we train them as best we can for the wage we pay them.'

The major shops in malls are generally clothiers

Cheaper in the States

While you'll have trouble finding Vegemite, the USA has the best prices in the world (with the possible exception of Hong Kong) on some items. They include:

- Jeans – New blue jeans in the USA (like unwashed Levi's 501) start at as low as $24 .
- Sunglasses – Ray Bans can be had for as low as $40.
- Zippo lighters – These babies start at about $12.
- Running shoes – You can get a good pair of name-brand running shoes starting at $40.
- Camping equipment – Everything costs less here.
- Computers – Though you may get hit with an import tax when you get home, the USA is definitely a great place for computers: take the price in UK£ and switch the symbol to $ and you're about right. As we went to press, a 75 MHz multimedia Pentium desktop with monitor could be yours for about $1200.
- Cameras – We got a good quality Minolta 400 series Maxxum for just about $300 including two lenses.
- CDs and musical instruments – The average price for a new CD release is between $12 and 14; musical instruments, especially items like DATs, ADAM and digital samplers, are in the same category as computers.

Note that if you're buying electric or electronic appliances here (like coffee grinders, telephones, tape recorders, CD players, etc – they're cheaper here as well) you'll need a step-down transformer (not adapter) to allow the thing to work at home. ■

(Neiman-Marcus, Saks Fifth Avenue, Gap, Burdines) and general merchandisers (Sears, K-Mart, Wal-Mart, JC Penney), while all malls will have a food court (a collection of fast food joints), a Sunglass Hut, shoe shops, some specialty jean and womens' clothing shops and bookshops.

The major players in the area are:

- Aventura Mall
  19501 Biscayne Blvd in Aventura, with a Macy's, Lord & Taylor and some funky security stuff (☎ 935-1110)
- Bal Harbour Shops
  9700 Collins Ave in Bal Harbour, with really expensive stuff from people like Chanel, Tiffany, Louis Vuitton, Hermés, Zhiguli and others
- CocoWalk
  3015 Grand Ave in Coconut Grove in the heart of a formerly charming neighborhood, cafés, Gap, Victoria's Secret, a cinema and one redeeming feature, The Cheesecake Factory (☎ 444-0777)
- Dadeland Mall
  7535 N Kendall Drive in Kendall with Florida's largest Burdines department stores and over 150 other shops (☎ 665-6226)
- Loehman's Plaza
  2855 NE 187th St at Biscayne Blvd; also in Aventura, with smaller chain shops (☎ 932-0520)
- Miracle Center
  3301 Coral Way in Coral Gables with The Limited, Gap, Victoria's Secret and others (☎ 444-8890)
- Omni International Mall
  1601 Biscayne Blvd, in downtown Miami with Gap, an AMC cinema (with a good deal on matinees), a photo shop and a software shop (☎ 374-6664)

WHAT TO BUY

Antiques & Art

See the Gallery Walks section in the Entertainment chapter, and the Miami Design District section in the Things to See & Do chapter for information on many galleries and antique shops in both those locations, which should be your first stop if you're in the market.

Cash Machines

After you've gone out and shopped till you dropped, you'll be needing some cash. There are ATMs at most banks that are on several networks, but the most flexible are at Nationwide Bank, which accepts cards on the Cirrus, Plus, Green Machine, Mac, Magic Line, NYCE, Star System, MC and Visa networks. On South Beach there are two at 1234 Washington Ave. Another good bet for a machine on many networks is any 7-11 store, which accepts cards on networks we've never even heard of, but note that these machines attach a surcharge of between 50¢ and $1 per transaction. ■

Once a month (usually the third week) at the Coconut Grove Convention Center, Coconut Grove Cares (☎ 444-8454) holds an antique and jewelry show with dealers from all over the country. The proceeds go to assist Coconut Grove Cares, a social organization that runs youth and after-school programs, day camps and summer jobs and other laudable efforts.

Bicycles

See the Activities section in the Things to See & Do chapter for where to buy bicycles.

Books

General Bookstores The best locally owned bookshops – and we're not just saying that because they carry lots of Lonely Planet titles – are the two branches of Books & Books, at 933 Lincoln Road on Miami Beach (☎ 532-3222) and at 296 Aragon Ave in Coral Gables (☎ 442-4408). The shops are host to visiting authors, discussions, poetry readings and, in Miami Beach, there's even a café. They have excellent selections of literature, fiction and Florida-related books. They're open Monday to Thursday 10 am to 10 pm, Friday and Saturday 10 am to midnight, Sunday 10 am to 9 pm. There's an open poetry-reading night the last Friday of the month, which alternates between the Coral Gables and South Beach shops; they start at 7.30 pm and run until closing time.

Books by Us (☎ 532-6011) at 1665 Michigan Ave opened just as we went to press. The concept is great: books and readings by local writers in an intimate shop/café. We hope it works out.

A good place in downtown Miami is the Downtown Book Center (☎ 377-9938) at 215 NE 2nd Ave, which has a good selection of books and . . . will coincidences never cease? lots of Lonely Planet books.

Other than those, there are Waldenbooks and B Dalton Books at most shopping malls, and a Borders (☎ 935-4712) at 19925 Biscayne Blvd, in Aventura, with a café and an enormous Florida selection.

Gay & Lesbian Bookstores The Gay Emporium (☎ 534-4763) at 720 Lincoln Road sells gay and lesbian literature, as well as postcards, gifts, flags, magazines, condoms and leather, and they rent videos (two nights for $2.69). It's a good gay information source as well. The staff is very helpful and friendly. Sunday through Thursday 11 am to 10 pm, Friday and Saturday 11 am to 11 pm. Lambda Passages (☎ 754-6900) way north at 7545 Biscayne Blvd sells gay and lesbian books and videos.

Periodicals & Foreign Press The News Cafe (☎ 538-6397) at 800 Ocean Drive has a separate 24-hour newsstand between the restaurant and the bar. They've got a good selection of international (from countries considered to be fashionable) and domestic press, and some paperbacks.

You can get dailies from practically every Spanish-speaking country at a couple of places: in downtown Miami, try the one that sets up just across the street from the Gusman Center for the Performing Arts at 174 E Flagler St, and the larger more permanent one at the corner of SE 1st St and SE 2nd Ave.

Cameras & Photography

For equipment, we found that the salespeople at Wolf Camera & Video (☎ 931-5839) in the Omni International Mall (see Shopping Malls, above) were honest and the prices weren't bad, even though the selection isn't absolutely massive.

Of the many places to develop and buy film in the area, we think that the best are on Miami Beach: Tropicolor at 1442 Alton Rd (☎ 672-3729) and 1657 Washington Ave (☎ 538-1183), and LIB Color Labs (☎ 538-5600) at 851 Washington Ave. The Dark Room (☎ 532-2185) at 1024 Lincoln Road is a professional-oriented lab very popular with the modeling set.

Cell Phones & Beepers

Anyone who's anyone in Miami has a cellular telephone, and you can rent one as easily as you buy a soda from a soda machine. That's right, there are cell phone rental *vending machines* in many airport car rental offices. There are also cell phone rental places in larger hotels. You should make certain that you only have to pay for air time (not equipment rental), and find out if there's a daily minimum – it's usually about three minutes. Note that airtime on rentals is far more expensive than on normal cell phones – count on about $1.25 to $2 a minute on local and incoming calls, and much more for long distance outgoing calls.

Beepers are a good way to stay reachable, and there are literally hundreds of shops selling them. You can buy a reconditioned basic Motorola pager (beeps, vibrates and holds seven numbers) for about $25 to 30, but you can spend much more than that on flashier models. Count on an average of $12 a month for the airtime.

Cosmetics

South Beach Make-up (☎ 538-0805) at 439 Española Way has mostly natural make-up, essential oils, soaps, etc – sort of a less activistic Body Shop.

It may be expensive, but the best selection of soaps from around the world, cosmetics, beauty and skin products, shower gels and wooden combs is Brownes & Co Apothecary (☎ 532-8703) at 841 Lincoln Road. They also do make-up lessons and analyze skin and hair problems. It's sort of like walking into the 1980s.

Eyeglasses & Contact Lens Supplies

You can get saline solution and other contact lens supplies at pharmacies like Eckerd, Walgreens or Lee Ann. There are express optometrist offices in every shopping mall. Pearle Vision Center is probably the largest, with five express shops in town; call ☎ 665-8660 for the closest location to you.

Fashion

The casting directors of *Beverly Hills Cop* must have drafted the guy who played Serge from the staff at Versace Jeans Couture (☎ 532-5993), at 755 Washington Ave, where discerning fashionplates can purchase Fabulous things like a $365 bathrobe or, for those with more meager budgets, a pair of blue jeans for $145. Frighteningly friendly staff may offer you an 'issprayso widda leetle laymon tweest, you'll lahk it, ah make it mahself.'

Not to be outdone, Armani has his own A|X Armani Exchange (☎ 531-5900) at 760 Collins Ave, with similarly priced merchandise.

Betsey Johnson has two shops in the area: one at 805 Washington Ave (☎ 673-0023) and another at 3117 Commodore Plaza in Coconut Grove. These sell hugely popular womens clothing – some pieces are so revealing that they may as well be ribbons with pockets.

Flowers

Flora Flora (☎ 672-5075), an outdoor stand run by a very friendly English guy, has reasonably priced large plants, flowers and pots. It's at 1520 Lenox Ave (behind Blockbuster Video), open Tuesday to Saturday 10 am to 6 pm.

Frugal Flowers (☎ 534-1159) at 1330 Collins Ave was closed when we visited; through the window it looked cute, they have different flowers every day, the price list is posted in the window and they also sell candle holders, cards and plant pots.

Designs by Rodney (☎ 673-4233, 800-754-9598) at 1623 Michigan Ave has natural flower baskets and they even do edible flower arrangements. Open Monday to Thursday 10 am to 9.30 pm, Friday, Saturday and Sunday 10 am to 11 pm.

Flowers & Flowers (☎ 534-1633) at 925 Lincoln Road has hands down the best selection of exotic flowers, and does the best arrangements, on the beach. But, uh, they're also by far the most expensive. But this is the place to come to get an arrangement that will impress a date, and it's always nice to walk in here and look, even if you're not buying.

Food & Drink

For a (somewhat) moderately priced picnic of extraordinary delights, hit two shops on Alton Rd: the grand gourmet hangout Epicure Market (☎ 672-1861) at No 1656 for some of their excellent delicatessen items, prepared Italian sauces and pasta dishes (they'll heat them up for you if you want) for $5 to 8, and then up the street a block or so to Biga Bakery (☎ 538-3335) at No 1710, where you can choose from some of the best bread in the USA – rosemary reggiano ($7.50), their incredible onion rye ($4.75) and heavenly black olive ($6.25). The prices are a bit high but the loaves are large and delicious.

There are only a couple of choices in real, honest-to-goodness American-style supermarkets in the local area. On Miami Beach there's a somewhat gigantic Publix (☎ 538-7250) that's been transported from the 1950s to 1045 Dade Blvd; there's also a pretty good Hyde Park Market open 24 hours at the corner of 5th St and Collins Ave. There are Publix, Winn-Dixies and Hyde Park markets scattered all over the area and the state.

For natural foods, the huge 5th St Natural Food Market in South Beach (☎ 535-9050) was in the process of opening when we were researching, probably worth checking out; it's at 1011 5th St at Michigan Ave. We liked the smaller but still well-stocked Apple A Day Food Market (☎ 538-4560) at 1534 Alton Rd, which has a good selection of oils and homeopathic cures and a good prepared food section as well.

Gifts & Knickknacks

Fabulous (☎ 532-1856) at 1251 Washington Ave has postcards, gifts, wrapping paper, picture frames and balloons; it's a nice place if the service doesn't get snooty.

Beachwear (☎ 538-3310) at 1602 Washington Ave has recycled Levi's, army surplus stuff and, for a neat gift idea, US license plates for $10.99. Details (☎ 672-0175), 1149 Washington Ave, is a knickknack store with somewhat eclectic stuff (jewelry, gifts, furniture, scent oils, etc) and free gift wrapping. They have another location at 1031 Lincoln Road (☎ 531-1325) with more furniture; both are open Monday to Friday 1 to 10 pm, Saturday 1 to 11 pm and Sunday 1 to 9 pm.

Studio Russo (☎ 534-3711) at 417 Española Way is one of our favorite shops on the Beach – actually it's an art gallery. Michael Russo is an artist who works with recycled rubbish, turning it into really creative works like scary faces in paper bags and a tremendous sculpture in the window that's just got to be seen to be believed. Russo sells most of the works in his place, and you can get something for under $20.

Ba-BaLú! (☎ 538-0679) at 432 Española Way, has a very eclectic collection of Cuban mementos, including postcards showing air routes between Miami and Havana, cigar box labels, concert posters, and a limited collection of music CDs.

Sunglass Hut (☎ 674-9977) at 948 Ocean Drive has a great selection of high quality sunglasses (all name brand) at very good prices, even for the States.

Motorcycles

Each year, hundreds of Europeans come to Miami Beach to buy Harley Davidsons at significant savings over buying them back home, even when including shipping charges. But the Beach is probably not the best place to do it: though selection is good, prices are higher than if you bought the bike somewhere else in the USA that's less fashionable – if you can get to another city you can probably do better. If not, Wings of Steel (☎ 672-4294) at 280 Española Way specializes in Harley sales and export. For other types of motorcycles, check out the *Pennysaver*, or classified advertising in the *Miami Herald*.

Music

Y & T Music (☎ 534-8704) at 1614 Alton Rd has records (can you believe it), tapes and CDs; used CDs are $7.99, music magazines are also available, Monday and Tuesday noon to 8 pm, Wednesday to Saturday noon to 9 pm and Sunday 1 to 7 pm.

Used CDs & Records (☎ 673-3293) at 1622 Alton Rd, is open Monday to Saturday noon to 8 pm, Sunday noon to

6 pm; all used CDs are $7.99 or less. This one is smaller but friendlier. Boom Records (☎ 531-2666) at 1205 Washington Ave has knowledgeable staff and a very good selection of new and used CDs.

Spec's Music (☎ 592-7288) has almost 20 record supershops around Miami and the Beach with a good selection of CDs and a smaller one of cassettes. They're pretty much the Tower Records of Miami right now.

Power Records has two locations: 1419 Calle Ocho (☎ 285-2212) in Little Havana, and 1549 Washington Ave (☎ 531-1138) on South Beach. Both have great selections of Latin, salsa, rhumba, Cuban and South American music at decent prices. Do Re Mi Music Center (☎ 541-3374) at 1829 Calle Ocho has a good selection of Latin cassettes, records, CDs and musical instruments.

Extremes Music (☎ 534-2003) at 513-15 Lincoln Road has a good selection of Latin, rock, pop, jazz and some classical, as well as some international newspapers.

Borders (☎ 935-4712) at 19925 Biscayne Blvd in Aventura has a good selection of pop, rock, jazz and classical music in this book superstore. There's also a café.

Adults Only

While Condomania of South Beach (☎ 531-7872), 758 Washington Ave, has many sex-related items like funky and functional condoms (glow in the dark, ribbed, spiraled, tickler-ed, extra large or just something so you'll have a different color every day), it's not a sex shop in that they don't sell any sex toys (other than a few vibrators) per se.

Given the amount of outrageous sexual openness and lewd behavior you'll witness on South Beach even when, say, walking to the store, it's surprising that real sex shops are very hard to come by in this neck of the woods. There's one on 15th St, just west of Washington Ave, but in the year we lived on the beach we never saw it open even once. We saw another one way up past the Aventura Mall, opposite the Circuit City that's at 20669 Biscayne Blvd. It sells videos and adult toys. For gay and lesbian videos, check out the Gay Emporium in Gay & Lesbian Bookstores, above, or New Concept Video (☎ 674-1111) at 749 Lincoln Road, which has gay, foreign, Japanese animation and XXX movies as well. And if you didn't come prepared, they'll even rent you a video player for $9 a night with a $150 deposit. ■

New Age

Sweet Earth Medicine (☎ 538-0927) is a healing arts center in the heart of South Beach with a very good selection of books, oils, crystals, CDs and cassettes. They also hold a range of classes and meetings throughout the week. Call for an appointment.

The Age of Innocence (☎ 673-8119) at 406 16th St has books, oils, crystals, cards and incense. They're open Monday to Friday 11 am to 9 pm and Sunday 11 am to 7 pm.

Versani (☎ 674-9595) doesn't really belong in this category, but it's a very nice, calm and peaceful place that has tons of jewelry, and also sarongs, little boxes, candles, etc – it smells very good in here. It's at 201 11th St.

New & Used Clothing

The Beach is a great place to buy cheap used clothing. Try one of the two Recycled Blues locations at 1507 Washington Ave (☎ 538-0656) and 945 Lincoln Road (☎ 531-0349), which have used Levi's jeans for $12, shorts for $8 and jackets at $20.

South Beach USA (☎ 674-0075) at 923 Lincoln Road sells really comfortable and soft cotton shirts, plus T-shirts and other really nice stuff. Very friendly owners and a good selection.

If you're female, Meet Me in Miami (☎ 538-8780) at 233 12th St is *the* place to get that ultimate SoBe outfit: glitzy plastic, piggy pink and polyester – they've got it all.

Mars (☎ 673-8040) at 1035 Washington Ave sells contemporary American clothing – Corinna really likes their colorful dresses ($40 to 140); men's shirts are around $60 and they also have sunglasses, backpacks and watches.

Miami Surf Style II (☎ 532-6928) at 421 Lincoln Road is great for cheap jeans, hats and T-shirts. Motor Oil (☎ 673-1968) at 530 Lincoln Road does Calvin Klein Jeans for $38, and a lot of other colorful but not totally unique new clothing. And Deco Denim (☎ 532-6986) at 645 Collins Ave has Levi's from $20, Ray Bans for about $60.

Photocopies

The Mail Boxes Etc (☎ 538-5076) in the Blockbuster Plaza at 1521 Alton Rd, has excellent self-service photocopiers, including color and large-scale copies, as well as the standard shipping, mailing and mailbox services.

In downtown Miami, Office Depot (☎ 372-3311) at 100 NE 1st St has a full-service copy shop in its basement as well as self-serve copiers; and south of the Brickell

Ave Bridge, Kinko's Copies (☎ 373-4910) is a copy supercenter open 24 hours a day at 600 Brickell Ave.

Piercing & Tattoos

Everyone and their dog in Miami Beach seems to have a tattoo, and while piercing isn't as popular here as it is in some other large cities, Beach piercers can put a pin through it with the best of them. Piercing is available, of course, at many jewelry stores in the area, but that's for ears, right? Bejeweled noses, eyebrows, lips and tongues are frequently seen, and nipples and navels are the most popular 'below the neck' piercings, though men can consider a half a dozen ways of putting a pin through their genitals. If you want to learn more, pick up a magazine called *PFIQ*, Piercing Fans International Quarterly. There aren't so many genital possibilities for women, but for the very brave a clitoral piercing is possible.

Tattoos by Lou (☎ 532-7300) at 231 14th St is probably the most famous place on the beach for tattooing, and it's been here the longest. You have to be at least 18 years old (bring your ID). They're open Monday to Thursday noon to 1 am, Friday and Saturday noon to 2 am, Sunday noon to midnight.

Art Attack (☎ 531-4556) at 1344 Washington Ave does tattoos and body piercing ($50 minimum). They're very friendly, seem to have experience (one rather dreads the word 'oops' during a clitoral piercing) and definitely have clean equipment. They're open Sunday through Thursday noon to midnight, Friday and Saturday till 2 am.

South Beach Tattoo Company (☎ 538-0104), 861 Washington Ave, also offers body piercing and tattoos for a minimum of $50, and they have a good selection of T-shirts that sell for $15. They're open Monday to Thursday noon to midnight, Friday and Saturday noon to 2 am and Sunday noon to 10 pm.

Excursions

CRUISES

The Port of Miami is the largest cruise ship port in the world, with over three million passengers a year. You can find anything from daytrips to top-end round-the-world voyages, with a whole spectrum in between, including the very common three-day Bahamas cruises, and four-day to one-week trips to ports of call like San Juan, Puerto Rico, St Thomas, St John and St Martin. Ships leave from the Port of Miami Cruise Passenger Terminals on Dodge Island.

Rates change almost daily, and there are any number of discounts that apply – even quoted fares when you call are subject to discounts just for the asking . . . so ask. Port charges are not included in most of these prices.

The major cruise operators include:

Carnival Cruise Lines
The most popular line, it does three-night tours on the *Ecstasy* from Friday to Monday to Nassau, Bahamas; an inside cabin (category four) was at the time of research $449, or suites from $879. A four-night cruise (from Thursday to Saturday) on the

KENNETH DREYFUSS

NICK SELBY

When you're bored of the deckside pools, you can always take a dip in the jambalaya.

Fantasy to the Bahamas starts at $399 for an inside cabin, $869 for a suite. (☎ 599-2600)

Norwegian Cruise Line

Three-night tours aboard the *Leeward* to the Bahamas run from $329 to 1189; four-night voyages to Mexico run from $449 to 1439. (☎ 447-9660)

Royal Caribbean Cruise Line

Three-night Bahamas weekends on the *Nordic Empress* run from $629 to 1869; a four-night cruise is $779 to 2029 and the seven-night Eastern Caribbean aboard the *Grandeur of the Seas* is $1399 to 3999. (☎ 539-6573)

Discovery Cruise Line

This line does one-day cruises out of Miami for $75 (standard), $90 (superior), $100 (double) or $135 (suite) to the Bahamas; they leave on Monday, Tuesday and Thursday to Saturday on the *Discovery Sun*. Cruise times vary; their casino (which is why most are here) usually opens 45 minutes after departure. You can also do a 'cruise 'n' stay package' for one to four nights; rates here are $99 to 309 depending on location and nights. (☎ 467-5777)

THE EVERGLADES

☎ area code 941 west of Shark Valley
☎ area code 305 Shark Valley and east

The second-largest US national park (after Yellowstone) and largest subtropical wilderness in the continental USA, the Everglades is a unique and delicate ecosystem made up of swamps and marshes at the southern tip of the Florida peninsula.

Though the threat to the Everglades is very real (see below), it is an absolutely spectacular place to get into the real nature of South Florida. In the park you'll see an amazing variety of flora & fauna. From the brackish waters of the mangrove and cypress swamps, to hardwood hammocks, sawgrass flats, Dade County pinelands and marshes to fascinating creatures like crocodiles and alligators, bottle-nosed dolphins, manatees, snowy egrets, bald eagles and ospreys, there is simply no place in the entire world like the Everglades.

Whether you just visit for an afternoon at the Main Visitor Center west of Florida City, take the Shark Valley

High Season & AAAHHH Season

The Everglades' seasons can be described as the dry season (roughly November to May), and the mosquitoes & no-see-ums (so called because of their disturbing tinyness in size and hugeness in biting power) season, which is the rest of the time. While the park is open year round, the best time to visit is in the dry season. ■

Tram Tour or get full into the canoeing and free camping possibilities in the 10,000 Islands and along the Wilderness Waterway, we can't urge you enough to come here.

History & Ecology

The Calusa Indians called the area Pa-Hay-Okee, or grassy water. Marjory Stoneman Douglas called it the River of Grass, but says in her book that Gerard de Brahm, a surveyor, named it River Glades, which on later English maps became Ever Glades.

The Everglades is a 'sheet-flow ecosystem', beginning at the Kissimmee River, which empties into Lake Okeechobee, which, before humankind's meddling, overflowed and sent sheets of water through the Everglades and finally into the Gulf of Mexico. The resulting ecosystem was home to thousands of species of flora, and wildlife flourished, including wading birds, amphibians, reptiles and mammals.

Enter business. Sugar growers, attracted by muck as they are, swarmed into the area and pressured the government to make the land available to them. In 1905, Florida Governor Napoleon Bonaparte Broward personally dug the first shovelful of dirt out of what would become one of the largest and most singularly destructive diversions of water in the world. The Caloosahatchee River was diverted and connected to Lake Okeechobee; hundreds of canals were dug directly through the Everglades to the coastline in order to 'reclaim' land. The flow of water from the lake had been restricted by a series of dikes, and farmland began to sprout up in previously uninhabited areas.

Efforts to save the Everglades were begun as early as the late 1920s, but they were put on the back burner by the Depression. In 1926 and 1928, two major hurricanes allowed Okeechobee to break free and the resulting floods killed hundreds, so the Army Corps of Engineers came in and did a *really* good job of damming the lake – the Hoover Dike was constructed.

What the farming was doing was a) diverting the fresh water desperately needed by nature in the Everglades, and b) producing fertilizer-rich waste water that created explosions in growth of foliage, which clogs waterways and further complicates matters. And with all the chemicals and other crud we're pouring into the Glades and local waters, the Florida aquifer, the source of Florida's fresh water supply, is in great danger of being contaminated. Autopsies of local animals, including Florida panthers, have shown that mercury levels are extremely high.

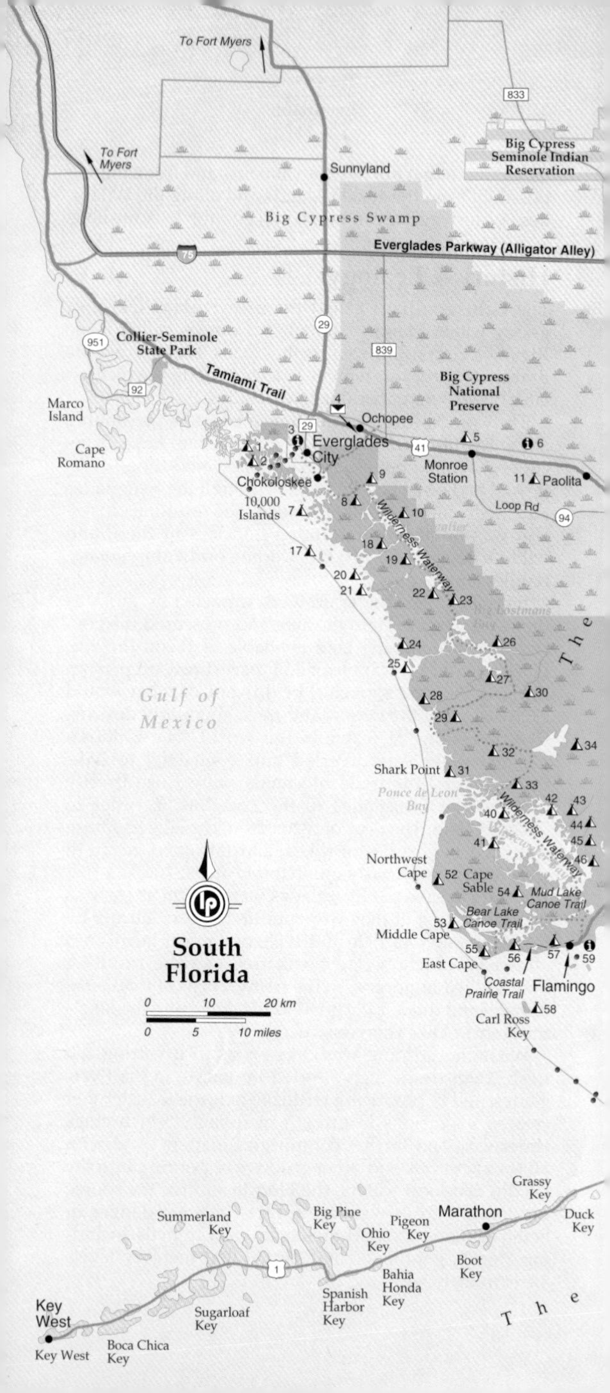

To Fort Myers
To Fort Myers
833
Big Cypress Seminole Indian Reservation
Sunnyland
Big Cypress Swamp
Everglades Parkway (Alligator Alley)
75
29
951
Collier-Seminole State Park
839
Big Cypress National Preserve
Tamiami Trail
92
Marco Island
Cape Romano
Ochopee
Everglades City
Chokoloskee
10,000 Islands
Monroe Station
Paolita
Loop Rd
94
41
Wilderness Waterway
Gulf of Mexico
Shark Point
Ponce de Leon Bay
Northwest Cape
Cape Sable
Mud Lake Canoe Trail
Bear Lake Canoe Trail
Middle Cape
East Cape
Coastal Prairie Trail
Flamingo
Carl Ross Key
South Florida
0 10 20 km
0 5 10 miles
Grassy Key
Summerland Key
Big Pine Key
Pigeon Key
Marathon
Duck Key
Ohio Key
Boot Key
Bahia Honda Key
Spanish Harbor Key
Sugarloaf Key
Key West
Key West
Boca Chica Key
1
The
The

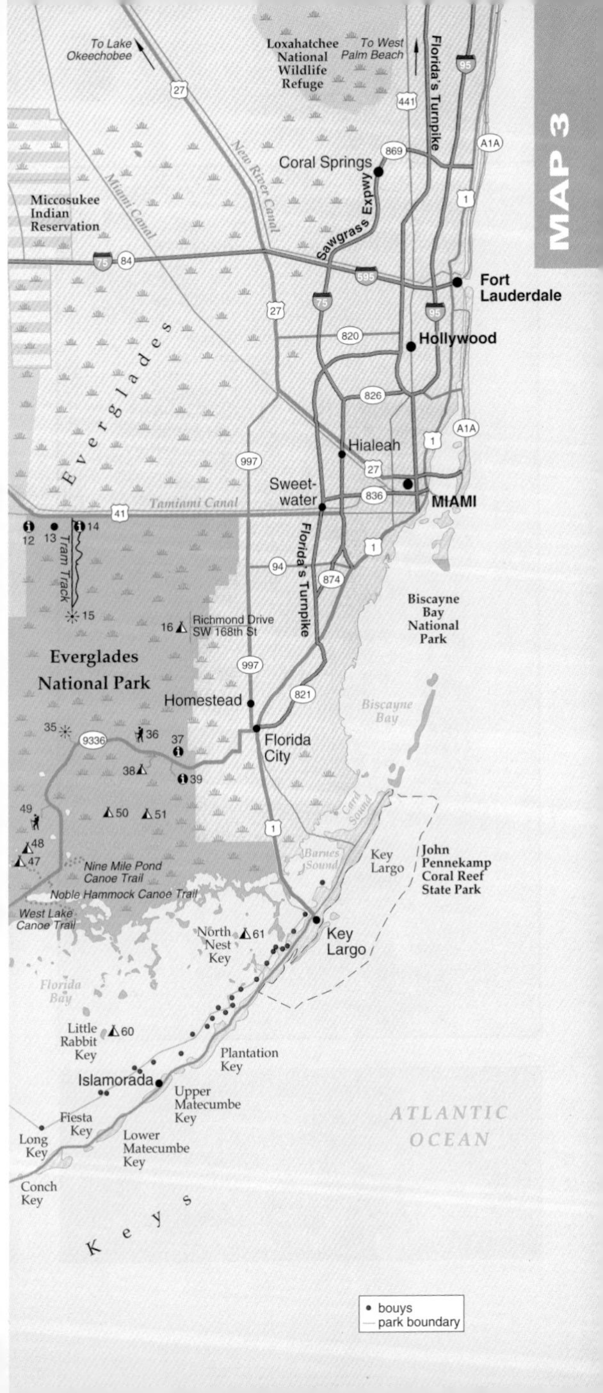
MAP 3
To Lake Okeechobee
Loxahatchee National Wildlife Refuge
To West Palm Beach
Florida's Turnpike
Coral Springs
Sawgrass Expwy
Miccosukee Indian Reservation
Miami Canal
New River Canal
Fort Lauderdale
Hollywood
Everglades
Hialeah
Sweet-water
MIAMI
Tamiami Canal
Tram Track
Richmond Drive SW 168th St
Biscayne Bay National Park
Everglades National Park
Homestead
Florida City
Biscayne Bay
Card Sound
Barnes Sound
Key Largo
John Pennekamp Coral Reef State Park
Nine Mile Pond Canoe Trail
Noble Hammock Canoe Trail
West Lake Canoe Trail
North Nest Key
Florida Bay
Little Rabbit Key
Plantation Key
Islamorada
Upper Matecumbe Key
Fiesta Key
Long Key
Lower Matecumbe Key
Conch Key
Keys
ATLANTIC OCEAN
bouys
park boundary

CAMPGROUNDS

1	Tiger Key
2	Picnic Key
5	Monument Lake
7	Rabbit Key
8	Lopez River
9	Sunday Bay Chickee
10	Sweetwater Bay Chickee
11	Midway
16	Chekika
17	Pavilion Key
18	The Watson Place
19	Darwin's Place
20	Mormon Key
21	New Turkey Key & Turkey Key
22	Plate Creek Bay Chickee
23	Lostmans Five Bay
24	Hog Key
25	South Lostmans
26	Willy Willy
27	Roger's River Bay Chickee
28	Highland Beach
29	Broad River
30	Camp Lonesome
31	Graveyard Creek
32	Harney River Chickee
33	Shark River Chickee
34	Cane Patch
38	Long Pine Key
40	Oyster Bay Chickee
41	Joe River Chickee
42	Watson River Chickee
43	North River Chickee
44	Robert's River Chickee
45	Lane Bay Chickee
46	Hells Bay Chickee
47	Lard Can
48	Pearl Bay Chickee
50	Old Ingraham
51	Ernest Coe
52	Northwest Cape
53	Middle Cape
54	South Joe River Chickee
55	East Cape
56	Clubhouse Beach
57	Eco Pond
58	Carl Ross Key
60	Little Rabbit Key
61	North Nest Key

OTHER

3	Gulf Coast Visitor Center
4	Ochopee Post Office
6	Big Cypress National Preserve Visitor Center
12	Tamiami Ranger Station
13	Miccosukee Cultural Center
14	Shark Valley Visitor Center & Trails
15	Shark Valley Observation Tower
35	Pay-hay-okee Overlook
36	Pinelands Trailhead
37	Main Visitor Center
39	Royal Palm Visitor Center
49	Mahogony Hammock Trailhead
59	Flamingo Visitor Center

KENNETH DREYFUSS

Through the efforts of conservationists and prominent citizens, notably Douglas, the Everglades was declared a national park in 1947, but the threat to the Everglades is far from over. Pollution running into the area from industry and farming in the north is killing foliage and because of the diversion of the area's water, salt water from the Gulf of Mexico is flowing deeper into the park than ever before. There are 16 endangered and five threatened species of animals within the park.

Information

The main points of entry to the park all have visitors centers where you can get maps, camping permits and information from rangers. The **Gulf Coast Visitor Center** (☎ 695-3311), on Hwy 29, is the northwesternmost ranger station, and provides access to the 10,000 Islands area. The **Shark Valley Visitor Center** (☎ 221-8455) is just off the Tamiami Trail (US Hwy 41). The **Main Visitor Center** (☎ 242-7700) and the **Royal Palm Visitor Center** (same ☎) are both off Hwy 9336 just inside the eastern border of the park, about 20 miles from Florida City. The last visitor center is the **Flamingo Visitor Center** (☎ 695-3094) on the park's southern coast.

Regulations

All the resources in the park are protected, including the plants, shells, artifacts and buildings. You can fish, but only with a state fishing license; check with the ranger stations for more information. Free permits, available at the ranger stations, are required for all overnight stays. In areas that do not have toilets, you'll need to dig a hole at least six inches deep to bury waste. Campfires are prohibited except at several beach sites: use dead and down wood only, and build below the high-tide line. Remove all your garbage from the park when you leave.

Planning a Trip

Books & Maps For all trips, you can work out specific itineraries with the assistance of the rangers, and the *Backcountry Trip Planner* guide to the park published by the NPS. Dennis Kalma's *Boat & Canoe Camping in the Everglades Backcountry and Ten Thousand Island Region* (Florida Flair Books, Miami) is an excellent guide to trails. For nature information and identification, the rangers themselves use *Florida's Fabulous Birds* by W Williams; *Florida's Fabulous Reptiles & Amphibians*; the National Geographic's *Field Guide to Birds of North*

America; and *Peterson Field Guide to the Birds* by Roger Tory Peterson.

The Gulf Coast Ranger Station sells the charts you'll need while canoeing in the 10,000 Islands (National Oceanic & Atmospheric Administration (NOAA)'s *Coast & Geodetic Survey*): paper is $14.86, waterproof (we recommend this) $16.91 including tax. See the Everglades map for the correct chart for the region you intend to visit.

What to Bring Things you'll need to bring for individual canoe trips (obviously the overnight stuff is only if you plan to camp) include:

- good, sightable compass and/or GPS (Global Positioning System)
- good flashlight (we like Petzl headlamps and Mini Mag brands)
- nautical charts & tide chart
- tent with no-see-um – not just mosquito – netting
- sleeping bag
- one gallon of water per person per day
- as much food as you'll need plus an extra day
- a solid plastic sealable cooler, like a Coleman or Eskimo – *not* Styrofoam – for food storage
- portable cooking stove, pot and utensils
- Avon Skin So Soft or industrial-strength insect repellent like REI Jungle Juice
- sunscreen, sunglasses and a hat
- strong plastic garbage bag
- biodegradable toilet paper and a small spade to dig waste pit
- binoculars (to see route markers) and camera
- dry change of clothes for *when* you fall in the water
- good shoes or boots

Camping

Three types of campsites are available at no cost with a reservation from the Gulf Coast Ranger Station (☎ 695-3311): beach sites, on coastal shell beaches and in the 10,000 Islands; ground sites, along the interior bays and rivers, which are basically mounds of dirt built up above the mangroves; and chickees, wooden platforms built above water on which you can pitch a free-standing (no spikes) tent.

Chickees, which have toilets, are the most civilized of the three, and certainly are unique: there's such serenity inherent in sleeping on what feels like a raft levitating above the water in the middle of a natural wonder. We found the beach sites to be most comfortable, though in all three biting insects – like mosquitoes and no-see-ums are rife, even in winter. The ground sites tend to be the most bug-infested of all.

Canoe Rentals

There are rental outfits at Everglades City and Flamingo. In Everglades City, we recommend North American Canoe Tours (NACT; ☎ 695-3299) at the Ivey House Hotel, 107 Camilla St, which rents out first-rate canoes for $20 for the first day, $18 each additional day, or $16 for eight hours; Sea Lion kayaks for $35 a day, or Sea Lions with rudders and upgraded paddles (which make going against the current a whole lot easier) for $45 a day. NACT has a representative office at Glades Haven Recreational Resort, 800 SE Copeland Ave, right across the street from the Gulf Coast Ranger Station.

A good deal they have is a shuttle service for those willing to make the five-day trip between the Gulf Coast and Flamingo Ranger Stations: for a $140 fee NACT will drive your car to Flamingo; when you arrive, turn in the canoe or kayak to the dockmaster, who will give you the keys to your car, and you can drive away. It is possible to work out a shuttle schedule for a Flamingo to Everglades City trip, but you'll need to negotiate that with NACT.

Just next to Glades Haven, Huron Kayak Adventures (☎ 695-3666) rents canoes for $15 for eight hours, $20 a day, and sea kayaks for $20/35.

Everglades National Park Boat Tours (☎ 695-2591) in the Gulf Coast Visitor Center, is most expensive for overnights: it's $18 from 8.30 am to 5 pm or $36 for an overnight rental. They'll take your car to Flamingo for $150.

At the Flamingo Lodge Marina & Outpost Resort (☎ 695-3101, 800-600-3813) TW Recreational Services rents canoes for $22 for four hours, $27 for eight and $30 for overnight. They also rent kayaks – a single is $25/40, a double is $35/50, no overnights on kayaks. They rent bicycles as well for $2.75 an hour, $7.75 for four hours, $13 for eight and $16 overnight.

Dangers & Annoyances

NICK SELBY

The main dangers you'll encounter will be weather and insects. Thunderstorms and lightning are more common in the summer – but in summer the insects are so bad you won't want to be out here anyway. In emergency weather, rangers will search for registered campers. But note that, under ordinary circumstances, unless rangers receive a call from someone saying you're missing, they will not keep track of campers. If you're camping, have a friend or family member ready to contact rangers if you do not report back by a certain day.

Mosquitoes are about half of the insect problem – and in summer the Everglades would appear to be the world's central mosquito manufacturing facility. The other half is made up handily at dawn and dusk by the insidious no-see-ums: tiny (almost invisible) yet ferocious and really God-awful biting insects. Avon Skin So Soft or REI Jungle Juice are key equipment. But note that the insect problem in the dry season isn't so bad.

While alligators are common in the park, they're not very common in the area of the 10,000 Islands, as they tend to avoid salt water. If you do see an alligator, it probably won't bother you, unless you do something overtly threatening or try and angle your boat between it and its young. If you hear an alligator make a high-pitched squeal, get the hell out of Dodge – that's a call to other alligators when a young gator is in danger. Finally, never, ever, *ever* feed an alligator – it's stupid, selfish and illegal. See Dangers & Annoyances in the Facts for the Visitor chapter for more information.

There are four types of poisonous snakes in the Everglades: diamondback rattlesnake *(Crotalus adamanteus)*, pigmy rattlesnake *(Sistrurus miliarius)*, cottonmouth or water moccasin *(Agkistrodon piscivorus conanti)* that swims along the surface of water, and the hugely

Air Boats & Swamp Buggies

Air boats are flat-bottomed boats that use powerful fans to propel themselves in the water. While they are capable of traveling in very shallow water, they are very loud, and their environmental impact has not been determined. One thing is clear: while air boats in the hands of responsible operators, like naturalists and geologists, have little impact, irresponsible operators can cause lots of direct and collateral damage to the surrounding wildlife.

Swamp buggies are enormous balloon-tired vehicles that can go through swamps. They definitely cause rutting and damage wildlife.

You'll be offered air boat and swamp buggy rides at stands all along US Hwy 41. Please assess the motive behind the operator's existence before just getting on a 'nature' tour: you may be helping to disturb the Everglades' delicate balance. ■

colorful coral snake *(Elaps fulvius)*. Wear long, thick socks and lace up boots and keep the hell away from them.

Less dangerous but very annoying are raccoons and rats who will tear through anything less than a solid and sealed plastic cooler to get to your food. Keep your food and food garbage inside the sealed cooler, and your water bottles sealed and inside your tent (open water can be smelled through your tent and the last thing you want at 4 am is a raccoon slashing through your sleeping bag in search of a sip).

10,000 Islands

We think that the finest way to experience the serenity and unique beauty – which is at the same time desolate and lush, tropical yet foreboding – of the Everglades is by canoeing or kayaking through the excellent network of waterways that skirt the southwest portion of the reserve.

The 10,000 Islands are made up of a lot (but not really 10,000) of tiny islands and mangrove swamp that hug the point of the southwesternmost border of Florida's peninsula. On the habitable islands, the US National Park Service allows free camping. These islands offer some amazing opportunities to enjoy the Everglades on an intimate basis.

Most of the islands are fringed by narrow beaches with sugar-white sand, though note that in most of the area, the water is brackish, not clear, and very shallow – it's not Tahiti, but it is a fascinating area. The best part is that you can get your own island for up to a week for nothing. That's right, free.

The **Wilderness Waterway**, a 99-mile path between Everglades City and Flamingo, is the largest canoe trail in the area, but there are shorter canoe trails as well, near Flamingo (see below).

Near Everglades City at the park's northwest border, you can take a downstream trip on the **Turner River** alone or with a group, and make it either an easy with-the-current drift to Chokoloskee Island, or add a bit of a challenge at the end and go upstream in the boating canal to the Gulf Coast (Everglades City) Ranger Station. You can also canoe around the 10,000 Islands for any period of time you wish, and we highly recommend it!

Suggested Itineraries Note that despite what it says on Everglades National Park maps, Comer Key is permanently closed – it washed away in 1995. Getting around in the 10,000 Islands is pretty straightforward if you religiously adhere to the NOAA charts, and rangers will help you develop an itinerary based on what you'd most like to see. For all these journeys, it is absolutely imperative that you have a nautical chart and a tide chart (see Books & Maps, above). Going against the tides is the fastest way to make it a miserable trip.

For an easy day of paddling around the islands, just get a boat and cross the bay from the Gulf Coast Ranger Station and out and around the mangroves.

For an easy overnight, or two-night, trip, you'll be wanting the islands closest to the ranger station: Tiger, Picnic, Rabbit, New Turkey, Turkey and Hog Keys, all with beach campsites.

For a nice few days (three to four) of canoeing, head south from the Gulf Coast Ranger Station, past Chokoloskee and up the Lopez River, north near Sunday Bay, then southeast to Sweetwater Bay, where you spend the night at the chickee there; the next morning head out towards The Watson Place and southwest to Pavilion Key for a second overnight at the beach campsite; then north to Rabbit Key for a final night on the beach; in the morning, head back north to the Gulf Coast Ranger Station.

There are literally hundreds of other combinations; see the rangers for more information.

Organized Tours Rangers lead free 5½-hour canoe trips through the overhanging mangrove tunnels along the Turner River on many Saturdays during the dry season. They leave the Gulf Coast Ranger Station at 9 am. David Harraden's NACT (see Canoe Rentals above) is the best outfit in the whole park for regular guided tours. For $40 per person, you can get a guided canoe trip down the Turner River, including an excellent lunch. The tours start daily at 9 am and return at 3 pm. You can also get day tours from NACT within the 10,000 Islands for about the same price.

For longer excursions, though, it gets very expensive: a four-day, three-night camping journey through the islands is $450 per person.

The simplest of all is a **boat tour** from Everglades National Park Boat Tours (☎ 695-2591, 800-445-7724). Tours on the large pleasure boats leave from the dock in front of the Gulf Coast Ranger Station in Everglades City from December 20 to April 15 aboard the *Panther I* (at 9 and 11 am and 1 and 3 pm); *Panther II* (10 am, noon, 1.30 and 3.30 pm); *Manatee I* (9.30 and 11.30 am and 1.30 and 3.30 pm) and *Manatee II* (10.30 am, 12.30 and 2.30 pm, and a special two-hour sunset tour at 5 pm in December and early January). From April 15 to December 20, boats leave the dock every half hour between 9.30 am and 5 pm. All tours (except the special sunset tour) are

KIM GRANT

Ochopee Post Office, the smallest in the USA

KENNETH DREYFUSS

Boardwalk at Pa-hay-okee Overlook

KENNETH DREYFUSS

Don't be fooled: it's the oldest trick in the book.

1¾ hours through the 10,000 Islands. The cost is $11.66 for adults, $5.83 for children aged six to 12 including tax. A Mangrove Wilderness tour costs $14.84/7.42.

Getting There & Away By far the easiest and cheapest way to get out here is by car; Greyhound only serves Naples, about 25 miles north of the Gulf Coast Visitor Center. Take the Tamiami Trail (US Hwy 41) due west. On the way, you'll pass the **Miccosukee Cultural Center**, a collection of tourist shops and pointless, inhumane alligator wrestling displays tended by morose and insolent staff, and the entrance to the **Big Cypress National Preserve**. For a nice but time-consuming detour, take a left turn just past the Tamiami Ranger Station onto **Loop Rd**, an unpaved trail through the southern section of Big Cypress National Preserve. It will take you about an hour and a half for the loop, which ends at Monroe Station. Further west there's a picnic area at **Kirby Storter Roadside Park**, and probably the brightest attraction on the way, the **Ochopee US Post Office**, the USA's smallest – it's about the size of an outhouse, and they're used to tourists stopping for photographs. For the cost of a stamp, you can send a postcard or letter from here, though be certain that the postmaster cancels the stamp nicely – some of ours were as smudged as a Russian visa stamp.

Turn south on Hwy 29 to Everglades City; go until you're forced to turn right (you'll see the Captain's Table Hotel & Restaurant in front of you), then make a left at the traffic circle (note the fine city hall building but ignore the not-so-fine Susie's Station restaurant on the right hand side of the street) and follow that road to the ranger station, which will be on the right hand side of the road. The trip from Miami takes a little less than two hours on the Tamiami Trail, 3½ to four if you do Loop Rd.

Shark Valley

At the northern border of the park, accessed just off the Tamiami Trail (US Hwy 41), the Shark Valley Visitor Center (☎ 221-8455) is a very popular way to get yourself easily and painlessly immersed in the middle of the Everglades prairie. You can bike or walk the 17-mile trail between the entrance and the 50-foot-high Shark Valley Observation Tower, which gives a pretty spectacular overview of the park. You will see a lot of flora and fauna – the last time we went there was a 10-foot alligator in the main parking lot, lazily sunning himself with his mouth wide open. We gave him a wide berth. Bicycle rentals (they're one-speeds but the ground is pretty flat) are available from the cash desk in the entrance to the park; the cost is $3.25 per hour including tax, or you can take the Shark Valley Tram Tour, led by rangers or 'experienced tram drivers'; the journey over the paved 15-mile tram road takes two hours. The cost is $8 for adults, $7.20 for seniors over 62 and $4 for children under 12. There's also a park entry fee of $4 per carload or $2 for pedestrians.

The trams leave every hour on the hour between 9 am and 4 pm in high season, and at 9.30 and 11 am and 1 and 3 pm in low season. Reservations are recommended in high season. There's no public transportation to this point. Driving, it's about 18 miles from the western border of the city of Miami, south of the Tamiami Trail.

Main Visitor Center

The Main Visitor Center (☎ 242-7700) for the Everglades Park is just southwest of Homestead, a 30-minute drive from downtown Miami. This is the fastest and easiest way to see the Everglades, or at least some of it, and the visitors center is packed with excellent information on everything in the park. Very close to the entrance, the Royal Palm Visitor Center (same ☎) is the entryway to the three-quarter-mile **Gumbo-Limbo Trail** with gumbo-limbo and royal palm trees, orchids and lush vegetation, and the **Anhinga Trail**, named for the odd anhinga birds (also called the snake bird, for the way it swims with its long neck and head above water), a half-mile route on which you'll probably run into alligators, turtles, waterfowl, lizards, snakes and . . . well, be prepared for anything. You can drive the 30-odd-mile main road that runs between the entrance and Flamingo; along the way are walking trails including: the **Pinelands**, a half-mile trail through Dade County pine forest – look for exposed limestone bedrock; **Pa-hay-okee Overlook**, a very short (quarter-mile) boardwalk trail with an observation tower; **Mahogany Hammock**, a half-mile boardwalk that leads into totally lush and overgrown vegetation; and **West Lake Trail**, a half mile through red, white, buttonwood and black mangroves. The longest series of trails is at **Long Pine Key**, the starting point of a 15-mile series of walking trails that contain many species indigenous to the Everglades, and even the Florida panther.

Admission to the park at this entrance is $5 per carload, or $3 for pedestrians. The main gate is open 24 hours, the Main Visitor Center from 8 am to 4.30 pm daily, Royal Palm Visitor Center from 8 am to 4.15 pm daily. Camping is $8 for tent sites and $10 for RVs and camper vans.

Getting There & Away The only way to do this by public transport is idiotic: you can take Metrorail to Dadeland North ($1.25), then Bus No 1 to the Cutler Ridge Mall ($1.25) and then No 35 or No 70 to Florida City (25¢ transfer). Greyhound serves Florida City three times a day (1½ hours), tickets are $8/16. The last Greyhound out of Florida City leaves at 8.25 pm. But once you're in Florida City still have to get a taxi to the park, which costs at least $10 but up to as much as $20.

By car, which, face it, is how you have to get here, take Florida's Turnpike Extension (toll) or US Hwy 1 to Florida City and take Hwy 9336 to the entrance of the park.

Flamingo

Flamingo, at the southernmost tip of the mainland of the Everglades Park is more developed than the 10,000 Islands, and the least authentic Everglades experience you can get; it's really geared to holidaymakers, with sightseeing and bay cruises. There are nature and bike paths, picnic tables, a bar, tourist trap . . . er . . . gift shops, tram tours, etc, as well as short **canoe trails**, which include West Lake, a one-way 7.7-mile path; Nine Mile Pond, a 5.5-mile circuit; Hells Bay, also a 5.5-mile circuit; Mud Lake, a 5.8-mile loop and Bear Lake, two miles one way.

And in Flamingo, everything's more expensive, including canoe rentals (see Canoe Rentals, above). You can stay in the *Flamingo Lodge* for $72 in low season (May to October), $82 in fringe seasons (October to December and April to May) and $97 in high season. Rooms are all identical, and have two double beds, TV and air conditioning. You can camp at the *campground* here, run by the Flamingo Visitor Center (☎ 695-3094); sites with no hookups are $8 for tents, $10 for RVs.

Entry to Flamingo is through the Main Visitor Center road, Hwy 9336.

THE KEYS & KEY WEST

• *pop Keys: 78,000, Key West: 25,000 ☎ area code 305*

The string of islands to the south of Miami has held a fascination to visitors since the original Spanish landings in the 16th century. But what most people are heading to is Key West. About 90 miles north of Havana, Cuba, Key West is the legendary land of Hemingway, sunset celebrations, Jimmy Buffet's *Margaritaville* and Key Lime Pie.

Early settlers in the Keys grew limes, tamarind and breadfruit; the lower Keys saw pineapple farming, and over on Big Pine Key locals caught and skinned sharks, salted the hides and prepared them for processing into shagreen leather.

In Key West and Islamorada, the non-farming population found a rather unique way of supporting themselves: they became 'Wreckers', salvaging goods from sinking or sunken ships. But these guys weren't pirates – they were federally licensed workers who would work wrecks, bringing the cargo into Key West for auction.

In 1868, cigar makers fleeing Cuba's Ten Years War made Key West into a sort of an 'enlightened masses tobacco combine'. Key West would remain a powerful player in the cigar market until Vicente Martínez Ybor figured out that he could make the stogies for less money (and fewer labor problems) in Tampa, which put an end to Key West as a cigar power. Key West also saw sponge gathering, but tourism – especially after Flagler built his Overseas Highway – became the Keys' main moneymaker and is to this day.

The capital of the Conch Republic (see sidebar), Key West's reputation as a tropical paradise with gorgeous sunsets and sultry nightlife is well-earned. It's gotten overrun by tourists and its conchs have become cynical over the years, but if you look carefully you'll find fleeting images of the Key West of the past: walking through the narrow side streets away from the action along

The Conch Republic

Conchs are people who were born and raised in Key West. It's a difficult title to earn; even after seven years of living here you only rise to the rank of 'freshwater conch'.

You will no doubt hear (and see the flag) of the Conch Republic, and therein lies an interesting tale.

In 1982, the US Border Patrol and US Customs came up with a terrific, they thought, way of catching drug smugglers, illegal aliens and other riff-raff. They erected a roadblock at Key Largo. As traffic jams and anger mounted, many tourists decided they'd just as soon take the Shark Valley Tram in the Everglades, thanks very much, and disappeared.

Enter a bunch of outraged conchs, who came up with the brilliant idea of seceding from the USA. They formed the nation of the Conch Republic, the first act of which was to secede from the USA; the second, to declare war on the USA; and the third, to surrender and request $1 million in foreign aid. ■

Truman Ave or Duval St, you'll see lovely Keys architecture and get a sense of how the locals who aren't there to sell you a T-shirt or book you on a glass-bottomed boat ride live. However, if you're looking for Hemingway's Key West, you're several decades too late.

Orientation

The island of Key West is roughly oval shaped, with most of the action taking place in the west end. The main drags are Duval St, and Truman Ave (US Hwy 1). In the downtown area there's a grid street structure, with street numbers (usually painted on lampposts) in 100-block format counting upwards from Front St (100) down to Truman Ave (900) and so on. Mallory Square, at the far northwestern tip, is the site of the nightly sunset celebrations.

From north to south, the Florida Keys include: Key Largo, Plantation Key, Islamorada, Fiesta Key, Long Key, Conch Key, Duck Key, Grassy Key, Marathon, Bahia Honda Key, Big Pine Key, Summerland Key, Sugarloaf Key, Boca Chica Key, Key West.

It's *possible* to do it in one day, but . . . just. Most people spend a night. Lonely Planet's *Florida – a travel survival kit* has full coverage of the Keys.

Addresses on the Keys work on Mile Markers (MM) along the Overseas Highway: mile 0 is in Key West at the corner of Fleming and Whitehead Sts, and the final marker, MM 126, is one mile south of Florida City.

Maps There are free tourist maps everywhere; the best is published by the Key West Business Guild (☎ 800-535-7797), a gay- and lesbian-oriented business association that has excellent information on gay/lesbian/bi-owned and -friendly businesses.

Information

Tourist Offices The Greater Key West Chamber of Commerce (☎ 294-2587, 800-527-8539) at 402 Wall St in Mallory Square is an excellent source of information, brochures, maps and advice. They're open 8.30 am to 5 pm daily. The Florida Keys & Key West Visitor's Bureau (☎ 296-1552) runs an excellent website (see the Online Services appendix), packed with information on everything the Keys has to offer. Coming into town on US Hwy 1, you'll pass right by the Key West Welcome Center at 3840 N Roosevelt Blvd (☎ 296-4444, 800-284-4482), which has a discount ticket booth that gives 25¢ to 50¢ off admissions to museums.

Money Barnett Bank's main office (☎ 296-7845) is at 1010 Kennedy Drive; there's an Old Town office (☎ 296-7845) at 510 Southard St: dig the trippy decor. American Express (☎ 294-3711) is represented by Boulevard Travel, at 811 Peacock Plaza.

Media The *Key West Citizen* and *Key West: the Newspaper* are the local rags of record. *Solares Hill* is the local radical newspaper (though far less than it was in the '60s and '70s) focusing on community interest and real-estate development. NPR is at 91.3 FM, though reception is terrible.

Bookstores & Libraries Sand Castles by the Sea (☎ 292-3048), 1219 Duval St, is a very helpful and friendly store with gay and general literature, and they're really helpful for information and advice on nightlife and dining. They also give out copies of the business guild map/listing. Blue Heron Books (☎ 296-3508), 538 Truman Ave, has a small travel section (not enough but some Lonely Planet), gay studies section and also a decent nature section and *The New York Times* Sunday edition.

Toilets There are public toilets behind the chamber of commerce. Throughout the rest of the city you're at the mercy of restaurants and hotels, though people are pretty happy to let you go about your business.

Mallory Square

Many people get misty-eyed when discussing Mallory Square, the site of the nightly sunset celebrations. 'Ahh,' they say, 'the romance of it all – watching a bunch of jugglers, bed-of-nails-lyers-down and clowns leaping about as the sun dips past the horizon.' But we just don't get it. In fact, what we thought was that if you could imagine the state of Florida as a giant tourist funnel, the output nozzle is here: Mallory Square, the grandest tourist trap east of the Pecos. It's packed with sharks: seashell, wind-chime and other tourist-trap crap of the 'someone-went-to-blank-and-all-I-got-was-a-lousy-t-shirt' caliber. One saving grace is Pat's Pots, where you can watch a very friendly woman create pottery. Mallory Square is also home to the chamber of commerce, an aquarium and the Shipwreck Historium (see below).

The sunset celebration, which, okay, okay, *is* a fascinating thing (once), occurs nightly, at . . . well, you know. Show up about an hour beforehand to get the full effect.

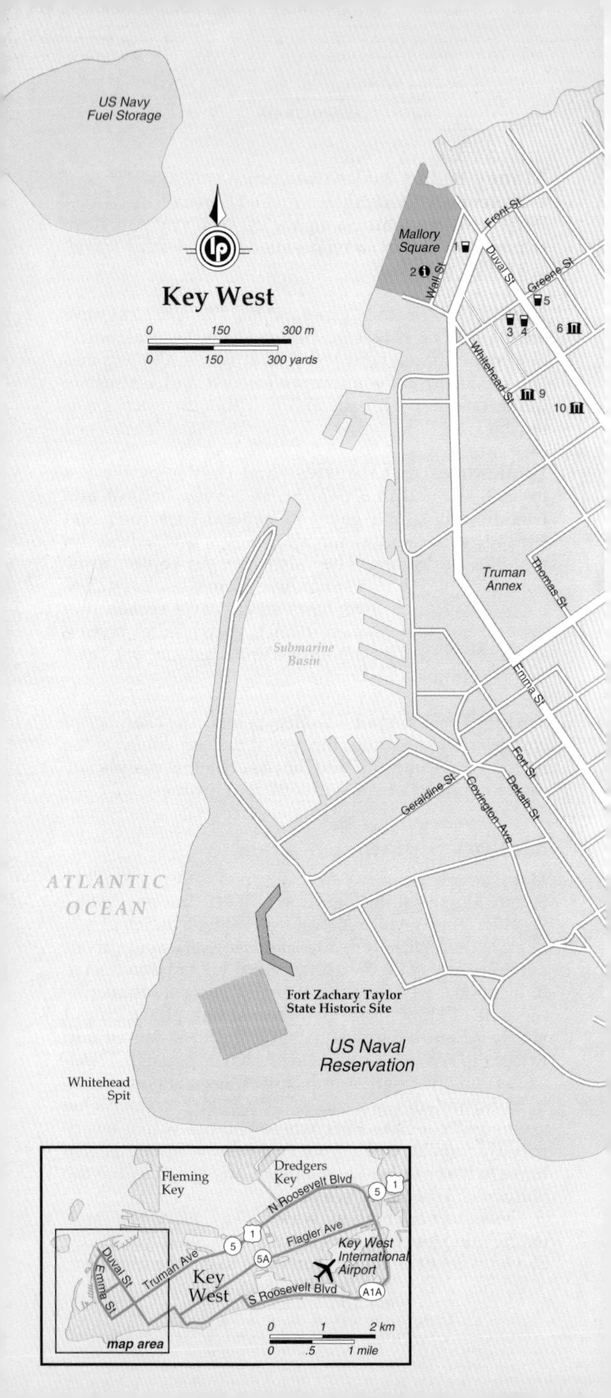

US Navy
Fuel Storage
Key West
0
150
300 m
0
150
300 yards
Mallory
Square
Front St
Wall St
Duval St
Greene St
Whitehead St
Truman
Annex
Thomas St
Submarine
Basin
Emma St
Fort St
Geraldine St
Covington Ave
Dekalb St
ATLANTIC
OCEAN
Fort Zachary Taylor
State Historic Site
US Naval
Reservation
Whitehead
Spit
Fleming
Key
Dredgers
Key
N Roosevelt Blvd
Flagler Ave
Key West
International
Airport
Truman Ave
Key
West
S Roosevelt Blvd
Duval St
Emma St
0
1
2 km
0
.5
1 mile
map area

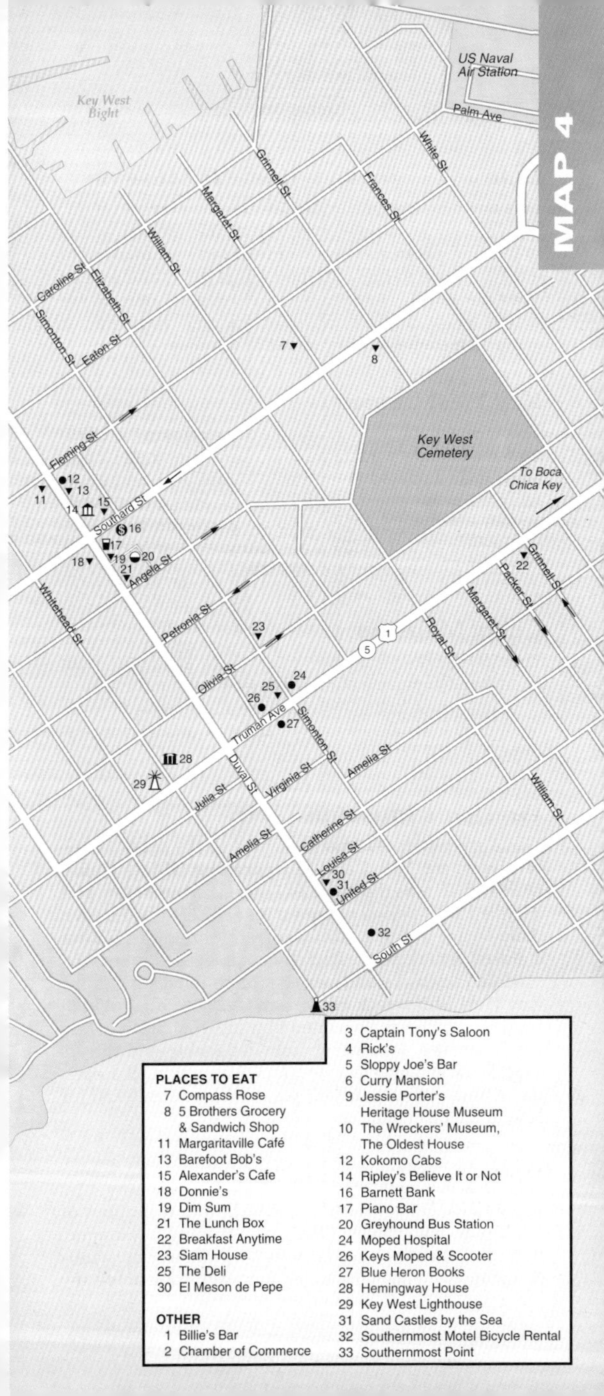
MAP 4
US Naval Air Station
Palm Ave
Key West Bight
White St
Frances St
Grinnell St
Margaret St
William St
Caroline St
Elizabeth St
Simonton St
Eaton St
Fleming St
Southard St
Angela St
Whitehead St
Petronia St
Olivia St
Truman Ave
Key West Cemetery
To Boca Chica Key
Packer St
Royal St
Amelia St
Virginia St
Julia St
Duval St
Catherine St
Louisa St
United St
South St
PLACES TO EAT
7 Compass Rose
8 5 Brothers Grocery & Sandwich Shop
11 Margaritaville Café
13 Barefoot Bob's
15 Alexander's Cafe
18 Donnie's
19 Dim Sum
21 The Lunch Box
22 Breakfast Anytime
23 Siam House
25 The Deli
30 El Meson de Pepe
OTHER
1 Billie's Bar
2 Chamber of Commerce
3 Captain Tony's Saloon
4 Rick's
5 Sloppy Joe's Bar
6 Curry Mansion
9 Jessie Porter's Heritage House Museum
10 The Wreckers' Museum, The Oldest House
12 Kokomo Cabs
14 Ripley's Believe It or Not
16 Barnett Bank
17 Piano Bar
20 Greyhound Bus Station
24 Moped Hospital
26 Keys Moped & Scooter
27 Blue Heron Books
28 Hemingway House
29 Key West Lighthouse
31 Sand Castles by the Sea
32 Southernmost Motel Bicycle Rental
33 Southernmost Point

Ernest Hemingway Home & Museum

This is, to us, one of Key West's great attractions. Hemingway lived in this lovely Spanish-Colonial house (☎ 294-1575) between 1931 and 1940, but kept ownership until his death in 1961. The house is at 907 Whitehead St, open daily from 9 am to 5 pm. Admission is $6.50 for adults, $4 for children, $5.50 for students. Tours depart every 15 minutes and last about 30 minutes.

Key West Cemetery

This is one of the more enjoyable cemeteries in the country for the odd characters buried here – tombstone epitaphs include 'I told you I was sick' and 'At least I know where he is sleeping tonight'. Guided tours are available on Saturday and Sunday at 10 am and 4 pm at the sexton's office (☎ 292-6829) at the Margaret St entrance; the cost is $5 for adults, $1 for children.

Curry Mansion

This 100-year-old Victorian mansion (☎ 294-5349), built by Milton Curry, one of Florida's first millionaires, functions as a guest house. You can take a self-guided tour of the antique-packed rooms for $5 for adults, $1 for children. It's at 511 Caroline St.

Wrecker's Museums

There are two museums dedicated to the study of the Wreckers; the **Wrecker's Museum/The Oldest House** (☎ 294-9502) was the home of Francis B Watlington, and it's filled with period antiques. It's at 322 Duval St, open daily 10 am to 4 pm, admission is $4 for adults, 50¢ for children, and there are friendly volunteer-led tours.

More expensive and perhaps more interesting is the **Key West Shipwreck Historium** (☎ 292-8990), 1 Whitehead St, which has a narrated film showing the lives and times of the Wreckers; knowledgeable volunteers explain how Key West developed as a port. It's open daily from 9.45 am to 4.45 pm, $7 for adults, $3.50 for kids aged four to 12.

Ripley's Believe It or Not

Ripley's (☎ 293-9694) began as the quirky collections of Mr Ripley, who traveled the world looking for 'unique' items like shrunken heads. Now it's a chain of museums featuring exhibits of the weird and wacky side of life; the

Believe It or Not part is up to you. Even if the answer's 'not', it still may be worth the admission price of $9.95 for adults, $6.95 for seniors and children aged five to 12 (under five are free). You can spend an hour here easily. It's at 527 Duval St, open Sunday to Thursday 10 am to 11 pm, Friday and Saturday 10 am to midnight.

Southernmost Point

This is, after all, the southernmost point in the continental USA, and there's a marker here at the corner of South and Whitehead Sts, along with some street performers and many photo-seeking tourists.

Jessie Porter's Heritage House Museum

This Caribbean-Colonial house (☎ 296-3573) at 410 Caroline St has the original furnishings and antiques of a Key West family that lived here, and a flower garden. The cost is $6 for adults, $5 for seniors, children are free. There are guided tours Monday to Saturday from 10 am to 5 pm, Sunday 1 to 5 pm.

Key West Lighthouse

The Key West Lighthouse (☎ 294-0012) is a still-functioning lighthouse at 938 Whitehead St. The lighthouse has a 3rd-order lens, but they also have a model of a 1st-order lens that you can walk into, and you can also climb the 88 steps to the top. Next door is the interesting lighthouse keeper's house. It's open daily 9.30 am to 4.30 pm; admission is $5 for adults, $1 for kids over seven.

Martello Towers

The **East Martello Tower** (☎ 296-3913), 3501 S Roosevelt Blvd, across the street from Key West airport, houses an art gallery and museum of Key West history. The central tower, reached by a 48-step staircase, affords a horrible view of the airport and a totally unimpressive view of the beach. Admission is $5 for adults, $1 for kids, open daily except Christmas from 9.30 am to 5 pm.

The **West Martello Tower** (☎ 294-3210), at Atlantic Blvd and White St, exhibits local plant life from the Key West Garden Club.

Fort Zachary Taylor State Historic Site

This fort (☎ 292-6713), in operation between 1845 and 1866, guarded blockade-running Union ships during the

CORINNA SELBY

CORINNA SELBY

Top: The view from the tower at Mallory Square
Bottom: A Key West guesthouse

Civil War. Today it's open as a state park, with a beach, showers, picnic tables and fishing (license required).

Admission is $3.75 per vehicle, $1.50 for pedestrians; it's open 9 am to 5 pm. There are ranger-led tours at noon and 2 pm. The fort is at the southwestern end of Southard St.

Beaches

There are three city beaches on the southern side of the island, all of them narrow, and the water is very calm

CORINNA SELBY

and clear here. **City Beach** is on the south side of the island at the end of South and Duval Sts. Close by, **Higgs Beach** has barbecue grills and picnic tables, and **Smathers Beach** is more popular with the vroom crowd of jet skiers and parasailers. There is also a beach at **Fort Zachary Taylor State Historic Site**.

Diving

While the coral reef here is the third-largest in the world (it's 200 miles long), it's terribly threatened by boaters, irresponsible divers, pollution and idiots. Don't touch the coral.

But there's obviously diving along the keys, and some of it can be excellent if you've got the right guide. A friend recommended Captain Billy Dean's Diving (☎ 294-7177, 800-873-4837), at MM 4.5. He's said to be the high-tech diving guru around here. Other dive companies set up kiosks around Mallory Square and in other places in town, notably the corner of Truman Ave and Duval St, to hawk to customers. Shop around carefully as prices vary greatly.

Organized Tours

Old Town Trolley Tours' (☎ 296-6688) narrated tram tours leave from Mallory Square and make a large, lazy circle around the city with stops including Key West Handprint Fabrics, Angela St Depot, Trolley Barn, Key West Welcome Center, East Martello Museum, and the Southernmost Point. The cost is $15 for adults, $6 for children for one full circle from any point on the route (you can get off and back on in the same direction for one rotation only), and it includes $1 off admission to the Hemingway House. The trolleys depart every half hour between 9.30 am and 6 pm.

The Conch Train Tour (☎ 294-5161) is pretty much the same thing, and is run by the same parent company. Trams leave every 20 minutes in high season, every half hour in low season between 9 am and 4.30 pm. The cost is $14 for adults, $6 for kids.

Kokomo Cabs (☎ 745-5652) at 519 Duval St offers a half-hour tour in a bicycle-powered rickshaw for $25.

Places to Stay

The *Key West International Hostel* (☎ 296-5719) is at 718 South St. Dorm beds are $17/20 for members/nonmembers; private rooms $40 to 50 in low season, $75 to 100 in high season.

The *Tilton Hotel* (☎ 294-8679) at 511 Angela St next to the Greyhound station has simple rooms (no air conditioning) for $40 to 75; free parking.

Frances St Bottle Inn (☎ 294-8530, 800-294-8530), 535 Frances St, is a very friendly B&B with rooms from $70 to 85 in low season, $90 to 110 in high season. We stayed at the *Wicker Guesthouse* (☎ 296-4275, 800-880-4275), 913 Duval St, a B&B with a great garden and a pool; rooms with shared bath are $63 to 75, rooms with private bath are $79 to 125. A breakfast buffet and use of the common kitchen is included.

Places to Eat

Don't miss Key Lime Pie, a sort of lime meringue made with Key limes, which are more lemony than standard issue limes.

Breakfast Anytime (☎ 292-2023) is a classic Key West find, and they take their grease seriously: try the triple-bypass omelet (three cheeses and bacon) for $5.75, or lighten up (a bit) and get eggs, home fries or grits and toast for $2. Lunch sees burgers ($2.50 to 3.75) and sandwiches ($2.75 to 5.75). It's at 934 Truman Ave, open 7 am to 3 pm every day, all year.

5 Brothers Grocery & Sandwich Shop (☎ 296-5205) is another local favorite, a Cuban market that does great sandwiches like midnite ($2.55), Cuban ($2.80) and pork (3.35); hamburgers/cheeseburgers $1.80/2.05; large café con leche $1.75; and, on Fridays, conch chowder ($2.75). They're at 930 Southard St.

We found the fabled real local hangout with good food and not so many tourists; it's *Compass Rose* (☎ 294-4394) at 532 Margaret St. Humongous burgers; all platters come with real mashed potatoes, veggies and garlic bread, and lunch specials, which change daily, are – hold onto your hats – $4.95 to 5.95; dinner has things like meatloaf ($6.95), roast turkey and stuffing ($8.95) and baby back ribs ($9.50). Drinks are served in large mason jars. Sassy service.

You gotta love *The Deli* (☎ 294-1464), at 926 Simonton St. It's been run by the same family since 1950, it's got really friendly service and extremely well-prepared food. Vegetarians can pile on side dishes like mashed potatoes, rice and beans, zucchini, carrots and other veggies for $1.20 each, and others can hit the meaty dinner specials ($6.50 to 9.15), steak ($12.95), half a rack of ribs ($4.75), or fish and chips ($5.95). Sandwiches go for $1.50 to 5.95. No beer or other alcohol is sold, and it's closed Wednesday.

The Lunch Box (☎ 294-5667) is a sandwich stand at 629 Duval St near the corner of Angela St with veggie chili for $2.25, 'very veggie' sandwiches for $3.25 and burgers for $3.95.

Alexander's Café (☎ 294-5777) is a very comfortable place with friendly service and reasonable prices. Their fresh fish sandwich is a bomb of a meal – huge and served with veggies and fries for $5.95. They're at 509 Southard St.

The *Siam House* (☎ 292-0302) has great food, excellent, friendly service and an all-you-can-eat buffet lunch ($6.95) Monday to Saturday 11 am to 3 pm. It's at 829 Simonton St.

A great backyard place is *Donnie's* (☎ 294-5620). It's got two large bars and live entertainment every night in addition to the restaurant, which is open 24 hours (!). Breakfasts are $3.50 to 5.95; at lunch, salads are $3 to 6.95, sandwiches $3.25 to 6.95, and hot dishes are more, like shrimp and veggies over pasta or rice for $12.95. Dinners can go as cheap as $9.95, but average $12.95. It's behind 618 Duval St.

El Meson de Pepe (☎ 296-6922) at 1215 Duval St is rustic, simple and Spanish-feeling, and is said to be excellent: they have a $7 chicken plate, or grilled steak for $9.90, and shrimp Creole at $12.50.

The pan-Asian food at *Dim Sum* (☎ 294-6230) is fantastic. It's very popular, and open only for dinner. Choose from Indonesian beef rendang ($16.95), veggie dishes ($12.95 to 13.95), chicken and shrimp in Thai green curry sauce ($17.95), Indian chicken curry ($15.95) and more. They're at 613½ Duval St.

Entertainment

For watering holes, most people head to one of a couple of places: *Sloppy Joe's Bar* (☎ 294-5717) at 201 Duval St, the Hemingway hangout-of-record with live

KIM GRANT

CORINNA SELBY

KIM GRANT

Key West style

entertainment every night, for a Hemingway Hammer ($6.50) made from 151-proof rum, banana and strawberry liqueur, blackberry brandy and a dash of white rum; and for drinks or a Cheeseburger in Paradise at Jimmy Buffet's *Margaritaville Café* (☎ 292-1435) at 500 Duval St. *Barefoot Bob's* (☎ 296-5858) at 525 Duval St is a bar/restaurant that has an outdoor garden; inside, it's kind of hippy-ish but not in an annoying kind of way.

Rick's (☎ 296-4890) – what a meat market! But people seem to really like it, if not just for their Wednesday and Thursday night specials: for $5 (low season) or $7 (high season) you get a wrist band allowing you to drink all you can from 9 to 11.30 pm (bring your ID). It's at *(hic!)* 202-208 Duval St.

Billie's Bar (☎ 294-9292) at 407 Front St has two bars, open until 4 am. Their sunset happy hour has $1 draft and $1.50 domestic beers, $2 well drinks, as well as sandwiches for $3.75 to 7, and entrees $10 to 20.

Captain Tony's Saloon (☎ 294-1838) at 428 Greene St has live music almost every night, and the *Piano Bar* (☎ 296-6625), 611 Duval St, is just that, with specials on frozen and sweet drinks.

Getting There & Away

Air At the time of writing one could count on spending from $150 to 180 for a roundtrip flight between Miami and Key West, but this changes drastically. American Airlines (☎ 800-433-7300), Chalk's International Air (☎ 800-424-2557), Gulfstream Air (☎ 871-1200, 800-992-8532) and USAir (☎ 800-428-4322) all have several flights a day (American has the most). Gulfstream, though, consistently has a better range of cheaper tickets than the others.

The airport is at the southeast end of the island off S Roosevelt Ave.

Bus Greyhound has three buses daily, they cost $26 one way, $50 roundtrip, with a weekend fare of $27/52. Buses leave Miami's Bayside Station for the 4¾-hour trip at 7.10 and 11.45 am and 6.15 pm. The Greyhound station (☎ 293-0410) is in the alley behind 615½ Duval St, between Angela and Southard Sts.

You can take the bus to any destination along the Florida Keys; there are official stops, but just tell the driver where you want to get off and they'll stop. If you're trying to get back to Miami from somewhere in the Keys, note that buses leave Key West at 8 am, 12.30 and 5.15 pm. Stand anywhere on the Overseas Highway (US Hwy 1) and when you see the bus in the distance, signal firmly and visibly, using all methods at your disposal – up to and perhaps including a flare gun – and the bus will stop to pick you up. If the driver sees you.

Shuttle Check with the Clay Hotel & International Hostel (see the Miami Beach section in the Places to Stay chapter) for information on the plethora of shuttle services that pop down to the Keys. Paradise Transport (☎ 293-3010) offers 15-passenger van service for $295 each way – which works out to about $20 per person each way if you fill the thing – putting a sign up on the bulletin board at the Clay is the best bet. For the flush (or flash), they also offer limo service for a mere $320 each way.

Car It's about 160 miles from Miami to Key West along US Hwy 1 on the Overseas Highway, a series of causeways built in the 1930s that connect the islands with the mainland. Take Florida's Turnpike Extension (toll) south and then pick up US Hwy 1 south at Florida City. The protected Key deer are an endangered species and reduced speed limits at various places along the route are keenly enforced; speeding fines are high, you'll get caught, and should you hit a Key deer, penalties are stiff. Slow down.

Getting Around

You can rent mopeds or scooters at several places on the island. Prices average $15 a day (from 8 am to 6 pm) or $25 for 24 hours. You don't need a motorcycle license. Bicycle rentals are also available in places listed below; prices average $7 to 10 a day. Try Keys Moped & Scooter (☎ 294-0399) at 523 Truman Ave; Scooter Rentals in the Southernmost Motel, 1319 Duval St; and Moped Hospital (☎ 296-3344) at 601 Truman Ave.

FORT LAUDERDALE

• *pop 150,000* ☎ *area code 954*

As recently as the late 1980s the sand in Fort Lauderdale was sticky from beer, the streets were full of bepimpled youths storming about drinking 1¢ plastic cups of draft beer, and celebrating that American university rite of passage, Spring Break.

Locals would watch in horror as their city was taken over by these yahoos, and finally they decided to do something about it. Over the last few years, the town has managed to divest itself completely of even fleeting images of the Spring Break scene. They've renovated, groomed and trimmed the whole place, and done an exceedingly good job of it.

Today Fort Lauderdale is known more as an international yachting center than a party spot. That's not to say that it's not a partying town: it decidedly is. These days you can party at dozens and dozens of clubs, bars, pubs and beach nightspots, as long as you dress respectably (meaning in clothes of some sort) and behave yourself. You can still party till you puke, but you'll puke in a sophisticated nightclub, in a toilet and not out on the beach. Thank you.

Orientation

Fort Lauderdale's about 25 miles north of downtown Miami. The city is set in a grid wherever physically possible (it's hard with all the water), and is divided into three distinct sections: the beach, on the east side of the Intracoastal Waterway; downtown, which is on the mainland, and Port Everglades, the cruise port at the south of the city. Federal Hwy (US Hwy 1) cuts through the downtown and passes under E Las Olas Blvd via the New River Tunnel. Hwy A1A runs along the ocean. Broward Blvd divides downtown into north and south sectors; Andrews Ave, just west of Federal Hwy, is the east-west line; as in Miami, streets and addresses are oriented by cross street and relation to Broward Blvd and Andrews Ave – N, S, E and W.

The main arteries between downtown and the beach are Sunrise Blvd to the north, E Las Olas Blvd in the center and the 17th St Causeway to the south, which connects the beach to Port Everglades.

Maps Of the two main free handout maps, the one published by the Las Olas Merchant Association is better on the whole than the one from the Convention & Visitors Bureau, which looks like a Find Waldo comic. Ask at a Barnett Bank branch if they happen to have any copies of the *Barnett Bank Map of Broward County*, which is a freebie version of the Dolph Map Company's *Map of Metropolitan Broward County* – the latter has no advertising, the former does, but the base map is the same.

Information

Tourist Offices The Greater Fort Lauderdale Convention & Visitor's Bureau (☎ 765-4466, see the Online Services appendix) is a bottomless source of practical information and assistance. Their offices are in Port Everglades, at 1850 Eller Drive, Suite 303. There's a very helpful activity line at ☎ 527-5600.

Gay & Lesbian The Gay & Lesbian Community Center of Greater Fort Lauderdale (☎ 563-9500) is an excellent source of information on gay and lesbian issues, events, health and community affairs, and maintains good lists of what's on with clubs and nightlife. They're at 1164 E Oakland Park Blvd, on the 3rd floor.

Money Barnett Bank has branches at 1 E Broward Blvd (☎ 765-1510) and 2404B E Sunrise Blvd (☎ 563-6500). American Express (☎ 565-9481) has an office at 3312-14 NE 32nd St.

Bookstores & Libraries Clark's Out of Town News (☎ 467-1543) at 303 S Andrews Ave (at the corner of Las

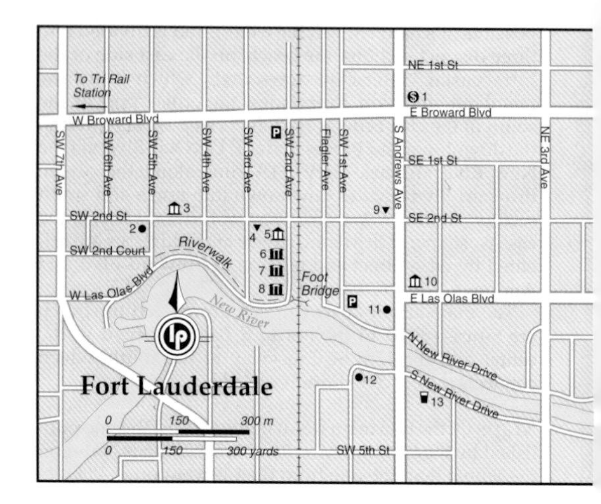

Olas Blvd) is an excellent source for out of town and foreign newspapers, travel books (though not enough Lonely Planet stuff) and local news.

MacCarthy's (☎ 467-7410), 1400 E Las Olas Blvd, has some international (German, British, Spanish) newspapers and magazines, it's open Monday to Saturday 8 am to 5 pm, Sunday 8 am to 3 pm.

Media The local daily is the *Sun Sentinel*. *XS* is a very well-done local weekly with music, club, restaurant, art and other entertainment. Check out their website (see the Online Services appendix). *Hot Spots* and *Scoop* are magazines on the gay and lesbian (though more gay) club scene. NPR is at 91.3 FM.

Museum of Art

Reopened in 1985 in brand new (and architecturally impressive) 63,800-sq-foot digs just off the New River, the Museum of Art, Fort Lauderdale is one of Florida's best.

The museum's permanent collection includes works by Pablo Picasso, Henri Matisse, Henry Moore, Salvador Dali, Andy Warhol and the core collection of works by William Glackens, as well as work by CoBrA (Copenhagen-Brussels-Amsterdam) artists Karel Appel, Carl-Henning Pedersen, Asger Jorn and Pierre Alechinsky. You can't ever really know, though, what you're going to see on a particular visit, as the enormity of the collection

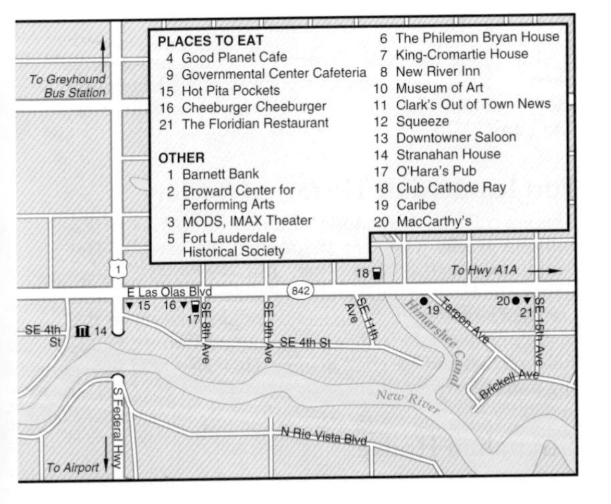

far outpaces the available space. Also not to be missed are the growing and equally impressive museum collections of Cuban and ethnographic art, including a large African and South American collection.

The museum (☎ 525-5550) is at 1 E Las Olas Blvd. Admission is $5 for adults, $4 for seniors (with ID), $2 for students (with ID) and free for children 12 and under.

Museum of Discovery & Science

Fronted by the 52-foot-tall Great Gravity Clock, Florida's largest kinetic energy sculpture, the Museum of Discovery & Science (MODS; ☎ 467-6637) is one of the best of its kind in the state, and worth a visit by children and adults alike. The environmentally oriented museum is very visual and very hands-on. It's at 401 SW 2nd St, and is open Monday to Saturday from 10 am to 5 pm, Sunday from noon to 5 pm. Admission to the museum is $6 for adults, and $5 for children aged three to 12 and seniors over 65.

In the same building, **IMAX** is $5 for adults, $4 for children/seniors, and a combination museum/film ticket is $8.50 for adults, $7.50 for children and seniors. In 1996, MODS became the fourth theater in the world to offer IMAX 3-D films with their bitchin' magic helmet. The helmet, which looks like a virtual reality gizmo, includes several speakers for totally rad sound placement, as well as high-tech 3-D goggles (no more plastic glasses).

Riverwalk

A strip along the New River, Riverwalk's just a very pleasant bit of green, and a lovely way to walk between the Museum of Art and the MODS. It's open daily from 5 to 1 am.

Fort Lauderdale Historical Society

This is a collection of historic buildings on the west of the railroad tracks just near the start of Riverwalk. The buildings are the New River Inn (1905), the King-Cromartie House (1907) and the Philemon Bryan House (1905). The museum (☎ 463-4431) holds exhibits on the history of Fort Lauderdale and Broward County, Seminole folk art and baseball history. They also hold walking tours by arrangement.

Stranahan House

One of Florida's oldest residences, the Stranahan House (☎ 524-4736) is now a registered historic landmark. Built as the home for Ohio transplant Frank Stranahan, the house, originally constructed in 1901 and expanded several times over the years, is a perfect example of Florida frontier design.

It's on the New River on SE 4th St, behind the Hyde Park supermarket. It's open Wednesday to Sunday 10 am to 5 pm, regularly scheduled tours run between 10 am and 4 pm. Admission is $5 for adults, $4 for students and seniors and $2 for children.

Bonnet House

This is a beautiful estate (☎ 563-5393) at 900 N Birch Rd in Fort Lauderdale Beach (enter through the west gate). Admission is $7 for adults, $6 for senior citizens, $5 for students under 18 and groups, children under six are free. Tours, which last about one hour and 15 minutes, leave at 10 am and 1 pm on Wednesday to Friday and at 1 and 2 pm on Saturday and Sunday. The property features native Southern Florida and imported tropical plants, including an extensive orchid collection.

Hugh Taylor Birch State Recreation Area

For almost a mile in the middle of the beach, this state-protected park contains one of the last significant maritime hammocks left in Broward county, mangroves, a freshwater lagoon system and several species of endangered animals, including the gopher tortoise, and golden leather fern. Oh, yeah, there's luscious peace and quite here as well. Admission is $1 for pedestrians and bicyclists, $3 per vehicle with up to eight passengers, $1 for each additional passenger. Ranger-guided tours are given on Fridays, weather permitting, at 10 am. The park is open daily from 8 am to 7.30 pm.

Organized Tours

The *Jungle Queen* BBQ & Shrimp Dinner Cruise (☎ 947-6597) is a kitschy Fort Lauderdale tradition. The narrated cruise itself is entertaining, as you get all the dirt on the rich folks who own houses on millionaire's row, and trivia and local lore on the way to the 'tropical' island on which you dine. After dinner, you'll see a show that is so Zen-like in the purity of its awfulness that it's a rollicking time for all.

For a good laugh, go on a Wednesday night, when patrons of the Downtowner Saloon (see below, Entertainment) arrange a group mooning of the boat.

The cruises leave from the dock at the Bahia Mar yacht center, just south of the Bahia Mar Resort at the southern end of town.

Diving

There are several dive shops in town, but if you're looking to get certified, the best deal that we know of in the entire state is through the HI International House (☎ 568-1615), 3811 N Ocean Blvd (Hwy A1A), which can get you certified in as quickly as three days (weather and seas permitting) for $135 per person.

Surfing & Water-skiing

Caribe (☎ 462-1130) rents and sells used and new surf and water-ski equipment at 1208 E Las Olas Blvd. Boogie boards are $5 an hour, $10 for four hours, $15 for 24 hours. Surfboards are $10 an hour with a four-hour minimum, $20 for 24 hours. Water-ski rental costs $20 a day but you'll need a boat to go with that – check the stands just south of the corner of E Las Olas Blvd and Hwy A1A for one.

Places to Stay

The cheapest beds in town are at *Floyd's Youth Hostel & Crew House* (☎ 462-0631; see the Online Services

appendix), with clean dorm beds at $11. Extras – like free barbecues (with beer) for guests every couple of weeks and free pick-up from airport, Greyhound and Amtrak stations – make the place a great value. The hostel's close to the port; call for the address, which he doesn't print.

The friendly, family-run *HI International House* (☎ 568-1615, fax 568-1595, HI reservations 800-444-6111), 3811 N Ocean Blvd (Hwy A1A), is one of the most popular hostels in the USA with dorm beds for $13.08/16.35 for members/nonmembers, one block from the beach with a swimming pool, huge kitchen, large rooms and common areas. There are free pick-ups from airport, Greyhound and Amtrak stations, and they even offer frequent dive trips and certification for beginners at the lowest prices in town.

The Winterhaven (☎ 564-5614, 800-888-2639, fax 565-5790), 2801 Terra Mar St, has two pools and is very clean, though furniture is of the large variety. Room rates start at $35/225 a day/week in low season, and $50 to 60 and $340 to 400 in high season.

The serene *Pillars Waterfront* (☎ 467-9639, 800-800-7666, fax 763-2845) at 111 N Birch Rd is a lovely and quiet resort tucked away at the end of Sebastian St, two blocks from the beach on the Intracoastal Waterway. There's an unbelievably helpful staff, a pool, barbecue area and tables lining a private pier. If you want to spend $49 to 110 in summer, $59 to 130 in fall and spring, and $99 to 159 in high season, this is the place to spend it.

NICK SELBY

Harbor in Fort Lauderdale

Places to Eat

Downtown & Mainland If you're in the area (like at the Museum of Art) and want to save a bit, try the open-to-the-public *Governmental Center Cafeteria* (☎ 462-8368) in room 308 of the Governmental Center Building at 115 S Andrews Ave, where you'll find the finest in administrative cuisine at taxpayer-subsidized prices. They're open Monday to Friday, 7 am to 3 pm.

It's worth the five-minute drive back south across the New River from E Las Olas Blvd to get to *Ernie's Bar-B-Q* (☎ 523-8636), a restaurant as famous for its squalor and good, cheap food as for the anti-government and -finance rantings that grace its walls. It's a 38-year-old tradition serving up enormous portions of conch chowder ($2 for a cup, $2.60 for a bowl). The soup itself can make a meal. They're at 1843 S Federal Hwy, open 11 am to 11 pm or midnight.

The laid-back folks over at the *Good Planet Cafe* (☎ 527-4663) ask that if you want service today you should request it with your order. Hippy dippy atmosphere (cactii on the tables) and health-oriented American cuisine: veggie melt ($4.75), burgers (about $5.95) and the interesting Posole del Buen Planeta at $2.75 a cup, 4.50 a bowl, $5.25 with half a sandwich. They're at 214 SW 2nd St, open every day from 11.30 am to about midnight.

Along E Las Olas Blvd The cheapest place we found on E Las Olas Blvd is *Hot Pita Pockets* (☎ 832-0301), and happily it turned out to be excellent; Middle Eastern pita sandwiches, with a large vegetarian selection. All foods are prepared on the premises and it's definitely good value. They are at 604 E Las Olas Blvd, open

Sunday to Thursday 11 am to 9 pm, Friday and Saturday 11 am to 11 pm and they deliver.

Cheeburger Cheeburger (☎ 524-8824), does excellent cheeseburgers (you can order one without cheese 'at no extra charge'). A quarter-pound sampler is $3.75. Free delivery. They are at 708 E Las Olas Blvd.

The Floridian Restaurant (☎ 463-4041) at 1410 E Las Olas Blvd, open 24 hours, is an upscale diner serving very good, if a bit pricey, diner food – but skip the coleslaw. Unique menu offerings, like their late night, 'Out too late, forgot to eat, I'm starving baby, can't make up my mind' special at $8.95, make the menu's fine print worth reading.

On the Beach There's not a whole lot on the beach that's worth jumping up and down about. A great new offering is the *Primanti Brothers* (☎ 565-0605, fax 537-4882) at 901 N Ocean Blvd (Hwy A1A), doing great New York-style pizza ($1.75 a slice) and Sicilian ($2 a slice).

Thai to Go (☎ 537-5375, fax 537-9001) at 3414D N Ocean Blvd (A1A) has decent Thai to go – there are no seats in the restaurant except for waiting – at $4.95 for lunch and $6.95 for dinner dishes. They're very close to the HI International House.

Entertainment

This is, if you hadn't noticed, a party town, and there are literally thousands of nightlife options available to suit a variety of tastes, persuasions, nuttiness and libidos. Cover charges vary incredibly and constantly, and coupons abound. Check in *XS* for listings when you get to town, or check out the listings on their website (see the Online Services appendix). These are but a few of the available options.

Dance *Baja Beach Club* (☎ 561-2432) at 3200 N Federal Hwy looks like an orgy at King Neptune's place. Dance music in an enormous multi-level place; Spring Break parties; retro ('80s) parties on Thursday; dance parties on Saturday.

Club Soda (☎ 486-4010) at 5460 N State Rd 7 does alcohol-free dances for clean and sober adults.

Alternative *Nemesis* (☎ 768-9228) in what was formerly a funeral home (now *that's* alternative) at 627 N Federal Hwy, is naturally very popular with the People in Black.

Crash Club (☎ 772-3611) at 4915 NE 12th Ave near Commercial Blvd and Dixie Hwy, does theme nights with weird themes (such as painted lady and tattoo contests). *The Edge* (☎ 525-9333) at 200 W Broward Blvd is a staggeringly huge and pretty minimalistic dance warehouse with seven bars, outside patio and balcony areas both with bars. There's live music a lot, with local and national bands.

Blues *Cheers* (☎ 771-6337) at 941 E Cypress Creek Rd has live blues. On Friday and Saturday, men must wear shirts with sleeves. *Dr Feelgoode's Boogie Woogie Emporium* (☎ 491-7440) 2471 E Commercial Blvd has live music Wednesday through Sunday.

Downtowner Saloon (☎ 463-9800), at 10 S New River Drive, does live blues Thursday through Saturday in the blues room. The best time to go is Wednesday evenings at 10.30 pm, when everyone heads out back to moon the *Jungle Queen* (get a T-Shirt – $12 – to commemorate your butt flapping in the breeze: 'I've been to the Moon at Downtowner Saloon').

Gay & Lesbian There are at least 20 gay bars and clubs in Fort Lauderdale, though the situation here is as in Miami – they go out fast! Check in *Scoop* and *Hot Spots*, or ask around.

The Copa (☎ 463-1507) has been around forever: it's a huge disco with an outdoor deck and drag shows several times a week. They're at 2800 S Federal Hwy. *Club Electra* (☎ 764-8447) is a high-energy dance club with nights for men during the week and women on Friday to Sunday at 1600 SE 15th Ave.

Club Cathode Ray (☎ 462-8611), 1105 E Las Olas Blvd, is kind of a guppie hangout. It's open Sunday to Friday 2 pm to 2 am, and Saturday 2 pm to 3 am.

Club Caribbean (☎ 565-0402) at 2851 N Federal Hwy and *The Everglades* (☎ 463-1507) at 1931 S Federal Hwy both do **Tea Dances** on Sunday evenings. Call them for more information.

The Other Side (☎ 565-5538) is a lesbian bar that's been around forever. There's a separate dance area and the bar has pool tables. It's at 2183 Wilton Drive.

Performing Arts The *Broward Center for the Performing Arts* (☎ 462-0222) at 201 SW 5th Ave does Broadway road shows and classical concerts. The box office is open Monday to Saturday 10 am to 6 pm, Sunday noon to 6 pm.

Getting There & Away

Air See the Getting There & Away chapter for information on the Fort Lauderdale-Hollywood International

NICK SELBY

Airport, which is just off I-595 at the southern edge of town.

Bus The Greyhound station (☎ 764-6551) is at 515 NE 3rd St at Federal Hwy, about 4½ blocks from Broward Central Terminal.

Train Tri-Rail stops in Fort Lauderdale. Call ☎ 728-8445, 800-874-7245 for ticket and scheduling information. The Fort Lauderdale station is located just south of Broward Blvd, just west of I-95 at 200 SW 21st Terrace.

Car I-95 is the main road between Miami and Fort Lauderdale. Florida's Turnpike also runs between those two cities, and I-595, the major east-west artery, connects Florida's Turnpike with downtown Fort Lauderdale, Port Everglades, the airport, I-95 and US Hwy 1.

Getting Around

Bus It's not a breeze, but it can be done without a car here. Frequent Broward County Transit (BCt) bus service runs between downtown and the beach, Port Everglades and surrounding towns and beaches. You can call BCt for information on specific routes at ☎ 357-8400, TTY 357-8302. One-way fares are $1, seniors, disabled or youth fares are 50¢, transfers are 15¢. Fare boxes on board accept dollar bills.

Car It's the easiest way to go, though parking is tight especially in high season, and you usually have to pay for it. Speed limits are enforced to such an extent that you may wonder if the cops get commission. See Car Rental in the Getting Around chapter for details.

Water Taxi The Water Taxi (☎ 565-5507) is a full-fledged transportation option in the canals and waterways of Fort Lauderdale; a $14 daily pass lets you ride as much as you'd like. Call from any commercial location downtown on the New River, or along the Intracoastal Waterway (anyplace with a dock) and they'll swing by and pick you up.

Taxi Yellow Cab Co's (☎ 565-5400, 565-8400) meter rates are $2.45 for the first mile, $1.75 for each additional mile.

Bicycle Fort Lauderdale's flatness makes it a great place to get around by bike. The St Tropez Resort (☎ 564-8468) rents bicycles for $4 an hour, $10 for a day (from 8.30 am to 8 pm), $15 for 24 hours or $40 a week with a $50 deposit. They're at 725 N Atlantic Blvd.

Appendix I
Online Services

For standard online services, the access numbers are:

America Online
☎ 800 827-6364, local access ☎ 621-8500
CompuServe
☎ 800-848-8990, local access ☎ 262-9325
Prodigy
☎ 800-776-3449, local access ☎ 471-1500, network symbol Q

ACCOMMODATIONS

Breakwater Hotel breakw@aol.com

Eden Roc Resort http://www.richnet.net/edenroc

Floyd's Youth Hostel & Crew House fecreamer@earthlink.net

Miami River Inn miami100@ix.netcom.com

AIRLINES

Aero Mexico http://www.wotw.com/aeromexico

Aero Peru http://ichu.rcp.net.pe:80/aeroperu

Air Canada http://www.aircanada.ca

Air France http://www.airfrance.fr

Alitalia http://www.alitalia.it

American Airlines http://www.amrcorp.com

British Airways http://www.british-airways.com

Carnival Airlines http://www.carnivalair.com

Continental Airlines http://www.flycontinental.com

Delta Air Lines http://www.delta-air.com

KLM Royal Dutch Airlines http://www.klm.nl

LAN Chile http://www.lanchile.com

Lufthansa http://www.lufthansa.de

TWA http://www.twa.com

United Airlines http://www.ual.com

USAir http://www.usair.com

ValuJet http://www.valujet.com

Varig Brazilian Airlines http://freesun.be/varig

Virgin Atlantic Airways http://www.fly.virgin.com

OTHER TRANSPORTATION

Alamo http://www.freeways.com/bookit

Amtrak http://www.amtrak.com

Avis http://www.avis.com

Greyhound http://www.greyhound.com

MISCELLANEOUS

American Police Hall of Fame & Police Museum
http://www.aphf.org

Beacon Council beacon1@gate.net

Black Heritage Museum http://gsni.com/bhm.htm

Council Travel http://www.ciee.org/cts/ctshome.htm

Discover Key West http://Discover.Key-West.FL.US/

Film Commission
http://www.hollywoodeast.com/mdtfp/expermit.html

Florida Citylink http://www.neosoft.com/citylink/fl.html

Florida Keys & Key West Visitor's Bureau
http://www.fla-keys.com

Florida Shakespeare Theatre http://www.afn.org/~theatre

Greater Fort Lauderdale Convention & Visitor's Bureau
http://www.co.broward.fl.us

Historical Museum of Southern Florida
natbrown@ix.netcom.com
http://www.gate.net/historical-museum

Holocaust Memorial Committee
http://wahoo.netrunner.net/~holomem/

Jerry Herman Ring Theatre http://www.miami.edu/tha

Mobility International USA miusa@igc.apc.org

Museum of Contemporary Art (MoCA)
http://gsni.com/moca-mia.htm

Queer Resources Directory http://www.infoqueer.org/qrd

Parrot Jungle & Gardens pjungle@aol.com
http://florida.com/parrotjungle

Single Source http://thesinglesource.com/eventguide/mia/

Virtua Cafe http://www.sobe.com/virtuacafe/

XS http://www.xso.com

Appendix II
Climate Chart

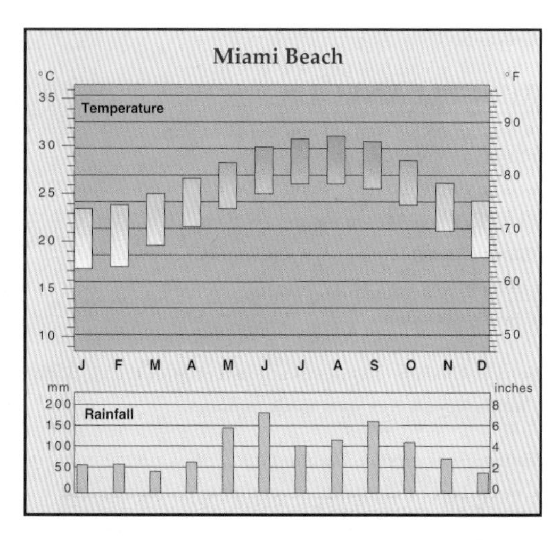

CORINNA SELBY

Index

Maps

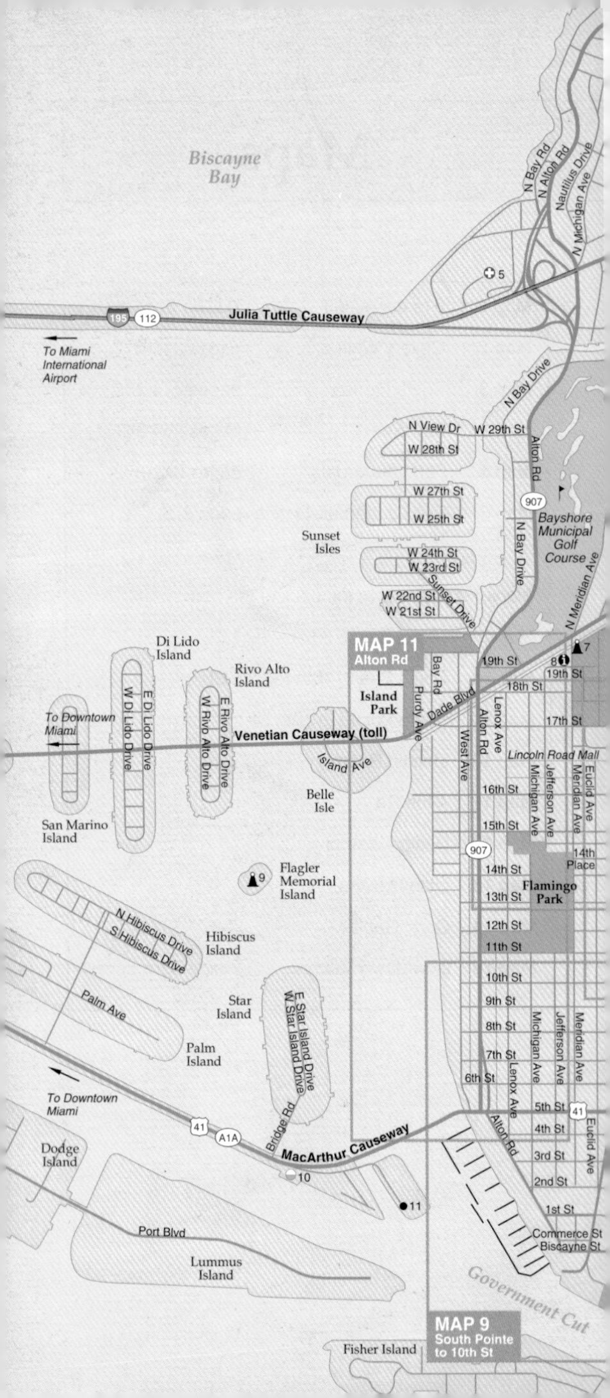

Biscayne Bay
N Bay Rd
N Alton Rd
Nautilus Drive
N Michigan Ave
5
195
112
Julia Tuttle Causeway
To Miami International Airport
N Bay Drive
N View Dr
W 29th St
W 28th St
Alton Rd
W 27th St
907
W 25th St
Bayshore Municipal Golf Course
Sunset Isles
N Bay Drive
W 24th St
W 23rd St
Sunset Drive
N Meridian Ave
W 22nd St
W 21st St
Di Lido Island
MAP 11
Alton Rd
7
19th St
8
19th St
Rivo Alto Island
Bay Rd
18th St
Island Park
Purdy Ave
Dade Blvd
Lenox Ave
17th St
To Downtown Miami
E Di Lido Drive
W Di Lido Drive
E Rivo Alto Drive
W Rivo Alto Drive
Venetian Causeway (toll)
Island Ave
West Ave
Alton Rd
Lincoln Road Mall
Belle Isle
16th St
Michigan Ave
Jefferson Ave
Meridian Ave
Euclid Ave
San Marino Island
15th St
907
14th Place
Flagler Memorial Island
9
14th St
Flamingo Park
13th St
N Hibiscus Drive
S Hibiscus Drive
Hibiscus Island
12th St
11th St
10th St
Palm Ave
Star Island
E Star Island Drive
W Star Island Drive
9th St
8th St
Michigan Ave
Jefferson Ave
Meridian Ave
Palm Island
7th St
6th St
Lenox Ave
To Downtown Miami
5th St
41
Bridge Rd
41
A1A
Alton Rd
4th St
Euclid Ave
MacArthur Causeway
Dodge Island
3rd St
10
2nd St
11
1st St
Port Blvd
Commerce St
Biscayne St
Lummus Island
Government Cut
MAP 9
South Pointe to 10th St
Fisher Island

MAP 7

Miami Beach

ATLANTIC OCEAN

PLACES TO STAY
1 Eden Roc Resort
2 Fontainebleau Hilton Hotel & Resort
6 Indian Creek Hotel
13 Roney Plaza Apartment Hotel

PLACES TO EAT
6 Pan Coast Restaurant
15 Casona de Carlitos

OTHER
3 Fontainebleau Mural
4 Fontainebleau Spa
5 Mount Sinai Medical Center
7 Holocaust Memorial
8 Miami Beach Chamber of Commerce
9 Flagler Memorial Monument
10 Fisher Island Ferry
11 Coast Guard Station
12 Groovejet
14 Paragon
16 Bass Museum
17 Miami Beach Public Library
18 De JaVu Showgirls

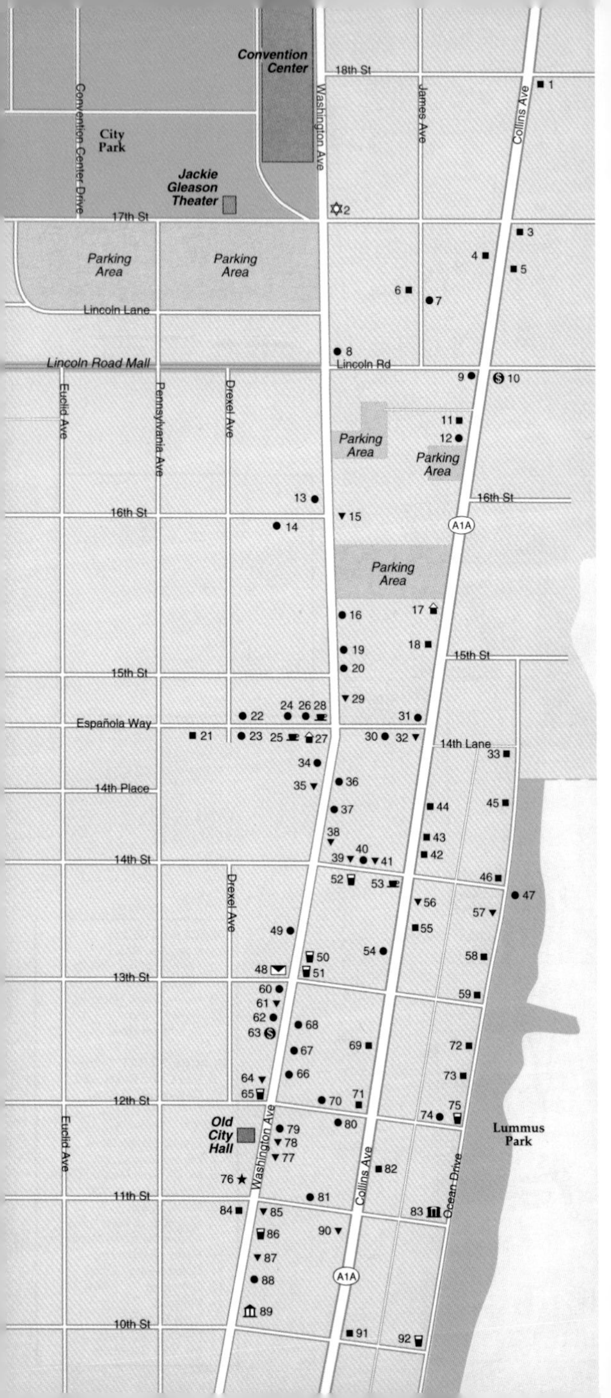

Convention Center
18th St
Washington Ave
James Ave
Collins Ave
City Park
Convention Center Drive
Jackie Gleason Theater
17th St
Parking Area
Parking Area
Lincoln Lane
Lincoln Road Mall
Lincoln Rd
Euclid Ave
Pennsylvania Ave
Drexel Ave
Parking Area
Parking Area
16th St
16th St
A1A
Parking Area
15th St
15th St
Española Way
14th Lane
14th Place
14th St
Drexel Ave
13th St
12th St
Old City Hall
Euclid Ave
Lummus Park
Collins Ave
Ocean Drive
11th St
A1A
10th St

South Beach 10th to 18th St

0 100 200 m
0 100 200 yards

ATLANTIC OCEAN

PLACES TO STAY
1 Raleigh Hotel
3 Delano Hotel
4 San Juan Hotel
5 National Hotel
6 James Hotel
11 Berkeley Shore Hotel
17 Tropics Hotel & Hostel
18 Parisian/Geneva Hotel
21 Matanzas Hotel
27 Clay Hotel & International Hostel
33 Betsy Ross Hotel
42 Brigham Gardens Guest House
43 Villa Paradiso Guesthouse
44 Carlton Hotel
45 Penguin Hotel
46 Winterhaven Hotel
55 Clifton Hotel
58 Cavalier Hotel
59 Cardozo Hotel
69 Hotel Impala
71 Marlin Hotel
72 Leslie Hotel
73 Ocean Front Hotel
82 Kent Hotel
84 Kenmore Hotel
91 Essex House Hotel

PLACES TO EAT
1 Raleigh Bar & Restaurant
15 Lincoln NYC Pizza
29 Pucci's Pizza
32 Grillfish
33 PaneCaldo Restaurant
35 Stephan's Gourmet Market & Café
38 Ciccio's Pizza
39 San Loco
41 La Sandwicherie
46 Renzi's Café
56 Sushi Rock Café
57 Mappy Cafeteria
59 Allioli Restaurant
61 Chrysanthemum
64 Toni's Sushi Bar
72 Leslie Hotel Café
73 Les Deux Fontaines
77 Sushi Hana
78 Thai House
85 11th St Diner
87 Lulu's
90 David's Cafe

ENTERTAINMENT
19 Club Madonna
25 Cosmic Cafe
28 Java Junkies, Edge Theater
31 Warsaw Ballroom
36 Cameo Theatre
50 Jam's Taverna & Grill
51 Virtua Cafe
52 Mac's Club Deuce Bar
53 Starbar Café
62 Sterling Club Billards
65 Mezza Notte
66 Glam Slam
75 The Palace Bar
86 Twist
92 Clevelander Bar

OTHER
2 Temple Emanu El
7 Pilar Tours
8 Tropicolor
9 Eckerd
10 Citibank
12 Travel Now
13 Beachwear
14 Age of Innocence
16 Power Records
20 Recycled Blues
22 South Beach Make-up
23 Ba-BaLú!
24 Studio Russo
26 Espanola Way Art Center
30 Wings of Steel
34 Travel by Design
37 Cycles on the Beach
40 Tattoos by Lou
47 Public Toilets
48 Post Office
49 Art Attack
54 Frugal Flowers
60 Gary's Megacycles
63 Nationwide Bank ATM
67 Club Body Tech Gym
68 Fabulous
70 Meet Me In Miami
74 Skate 2000
76 Miami Beach Police Station
79 Details
80 Coin Laundry
81 Versani
83 Casa Casaurina
88 Mars
89 Wolfsonian Foundation

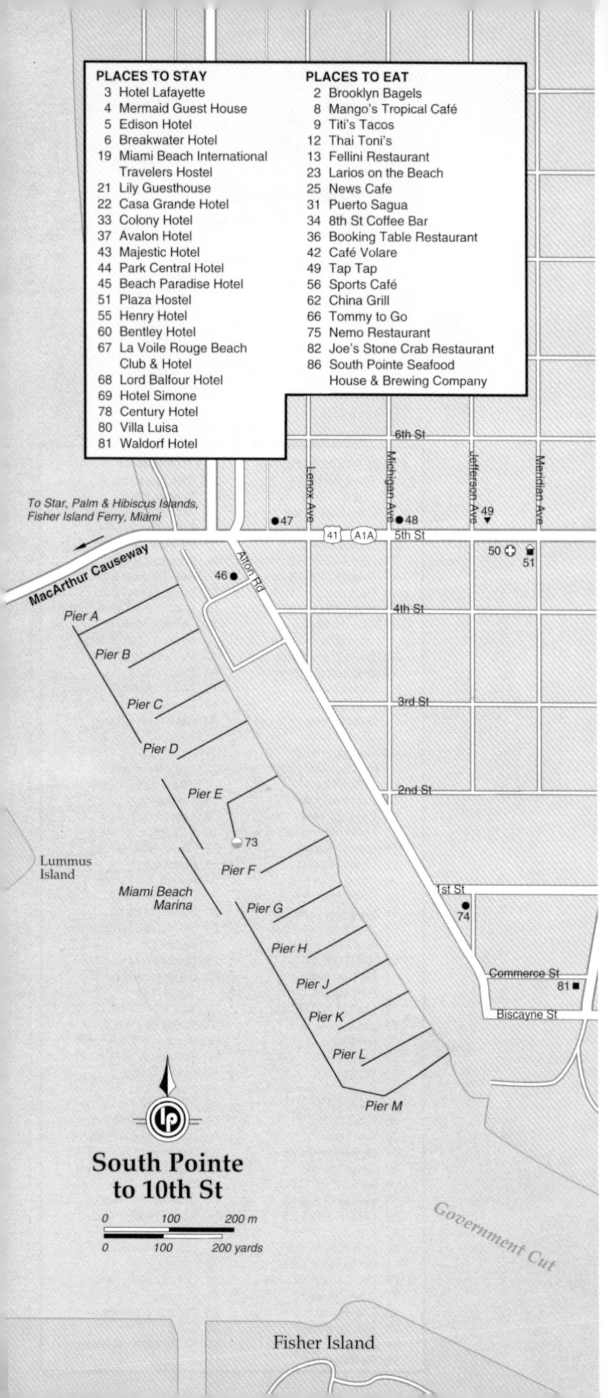
PLACES TO STAY
3 Hotel Lafayette
4 Mermaid Guest House
5 Edison Hotel
6 Breakwater Hotel
19 Miami Beach International Travelers Hostel
21 Lily Guesthouse
22 Casa Grande Hotel
33 Colony Hotel
37 Avalon Hotel
43 Majestic Hotel
44 Park Central Hotel
45 Beach Paradise Hotel
51 Plaza Hostel
55 Henry Hotel
60 Bentley Hotel
67 La Voile Rouge Beach Club & Hotel
68 Lord Balfour Hotel
69 Hotel Simone
78 Century Hotel
80 Villa Luisa
81 Waldorf Hotel
PLACES TO EAT
2 Brooklyn Bagels
8 Mango's Tropical Café
9 Titi's Tacos
12 Thai Toni's
13 Fellini Restaurant
23 Larios on the Beach
25 News Cafe
31 Puerto Sagua
34 8th St Coffee Bar
36 Booking Table Restaurant
42 Café Volare
49 Tap Tap
56 Sports Café
62 China Grill
66 Tommy to Go
75 Nemo Restaurant
82 Joe's Stone Crab Restaurant
86 South Pointe Seafood House & Brewing Company
6th St
Lenox Ave
Michigan Ave
Jefferson Ave
Meridian Ave
To Star, Palm & Hibiscus Islands, Fisher Island Ferry, Miami
47
48
49
41
A1A
5th St
50
51
MacArthur Causeway
Alton Rd
46
4th St
Pier A
Pier B
Pier C
3rd St
Pier D
Pier E
2nd St
73
Lummus Island
Pier F
Miami Beach Marina
1st St
74
Pier G
Pier H
Commerce St
81
Pier J
Pier K
Biscayne St
Pier L
Pier M
South Pointe to 10th St
0
100
200 m
0
100
200 yards
Government Cut
Fisher Island

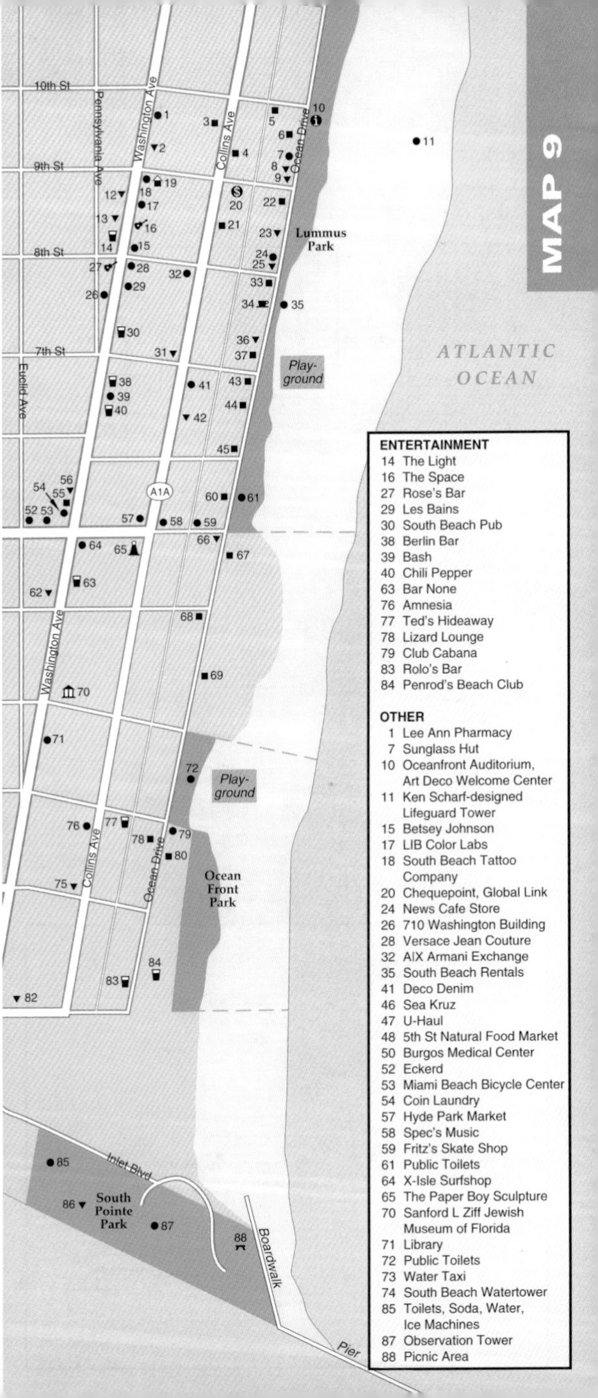

MAP 9

ATLANTIC OCEAN

ENTERTAINMENT

14 The Light
16 The Space
27 Rose's Bar
29 Les Bains
30 South Beach Pub
38 Berlin Bar
39 Bash
40 Chili Pepper
63 Bar None
76 Amnesia
77 Ted's Hideaway
78 Lizard Lounge
79 Club Cabana
83 Rolo's Bar
84 Penrod's Beach Club

OTHER

1 Lee Ann Pharmacy
7 Sunglass Hut
10 Oceanfront Auditorium, Art Deco Welcome Center
11 Ken Scharf-designed Lifeguard Tower
15 Betsey Johnson
17 LIB Color Labs
18 South Beach Tattoo Company
20 Chequepoint, Global Link
24 News Cafe Store
26 710 Washington Building
28 Versace Jean Couture
32 AIX Armani Exchange
35 South Beach Rentals
41 Deco Denim
46 Sea Kruz
47 U-Haul
48 5th St Natural Food Market
50 Burgos Medical Center
52 Eckerd
53 Miami Beach Bicycle Center
54 Coin Laundry
57 Hyde Park Market
58 Spec's Music
59 Fritz's Skate Shop
61 Public Toilets
64 X-Isle Surfshop
65 The Paper Boy Sculpture
70 Sanford L Ziff Jewish Museum of Florida
71 Library
72 Public Toilets
73 Water Taxi
74 South Beach Watertower
85 Toilets, Soda, Water, Ice Machines
87 Observation Tower
88 Picnic Area

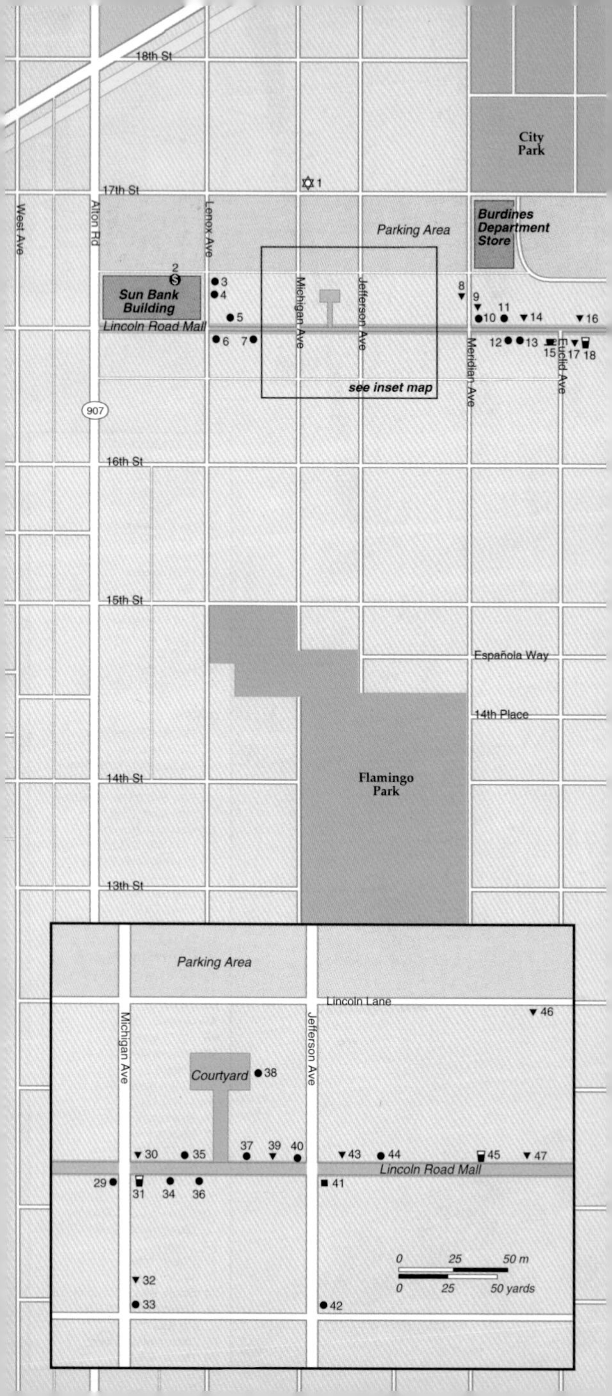
18th St
City Park
17th St
1
West Ave
Alton Rd
Lenox Ave
Parking Area
Burdines Department Store
2
Sun Bank Building
3
4
5
6
7
Michigan Ave
Jefferson Ave
8
9
10
11
14
16
Lincoln Road Mall
12
13
15
17
18
Meridian Ave
Euclid Ave
see inset map
907
16th St
15th St
Española Way
14th Place
14th St
Flamingo Park
13th St
Parking Area
Lincoln Lane
46
Michigan Ave
Jefferson Ave
Courtyard
38
30
35
37
39
40
43
44
45
47
Lincoln Road Mall
29
31
34
36
41
32
33
42
0
25
50 m
0
25
50 yards

MAP 10

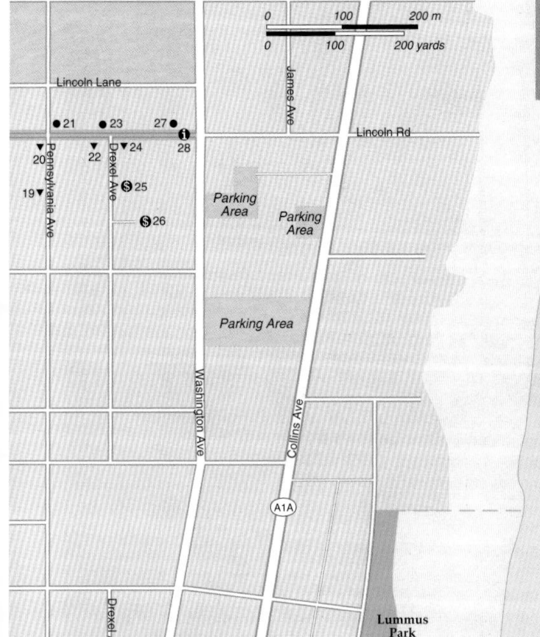

PLACES TO STAY
41 Van Dyke Hotel

PLACES TO EAT
8 David's Cafe II
9 Embers
14 World Resources Café
15 Hollywood Juice & Smoothie
16 Granny Feelgood's
17 Norma's on the Beach
19 El Rancho Grande
20 Lyon Frères et Compagnie
22 Café Papillon
24 Las Americas
30 Lincoln Road Café
32 Jeffrey's
39 Pacific Time
41 Van Dyke Hotel Restaurant
43 Canton Inn
46 Los Hispanos Restaurant
47 Da Leo

OTHER
1 Cuban-Jewish Congregation
2 ATM
3 Bar-Cinema Vortex
4 Common Space Exhibition
5 Details
6 Colony Theatre
7 Dark Room
10 New Concept Video
11 The Kremlin
12 Fritz's Skate Shop
13 The Gay Emporium
18 The Beehive
21 Lincoln Theatre, New World Symphony
23 Extremes Music
25 Barnett Bank
26 ATM
27 Miami Surf Style II
28 Tourist Information Kiosk
29 Idol's Gym
31 West End, The Club
33 Designs by Rodney
34 Recycled Blues
35 Books & Books
36 Lincoln Road Partnership Office
37 Flowers & Flowers
38 Alliance Cinema
40 Miami City Ballet Rehearsal Hall
42 Jefferson Coin Laundry
44 Brownes & Co Apothecary
45 821

CORINNA SELBY

KENNETH DREYFUSS

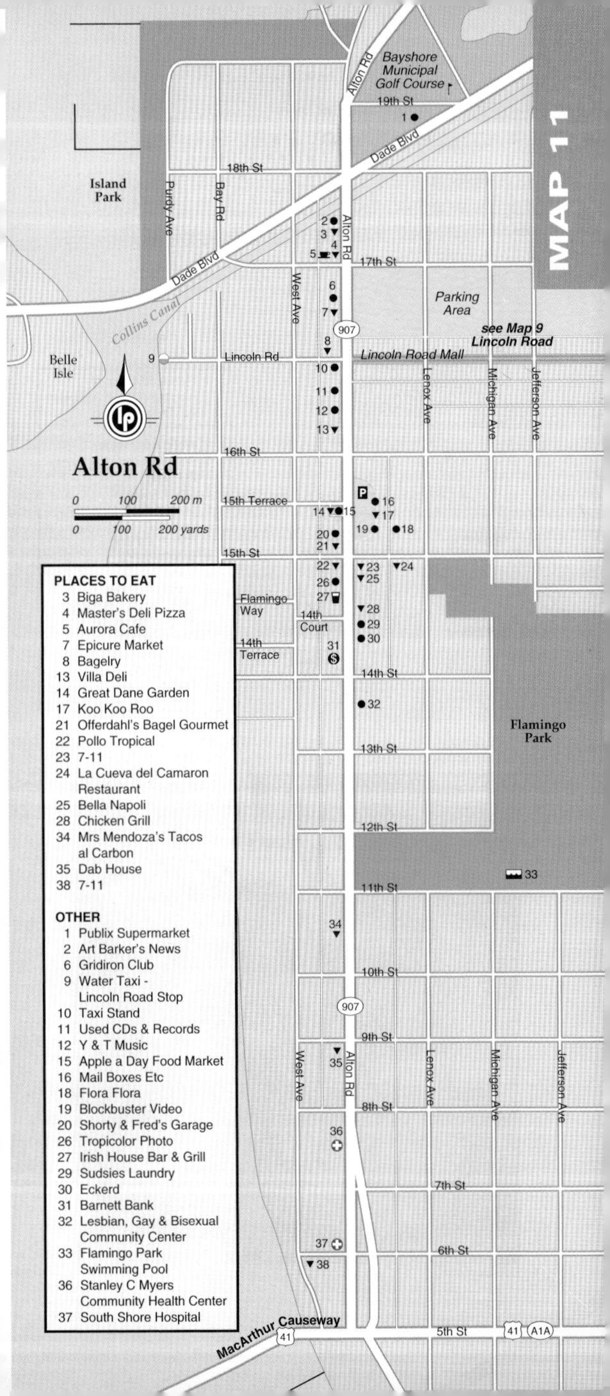
MAP 11
Alton Rd
Bayshore Municipal Golf Course
19th St
18th St
17th St
16th St
15th Terrace
15th St
14th St
13th St
12th St
11th St
10th St
9th St
8th St
7th St
6th St
5th St
Dade Blvd
Island Park
Belle Isle
Purdy Ave
Bay Rd
West Ave
Lenox Ave
Michigan Ave
Jefferson Ave
Collins Canal
Lincoln Rd
Lincoln Road Mall
see Map 9 Lincoln Road
Parking Area
Flamingo Way
14th Court
14th Terrace
Flamingo Park
MacArthur Causeway
907
41
A1A
0 100 200 m
0 100 200 yards
PLACES TO EAT
3 Biga Bakery
4 Master's Deli Pizza
5 Aurora Cafe
7 Epicure Market
8 Bagelry
13 Villa Deli
14 Great Dane Garden
17 Koo Koo Roo
21 Offerdahl's Bagel Gourmet
22 Pollo Tropical
23 7-11
24 La Cueva del Camaron Restaurant
25 Bella Napoli
28 Chicken Grill
34 Mrs Mendoza's Tacos al Carbon
35 Dab House
38 7-11
OTHER
1 Publix Supermarket
2 Art Barker's News
6 Gridiron Club
9 Water Taxi - Lincoln Road Stop
10 Taxi Stand
11 Used CDs & Records
12 Y & T Music
15 Apple a Day Food Market
16 Mail Boxes Etc
18 Flora Flora
19 Blockbuster Video
20 Shorty & Fred's Garage
26 Tropicolor Photo
27 Irish House Bar & Grill
29 Sudsies Laundry
30 Eckerd
31 Barnett Bank
32 Lesbian, Gay & Bisexual Community Center
33 Flamingo Park Swimming Pool
36 Stanley C Myers Community Health Center
37 South Shore Hospital

NW 42nd St
NE 43rd St
NE 42nd St
NW 41st St
NE 41st St
NW 40th St
NW 39th St
NW 38th St
NE 38th St
NW 2nd Ave
NW 1st Ave
N Miami Ave
NE 1st Ave
NE 2nd Ave
NE 4th Ave
Biscayne Blvd
195
1
NW 36th St
27
NW 35th St
NE 35th St
NW 34th Terrace
Roberto Clemente Park
NW 34th St
NW 33rd St
NW 32nd St
NW 31st St
NW 30th St
NW 29th St
NW 28th St
NW 27th St
NW 26th St

Design District

0 100 200 m
0 100 200 yards

1 Florida Museum of Hispanic & Latin American Art, Design Gallery of the Americas
2 World Resources
3 Picadilly Garden Lounge
4 EG Cody
5 David & Dash
6 Country Floors
7 Lord Jay
8 Palace Lighting
9 Brito Interiors
10 Dacra Design
11 Concept Casual
12 Art & Design District Association (ADDA)
13 Dacra Design
14 Evelyn S Poole
15 Post Office
16 Omian
17 Miami Art & Design Centre

CORINNA SELBY

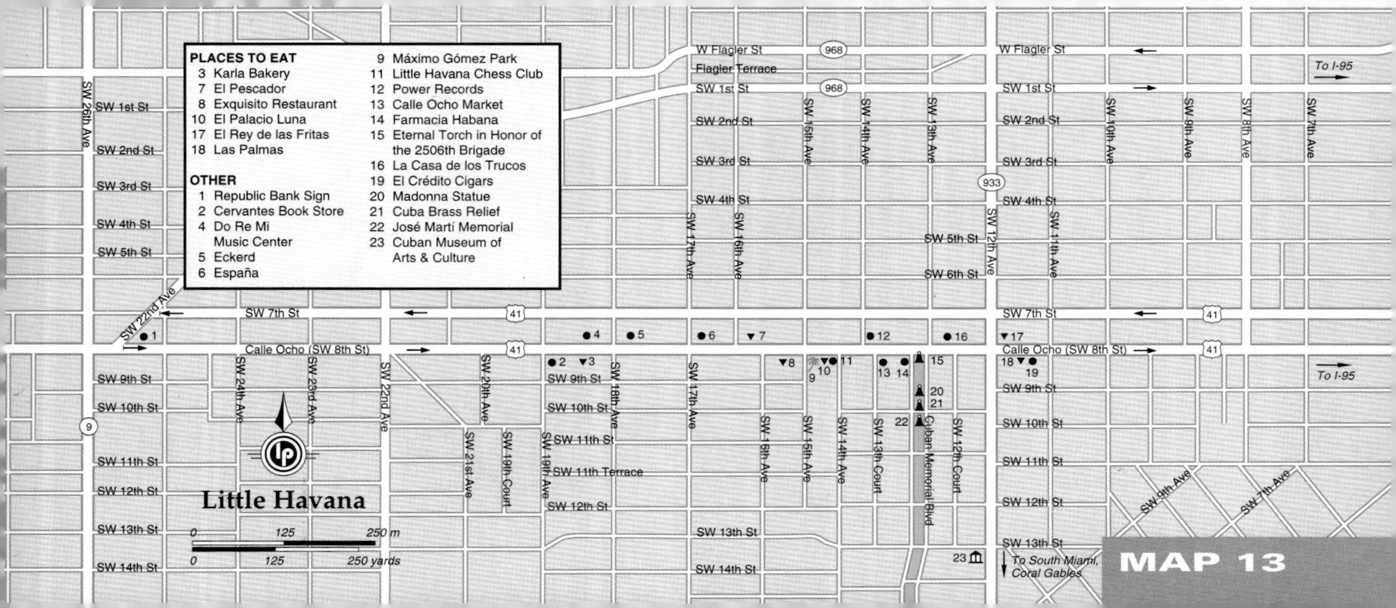
MAP 13
Little Havana
PLACES TO EAT
3 Karla Bakery
7 El Pescador
8 Exquisito Restaurant
10 El Palacio Luna
17 El Rey de las Fritas
18 Las Palmas
OTHER
1 Republic Bank Sign
2 Cervantes Book Store
4 Do Re Mi Music Center
5 Eckerd
6 España
9 Máximo Gómez Park
11 Little Havana Chess Club
12 Power Records
13 Calle Ocho Market
14 Farmacia Habana
15 Eternal Torch in Honor of the 2506th Brigade
16 La Casa de los Trucos
19 El Crédito Cigars
20 Madonna Statue
21 Cuba Brass Relief
22 José Martí Memorial
23 Cuban Museum of Arts & Culture
0 125 250 m
0 125 250 yards
W Flagler St
Flagler Terrace
SW 1st St
SW 2nd St
SW 3rd St
SW 4th St
SW 5th St
SW 6th St
SW 7th St
Calle Ocho (SW 8th St)
SW 9th St
SW 10th St
SW 11th St
SW 11th Terrace
SW 12th St
SW 13th St
SW 14th St
SW 26th Ave
SW 24th Ave
SW 23rd Ave
SW 22nd Ave
SW 21st Ave
SW 20th Ave
SW 19th Court
SW 19th Ave
SW 18th Ave
SW 17th Ave
SW 16th Ave
SW 15th Ave
SW 14th Ave
SW 13th Court
SW 13th Ave
Cuban Memorial Blvd
SW 12th Court
SW 12th Ave
SW 11th Ave
SW 10th Ave
SW 9th Ave
SW 8th Ave
SW 7th Ave
To I-95
To South Miami, Coral Gables

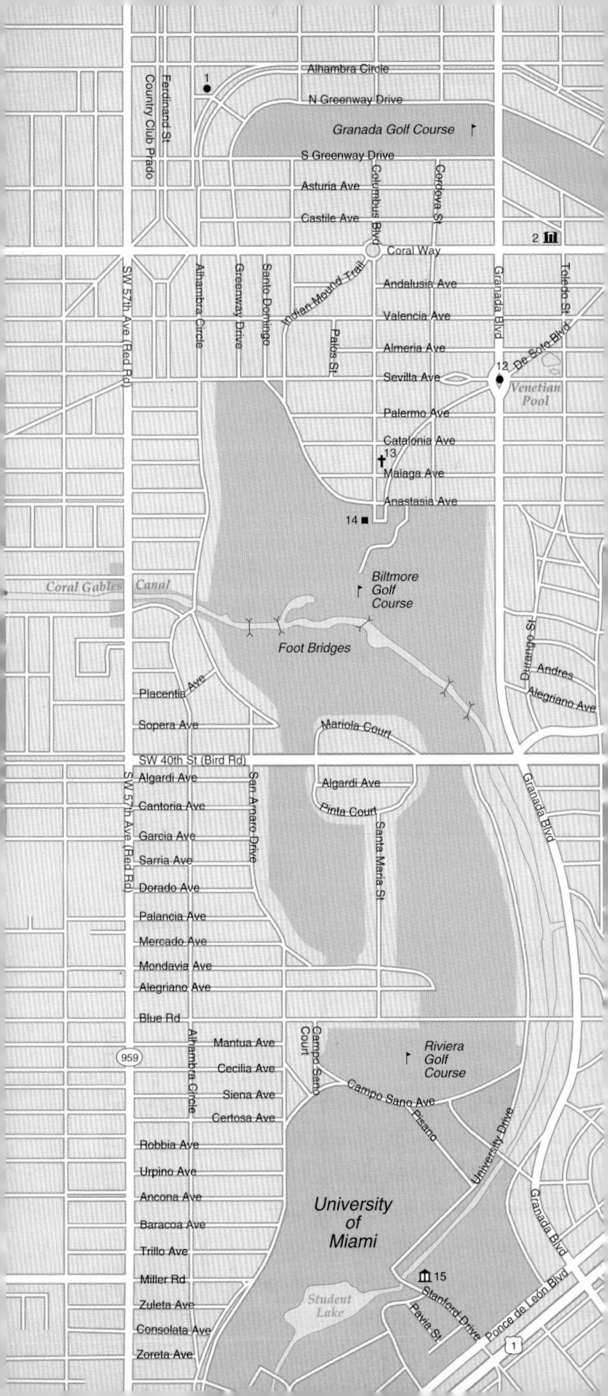

Alhambra Circle
N Greenway Drive
Granada Golf Course
S Greenway Drive
Asturia Ave
Castile Ave
Columbus Blvd
Cordova St
Country Club Prado
Ferdinand St
Coral Way
Andalusia Ave
Valencia Ave
Almeria Ave
Sevilla Ave
Palermo Ave
Catalonia Ave
Malaga Ave
Anastasia Ave
Indian Mound Trail
Alhambra Circle
Greenway Drive
Santo Domingo
Palos St
Granada Blvd
Toledo St
De Soto Blvd
Venetian Pool
SW 57th Ave (Red Rd)
Coral Gables Canal
Biltmore Golf Course
Foot Bridges
Placentia Ave
Sopera Ave
Mariola Court
Durango St
Andres
Alegriano Ave
SW 40th St (Bird Rd)
Algardi Ave
Cantoria Ave
Garcia Ave
Sarria Ave
Dorado Ave
Palancia Ave
Mercado Ave
Mondavia Ave
Alegriano Ave
Blue Rd
San Amaro Drive
Algardi Ave
Pinta Court
Santa Maria St
Granada Blvd
SW 57th Ave (Red Rd)
959
Alhambra Circle
Mantua Ave
Cecilia Ave
Siena Ave
Certosa Ave
Campo Sano Court
Riviera Golf Course
Campo Sano Ave
Pisano
University Drive
Robbia Ave
Urpino Ave
Ancona Ave
Baracoa Ave
Trillo Ave
Miller Rd
Zuleta Ave
Consolata Ave
Zoreta Ave
University of Miami
Student Lake
Stanford Drive
Pavia St
Ponce de León Blvd
Granada Blvd
1
2
12
13
14
15